LANDMARKS IN MODERN LATIN AMERICAN FICTION

LANDMARKS IN MODERN LATIN AMERICAN FICTION

Edited by

PHILIP SWANSON

ROUTLEDGE

London and New York

First published in 1990
by Routledge
11 New Fetter Lane, London EC4P 4EE

Simultaneously published in the USA and Canada by Routledge
a division of Routledge, Chapman and Hall, Inc.
29 West 35th Street, New York, NY 10001

Typeset by Columns of Reading
Printed in Great Britain by Richard Clay Ltd, Bungay

British Library Cataloguing in Publication Data

Landmarks in Modern Latin American Fiction
1. Fiction in Spanish. Spanish American Writers – Critical Studies
I. Swanson, Philip
863

Library of Congress Cataloging in Publication Data

Landmarks in Modern Latin American Fiction/edited by Philip Swanson.
p. cm.
Bibliography: p.
Includes index.
ISBN 0-415-01996-6. – ISBN 0-415-01997-4 (pbk.)
1. Spanish American fiction – 20th century – History and criticism.
I. Swanson, Philip
PQ7082.N7C675 1989
863–dc20

CONTENTS

CONTENTS

NOTES ON CONTRIBUTORS

Pamela Bacarisse teaches Spanish, Latin American and Portuguese Literature at the University of Pittsburgh. Her second book on the Argentine novelist Manuel Puig, *Impossible Choices. The Implications of the Cultural References in the Novels of Manuel Puig*, is in preparation.

Peter R. Beardsell is Senior Lecturer in the Department of Hispanic Studies, University of Sheffield, where he teaches courses in Latin American literature, history and politics. Publications include *Winds of Exile* (a monograph on the Ecuadorean poet Jorge Carrera Andrade), *Horacio Quiroga. Cuentos de amor de locura y de muerte* (a critical guide), *Ricardo Güiraldes. Don Segunda Sombra* (a critical edition), and articles on Güiraldes, Carrera Andrade, Quiroga, the Mexican dramatist Rodolfo Usigli and Spanish American literature of the 1960s.

Steven Boldy is Lecturer in Latin American Literature at Cambridge University. He has published a book on Cortázar and articles on other Latin American authors, especially Fuentes and Rulfo.

Robin Fiddian is Lecturer in Spanish and Latin American Studies in the University of Newcastle upon Tyne. His major interest is in the fiction of the modern period in Spain and Latin America, on which he has written numerous articles and two books. He is also interested in aspects of comparative literature and the Spanish cinema since the Civil War.

James Higgins is Professor of Latin American Literature at the University of Liverpool, and an Honorary Professor of the Universidad Nacional Mayor de San Marcos, Lima, Peru. In addition to numerous articles, he has published the following books: *César Vallejo: An Anthology of his Poetry*; *Visión del hombre y de la vida en las últimas obras poéticas de César Vallejo*; *The Poet in Peru*; *A History of Peruvian Literature*; *César Vallejo: A Selection of his Poetry, with Translations*.

Gerald Martin is Professor of Hispanic and Latin American Studies at Portsmouth Polytechnic. In addition to his work on Asturias he has published widely on Latin American literature and culture, most recently through his contributions to the Cambridge History of Latin America.

Donald Leslie Shaw, Brown-Forman Professor of Spanish American Literature in the University of Virginia, was formerly Professor of Latin American Studies in the University of Edinburgh. He has published books on Gallegos, Borges, Carpentier and the New Spanish American Novel, as well as numerous contributions to books and to learned journals on modern Spanish literature and Spanish American prose, drama and poetry.

Peter Standish is Head of Spanish at the University of Stirling. He studied at Bristol and as a Fulbright scholar at Tulane, going on to teach at the Universities of Essex and the West Indies. His early publications were on language teaching, but more recently he has been concerned with Latin American literature, and has written on Borges, Carpentier, Cortázar, Fuentes and Vargas Llosa. He is President of the European Association of Spanish Teachers.

Philip Swanson is Lecturer in Hispanic Studies at the University of Edinburgh, having taught previously at the National University of Ireland. His main interests are Latin American literature, modern theatre and language teaching methodology. In the Spanish American field he has published the book *José Donoso: The 'Boom' and Beyond* and articles on the novel, drama and poetry.

PREFACE

The aim of this book is to offer an overview of the evolution of modern fiction in Latin America via a study of key texts. It is hoped that in this way the book will provide a useful account of overall trends without the pitfalls associated with more general surveys, as well as giving detailed analyses by specialists of a number of central works. Nine chapters on individual texts form the core of the book, with a lengthy introduction and conclusion providing (again via studies of key works) the background to the Boom in the modern Latin American novel and charting developments since the Boom. The texts are approached in a roughly chronological order, though this pattern is sometimes modified to assist thematic unity and development of argument. No attempt is made to cover every author's entire literary production, and the study confines itself to authors from Spanish-speaking countries. Dates are provided for major Latin American authors and their works only where considered appropriate. A basic bibliography concentrating on the nine central texts examined is also included.

Inevitably this sort of study will involve some generalisations (particularly in the introduction and conclusion) and occasional reiterations of a similar point or slight differences of opinion on the same point from chapter to chapter. Equally there may be those who lament the exclusion or inclusion of certain figures from the nine central chapters or the choice of one or two of the texts therein. Nonetheless, it is felt that the survey presents an accurate picture of basic underlying patterns, while the selection of texts (both the central nine and those given special emphasis in the introduction and conclusion) is representative of the most significant works and of those that are most likely to be encountered by readers and students of Latin American fiction. It is hoped, in short, that the book will prove helpful both in its entirety as an introduction to modern Latin

American narrative and as a series of self-contained units on individual authors, works, or tendencies.

Finally, I should like to acknowledge the invaluable assistance of Elaine Edgar, whose patience and painstaking work on the word-processor have greatly eased the editor's task, and to thank Miranda France for her help with proof-reading.

P.S.

1

INTRODUCTION: BACKGROUND TO THE BOOM

PHILIP SWANSON

The two key terms in any discussion of modern Latin American fiction are those of the 'Boom' and the 'new novel'. The terms are sometimes confused but really the distinction is quite a simple one. The Boom is basically the sudden explosion of literary activity which occurred amongst Latin American writers in the 1960s when there was a marked increase in the production and availability of dazzlingly innovative and experimental novels. However, the more general term, new novel, recognises the fact that this type of fiction was being produced well before the Boom and has continued to be produced well after it. Indeed, some of the most important examples of the new novel were published in the 1940s and 1950s (with their forerunners written earlier still), while many critics point to great 'new novels' of the 1970s and 1980s.

Defining the so-called new novel is another problem altogether. A rich variety of differing narratives has come to be encompassed by this umbrella label; nonetheless, a number of basic points can be made. Essentially, the new novel can be seen as a reaction against and rejection of the assumptions and forms of traditional realism. In Latin America realism was associated with social observation (usually of backward, rural areas). The traditional novel in the early twentieth century attempted to document reality authentically so as to expose a variety of social ills, such as harsh natural conditions or the brutality of certain social groups and the exploitation of others (like the Indians, for example). In practice, this often tended to result in a simplistic, black-and-white presentation of reality: on the one hand there were villainous landowners and corrupt opportunists, while on the other hand there were idealised peasants and innocent victims. This is, of course, a contradiction of realism: literature cannot claim to be an objective document while steering its readers towards a subjective interpretation of reality. But given that the readers of the time were happy to accept fiction as a mirror of reality, this meant that they accepted a novel's distortions as truth. The generally omniscient, third-person narrator was seen as a kind of donor of truth or reality, with the reader acting as his acquiescent, passive recipient. The assumption of author and reader alike, then, was that reality was a readily comprehensible phenomenon which could be unproblematically captured and reflected in writing.

The new novel questions the suppositions of conventional realism and its Latin American equivalents, so that (local) social certainties give way to the (universal) metaphysical scepticism of the modern age. Modern man's crisis of faith in the values and systems which have traditionally guaranteed order and meaning in life has led to a repudiation of the Western view, rooted in Christianity, of a coherent world based on clear principles of right and wrong. Whereas the ordered structures of the realist text reflect a faith in an ordered, meaningful reality, the modern novelist feels that reality is much more problematic, contradictory and ambiguous. It is not something which can be clearly understood and transferred to the written page: therefore fiction must abandon its pretensions to mimesis and/or adopt complex techniques to express a vision of a complex reality. Hence, the subjectivity of reality is put across via the withdrawal of the narrator, interior monologues, stream of consciousness, multiple viewpoints, inner time scales; similarly, its complexity is stressed through structural fragmentation, chronological inversion, fantastic distortion and multifaceted symbolism. This introduction of difficult techniques inevitably changes the role of the reader: no longer a passive receptor, he has to engage actively in the text and piece its parts together, sharing the confusion of the characters as they attempt to find order in their chaotic existence.

Having said all of this, the switch from traditional novel to 'new' novel in Latin America should not be seen as too abrupt a process. It is not simply a question of unsophisticated, unambiguous social fiction being 'replaced' by ingenious, polysemic universal fiction. For a start, the early-twentieth-century Latin American novel is not as traditional as is often supposed (and indeed the new novelists were really reacting against a notional realist novel which may never have really existed in any pure form). As an illustration, it is worth examining briefly a few of the major examples of the Regionalist novel, as Latin America's rural social realist fiction was known. For example, the subcontinent's most famous traditional novel, *Doña Bárbara* (1929), by the Venezuelan Rómulo Gallegos (1884–1969) demonstrates considerable ambiguity. Conventional wisdom has usually seen the novel as an illustration of the conflict of civilisation-versus-barbarism.[1] The cruel and corrupt rural landowner, doña Bárbara, represents (as her name implies) the barbarism of the interior, while the sophisticated city-dweller, Santos Luzardo, who attempts to clean up the region, represents (as his name implies) the enlightening forces of civilisation. Yet a closer analysis reveals that each character contains something of the other. Bárbara (whose badness can in any case be explained by her traumatic past) oscillates between 'malos instintos' and 'sentimientos nuevos', ultimately sacrificing her own interests for the sake of love when she spares her daughter's life. Santos, meanwhile, is similarly prey to 'dos sentimientos contrarios' and flirts with the thrill of machismo and violence. So accommodation of the two traditions is made to seem more fruitful than the swamping of one by the other. The point is that, despite the novel's tendencies towards simplification and schematism, there is some degree of psychological complexity in the characters and an appreciation of the social complexity of the problem under consideration. Even if the novel does aim to teach its readers, its underlying sense of confusion provides a hint – albeit small – of things to come.

This process is carried a stage further by the two other great Regionalist novels of this period. Firstly, *Don Segundo Sombra*, published in 1926 by Argentina's Ricardo Güiraldes (1886–1927), reverses the civilisation-versus-barbarism equation, idealising the *gaucho* of the Argentinian *pampa* and opposing his values to sterile, modern European importations. But, as Beardsell has expertly shown,[2] the eponymous gaucho hero is dangerously prone to violence and irresponsibility. Moreover, don Segundo's young apprentice, Fabio, though remaining a gaucho at heart, becomes an educated member of a landowning elite. This is paralleled on a stylistic level too, where there is a similar blend of the rustic and the *culto*: for Güiraldes – himself a wealthy landowner with a European background – uses language inherited from French Symbolist and Latin American Modernist poetry to describe the rough, tough world of the outback. Thus the novel posits, not a simple opposition, but a complex – if vague – pattern of acculturation. In the same way, Mariano Azuela's (1873–1952) 1915 novel of the Mexican

Revolution, *Los de abajo*, presents its protagonist, Demetrio Macías, as a genuine peasant hero, but also as a man given to drunkenness, womanising and aggression. Even more interesting is the structure of the novel which strings together a series of only loosely related impressionistic scenes, suggesting the directionless bewilderment of characters grappling with a reality beyond their comprehension. The reality here, of course, is a social one rather than a metaphysical one, and there is no radical questioning of the nature of existence. The point is not that these novels were consciously experimental precursors of the new novel, but that they provide evidence of an unconscious sense of confusion before reality which, even at this early stage, was already threatening to subvert the novels' realism without their authors being aware of it.[3] Add to this the precedent of *modernismo* – a turn-of-the-century poetic movement which rejected naturalism and everyday reality[4] – and the stimulus of social development in the form of European immigration, rapid modernisation and urban migration, and some kind of major change on the literary scene was inevitable.

The bridge linking Regionalism and social realism with fantasy and formal innovation is the phenomenon known as Magical Realism (and the related phenomenon of Neo-Indianism): for both these styles involved the assimilation of the technical accomplishments of European writing in order to explore better the nature of an essentially Latin American reality. The term magical realism is much abused and misused (particularly since journalism's discovery of García Márquez, Vargas Llosa *et al.*, which has led to its being availed of to define almost any piece of fiction that is modern and Latin American). Essentially, magical realism is based around the idea that Latin American reality is somehow unusual, fantastic or 'marvellous' because of its bizarre history and because of its varied ethnological make-up. In other words, reality in Latin America is more akin to fantasy given its prodigious historical background, its incredible range of communities and living conditions, its spectacularly heterogeneous geography, and – above all – the indigenous population's view of life based on myth and legend. This was later to lead to a type of fiction (often associated with García Márquez) where fantasy was incorporated into realistic narratives, with incredible events presented in a deadpan manner as if they were really happening. However, at this point the debate concerning magical realism begins to widen out: now it becomes difficult to decide if the fantastic is pointing to the sheer exuberance of Latin American reality or if it is going beyond this to question or subvert the notion of reality in general.

Perhaps the author whose name should be most closely linked with magical realism is Cuba's Alejo Carpentier (1904–80). Though his story 'Viaje a la semilla' (1944) is plainly fantastic (most notably through its inversion of chronological time) and is therefore closer to the more typical elements of the *nueva narrativa*, his work is more often concerned with seeking out the magical or 'marvellous' in everyday reality. Indeed, he makes this clear himself in the famous prologue to his 1949 novel, *El reino de este mundo*, in which he coined the phrase 'lo real maravilloso'. The discovery of the 'marvellous real' evidenced in the prologue owes itself to a fusion of European and Latin American influences. Throughout the 1930s Carpentier had been in Paris and, along with Asturias, had come into contact with the French Surrealists. Following his return home at the end of the decade and a highly formative trip to Haiti in 1943, Carpentier began to apply the lessons of Europe purely to Latin America, seeing the surreal as a daily feature of life in his own subcontinent. Hence now, just as his earlier Afro-Cuban novel *Ecué-Yamba O* (1933) opposed black primitivism to white dominance, so the much more successful *El reino de este mundo* sees native values and voodoo as somehow superior to culture of European descent or influence.

But Carpentier's two most famous novels are probably *Los pasos perdidos* (1953) and *El siglo de las luces* (1962). In fact, the unnamed narrator of *Los pasos perdidos* embodies the Carpenterian dilemma of a Europeanised Latin American reviewing his impressions of his homeland.[5] He is of mixed parentage (Protestant Northern European and Catholic Latin American) and, though born in Latin America, has lived largely in Europe and the USA. Thus he is a perfect vehicle for an exploration of the decadence of the North in comparison to the elemental vitality of Latin America. Much influenced by Oswald Spengler's *The Decline of the West* (1918),[6] Carpentier characterises life in the USA and Europe as empty and alienating, the materialism and pretentiousness of New York society finding a more sinister echo in the references to war and concentration camps in Europe. However, when the narrator is given an opportunity to undertake a journey to a remote region of Latin America in order to unearth primitive musical instruments, he is brought face-to-face with a more authentic form of existence.

5

The contrast between inauthenticity and authenticity is underlined schematically by the opposition established between Mouche (the narrator's lover in the North) and Rosario (his lover in the South). Rosario accepts misfortunes with equanimity, while Mouche complains of minor discomforts; Rosario reads simple folk tales, while Mouche reads thinly disguised pornography posing as art; Rosario offers native herbal remedies, while Mouche exploits superstition for commercial ends through astrology. Similarly, almost all of the characters in South America are natural and down-to-earth while almost all the characters in North America are shallow and superficial.

Given that the modern world of the North is presented as a kind of perversion of natural norms, it is not surprising that the narrator's South American odyssey is portrayed as a journey back in time towards a more meaningful form of primitivism. His journey takes him ever further away from modern civilisation and, in particular, the river, which leads him deep into the jungle, is an obvious symbol of the backwards flow of history. For example, the narrator can say that: 'los años se restan, se diluyen, se esfuman, en vertiginoso retroceso del tiempo.'[7] This is, of course, partly what marvellous realism is all about: the idea that communities of vastly differing stages of development can exist side by side in this huge subcontinent, that '(el) hombre prehistórico' can be 'contemporáneo nuestro' (p.203). But it is also linked, as González Echevarría has pointed out,[8] with the quest for some sort of Edenic origin or paradise of authenticity prior to the trauma and devastation of the European invasion. And so the narrator asserts that:

Si algo me estaba maravillando en este viaje era el descubrimiento de que aún quedaban inmensos territorios en el mundo cuyos habitantes vivían ajenos, a las fiebres del día, y que aquí, si bien muchísimos individuos se contentaban con un techo de fibra, una alcarraza, un budare, una hamaca y una guitarra, pervivía en ellos un cierto animismo, una conciencia de muy viejas tradiciones, un recuerdo vivo de ciertos mitos que eran, en suma, presencia de una cultura más honrada y válida, probablemente, que la que se nos había quedado allá.

(p.126)

Interestingly though, despite his glorification of an aboriginal past which seems alive in the present, the narrator is ultimately incapable of fitting into it. Writing music (presumably for performance in the USA), waxing lyrical and engaging in intellectual speculation, the narrator is never really fully at home in the uncomplicated jungle community where he attempts to settle. Moreover, his failure to punish the leprous rapist is a symbolic reminder of his basic non-identification with the customs and practices of the community. His eventual departure and inability to retrace his steps reinforce the point. Yet this defeat need not be interpreted in wholly negative terms (a comment which could be equally applied to the protagonist of Carpentier' subsequent novel, *El acoso* (1956)).[9] At the end of the novel, the narrator comments that: 'hoy terminaron las vacaciones de Sísifo' (p.279). The image of Sisyphus, forever re-enacting the task of pushing his boulder uphill, suggests that change is an uphill struggle, for history seems to repeat itself unerringly in a frustrating cyclical pattern. This novel shows that escape into a world of timelessness is impossible though. Man must face up to his historicity and continue the struggle. There will be mistakes, there will be frustrations, there will be the sensation of always ending up back where one started. But history is a stuttering, stammering process and the only way to gain liberation is to work for change within that process.

This is the thrust of Carpentier's most acclaimed work, *El siglo de las luces*, which – now joined by Vargas Llosa's *La guerra del fin del mundo* (1981) – is one of the great historical novels to emerge from Latin America in modern times. Set between 1791 and 1808, it concerns the French Revolution and the attempts to export it to the Caribbean. At first, the novel may seem to be a polished reworking of the stock Latin American theme of the betrayal of the revolutionary ideal. The young protagonists Esteban and Sofía are initially charmed by the dashing entrepreneur, Víctor Hugues. Esteban joins him enthusiastically in the Revolution in France, but his growing apprehension about Hugues's fanaticism turns to complete disillusionment when he witnesses the Frenchman's creation of a tyrannical dictatorship in Guadeloupe. Likewise, Sofía, Hugues's one-time lover, is disappointed by the cruelty of his regime in Cayenne. The central irony is perhaps that Hugues, who returns to the Caribbean to liberate slaves, ends up as a slave-owner himself.

But the novel is not that simple. The basic symbol of the guillotine illustrates this. Presented to us in the prologue, it obviously represents the appalling cost in human suffering of revolutionary

7

change. Equally, however, it is 'una puerta abierta sobre el vasto cielo' opening up a path towards the stars and the heavens.[10] This all suggests that, despite setbacks, positive change, movement towards an ideal, can be achieved, albeit through a series of jerks and hiccups rather than smooth transitions. Thus, one of the novel's other central symbols, the painting of an explosion in a cathedral, is equally two-sided: negative in so far as the blast causes violence and the cathedral (old values) is not even fully destroyed; positive in that the explosion is not complete, but in action, ongoing like the Revolution itself which may construct a new cathedral of humanitarianism dedicated to 'el reino de *este* mundo' (my italics).

This, of course, raises the question of the novel's attitude to history. For Ortega, the revolutionary drive is a noble quest for a Utopia (represented by the story of the Caribs' search for a promised land) which is degraded by the demands of politics: history, therefore, is a series of flawed acts committed in the pursuit of a lost paradise. The emphasis on seafaring and travelling stresses the confusion and instability of history, its inability to lead us to firmer, solid ground. Moreover, the fact that the novel opens and closes with the bourgeois Carlos encloses the text in a circle, suggesting that the true beneficiaries of the Revolution are the middle classes, that the existence of a dominant class has been perpetuated.[11] González Echevarría, on the other hand, sees Carlos as a force for independence. Moreover, he shows that there is progress in the novel. Sofía's emergence in its later stages implies a shift from the power of reason (bourgeois revolution) to the power of emotion (revolution of the masses). Moreover, she refuses to be put off by her experience of Víctor and persuades Esteban to join her in supporting a popular revolution in Spain in 1808. The shift from Hugues to Sofía, therefore, is a development from bourgeois to popular rebellion. So, for González Echevarría, history is presented, not as a circle, but a spiral (hence the importance of the image of the spiralling shell).[12] Behind the pattern of repeated failures there is optimism for the future.

This positive outlook is clearer still in the relationship of two of Carpentier's later works, *El recurso del método* (1974) and *La consagración de la primavera* (1978). Though some critics have noted circular elements suggestive of futility in the former, it should be emphasised that the unscrupulous dictator at the centre of the novel is, in effect, deposed, while his bewilderment in the face of modern art points up his status as an outmoded phenomenon; and, even if he is not replaced by a genuinely progressive force, the dedication of the idealistic but realistic Estudiante indicates hope for the future. This hope materialises in the 1978 novel, which describes, in glowing terms, the triumph of the Cuban Revolution portended by the Estudiante. Thus, the occult reality of 'lo real maravilloso' (in a sense subverted in the denouement of *Los pasos perdidos*) has become the unseen movement of collective, popular feeling underlying the superficial pattern of history. Just how convincing all this is is a matter for individual readers. Certainly, *La consagración de la primavera* is at times corny and over-generous in its interpretation of Fidel Castro, while the self-indulgently baroque style of *El recurso del método*, coupled with a kind of haughty wit, fails to 'move' the uncommitted reader. Indeed, the entire Carpenterian notion of marvellous realism may foreclose reader involvement: rather than promoting a genuinely Latin American consciousness, the very idea of 'marvelling' at Latin American reality suggests non-participation, looking on from the outside, even a European perspective.[13] Carpentier's magical realism is ultimately contradictory, but so is its evolution throughout Latin America, alternating as it does between the local and the universal, the real and the unreal.

Two authors who more consciously attempted to avoid the trap of an external perspective were Guatemala's Miguel Ángel Asturias (1899–1974) and Peru's José María Arguedas (1911–69), both of whom explored Latin American society through the medium of Indian mythology. While Asturias (who will be dealt with in a separate chapter) was influenced by fantasy and Surrealism, Arguedas – whose first language was Quechua and whose contact with Europe was limited – stuck more rigidly to native models. Indeed, he is generally seen as a renovator of *indigenismo*, a movement concerned with the plight of the indigenous Indian population. And this is where the magical element comes in, for his originality lies in the way he presents reality from the magical-religious perspective of the Indian community. Whereas even the better examples of nativist fiction, such as *El mundo es ancho y ajeno* (1941) by fellow Peruvian Ciro Alegría (1909–67), were simplistic outsiders' views of the Indians, Arguedas's work gives a more complex vision, from the inside.

His most studied novel is, without doubt, *Los ríos profundos* (1958). Similar in content to his 1935 book of stories, *Agua* (which attempted to render Quechua syntax via Castillian Spanish), this later work is centred around a child narrator, Ernesto, who, though white and not poor, was brought up for part of his childhood in an Indian community or *ayllu*. As an adolescent, however, he is made to enter a white, religious school in Abancay. The school prepares young whites to take their dominant place in society, while the town itself is dominated by a large estate run by powerful landowners who keep their Indian labourers in a state of virtual slavery. Ernesto therefore feels a sense of confusion and not belonging, as his meaningful, harmonious Indian upbringing is contradicted by the divisiveness and cruelty of the established order.

Much of the novel is given over to developing the contrast between these two ways of life through the filter of Ernesto's experiences. For example, the school clearly stands for the harshness of white society. Here corrupt priests support the landowners and use religion to keep the Indians down, while racism effectively leads to the departure of a black brother. On a more symbolic plane, the underlying violence and degradation of 'civilised' society is reflected in the boys' constant fighting, bullying and rivalry, their guilty acts of masturbation and their sexual abuse of the subnormal servant woman, 'la opa'. But set against this environment is the magical world of Indian tradition into which Ernesto tries to escape. A key symbol here is the *zumbayllu*, a kind of supernatural spinning-top which he thinks will attract the harmony of the natural world to the hostile world of the school. His beliefs are reinforced in this respect by his visits to the local bars where he hears Quechua songs and his contemplation of the natural scenery of the surrounding countryside.

But the most interesting aspect of all of this is the absorbing way in which this mixture of the child's and the Indian's world view is presented. For here there is no conventional rationalist or humanist separation of man and nature, there is no gap between reality and any spiritual or supernatural order. Instead the viewpoint is the Indian, mystical-religious one of a harmonious universe where man and nature are integrated in a synthesised whole. Hence Rowe has been able to show how the novel portrays the same qualities in humans, animals and objects, often expressed by the same morpheme.[14] This is an important step forward from the facile, explanatory style of, say, Alegría and underlines the point that the 'new novel' was not just a sudden rejection of the old principles of traditional social fiction, but evolved gradually and, in large part, via the renovation of social fiction.

The move away from both didacticism and external observation is highlighted by Ernesto's response to the rebellions of the *chicheras* (female bar-owners) and the *colonos* (Indian serfs). He lacks the ideological framework to see these in political terms and so responds on a magical-religious level; he thinks that the leader of the *chicheras* (whom he associates with the river, the sun and the *zumbayllu*) is invulnerable to danger and that the Indians' march *en masse* will frighten off the 'fever' (which he conceives of as a kind of supernatural creature).[15] But this process results in a confusion of the social and political element of the novel (a recurring problem in modern Latin American literature as socially orientated fiction attempted to reconcile protest with the literary trend towards subjectivity and ambiguity). At the end it is not clear if the *colonos'* 'supernatural' victory presages meaningful change in 'real' terms. Throughout the novel the *colonos* are presented as timorous and cowering, while their uprising at the end is only to demand a special mass to ward off disease (which in some ways reiterates their submissiveness to an ambivalently presented Church). The question therefore is whether their traditions (which give them a certain moral superiority over the white man) also act as a block to genuine social progress on their part. The question remains open, but there is some hope. The parallel with the earlier *chicheras* revolt (where government salt supplies are raided and handed over to the needy) may hint that the Indians' conduct is the first step along a path that could one day lead to social or political action. Moreover, the conflict is not black and white: Ernesto, it should be remembered, is somewhere between the respective cultures of the whites and the Indians. This points to the presence of a process of transculturation and looks forward to the benefits of a mutually-enriching interchange of cultural values in a reformed Peru: in this instance ambiguity may be seen to sharpen rather than blunt the social message.

This combination of complexity and positiveness is developed in Arguedas's last two major works. *Todas las sangres* (1964) – building on his earlier *Yawar Fiesta* (1941) – expands the range of the typical *indigenista* novel, giving a panoramic view of Andean society in the 1950s as it undergoes a period of socio-economic change. In it the Indians – led by the Lima-educated Rendón Willka – become an effective workforce, go on strike and run estates themselves. In other words, they advance themselves by simultaneously adapting to the system while retaining their own identity. Whether such meaningful acculturation is endorsed by Arguedas's final novel is more problematic. The title, *El zorro de arriba y el zorro de abajo* (1971, posthumously), refers to the fusion of Andean society (*arriba*) and coastal society (*abajo*), anticipating a new nation transformed by transculturation. However, the novel as a whole seems deeply pessimistic: Chimbote – a newly industrialised port attracting rural immigrants – really represents the annihilation of Indian values by the all-powerful claws of capitalism. Indeed, the novel itself, though attempting to use traditional oral forms in an original way, ends up as a kind of monstrous labyrinth ultimately leading nowhere. It was never finished, and Arguedas committed suicide in 1969: his dream of a new Peru died with him.

A similar dream, equally clouded by uncertainty, is shared by Paraguayan novelist Augusto Roa Bastos (b.1917). His first novel, *Hijo de hombre* (1960),[16] is a good example of the marriage of the so-called magical realism and social protest, while at the same time it takes the process a stage further by incorporating some of the structural techniques associated with the new novel. The central technical feature of the novel is its inversion of the Biblical motif of Jesus Christ as saviour, replacing it with the notion of salvation by the common Guaraní-speaking peasant. Such inversion (visible also in novels by Asturias, Rulfo, Donoso and García Márquez) is typical of magical realism in that it underscores the fantastic disproportions of Latin American history and asserts an alternative viewpoint based on Indian or peasant cultures. But while Carpentier, especially in his earlier works, marvels and waxes intellectual, while Arguedas posits the rather unpromising notion of an Indianist cultural impregnation of Peru, Roa grasps the theme of a revolutionary guerrilla war more firmly by the horns, in a way that links him – to some degree – to the brand of committed literature wrapped in the new novel formula expounded by Argentina's David Viñas (b.1929). Just how practical such a revolution is, though, remains, in the case of Roa, an unresolved issue.

The substance of the Biblical allegory in Roa's novel is that the plight of the descendants of the natives of Paraguay – a kind of charred and desolated Garden of Eden[17] – corresponds to an expulsion from paradise to a world of suffering and hardship where, like the descendants of Adam and Eve, they await a saviour – not a divine saviour but a human one, an 'hijo de hombre'. That is, only man can save man: in other words, by taking collective action.

Hence the novel presents us with a series of Christ figures emblematic of this potential redemption, the most important being the aptly named *Cristóbal* Jara (whose characterisation is positively overflowing with Christian connotations). Jara, like Christ, eventually dies whilst bringing life-saving water to a sinner (the traitor, Miguel Vera). Moreover, having sacrificed his own life to bring the water of life to lesser mortals, the Christ figure undergoes a metaphorical resurrection by continuing to inspire others through the memory of his example (p.274).

So far, so good. But once again the positive thrust of magical realism runs into practical obstacles, for none of the Christ figures really seems to get anywhere. The statue carved by the leper Gaspar Mora – initially seen as 'una inversión de la fe, un permanente conato de insurrección' (p.14) – is blessed and institutionalised by a corrupt Church. The Christ-like doctor, Alexis Dubrovsky, succumbs to alcoholism and avarice and flees following an act of rape. Jara, finally, dies in a war that achieves nothing, in order to preserve a traitor (who goes on to acquire political authority). Yet, despite all of this, Dubrovsky's illegitimate son provides a glimmer of hope: 'Había algo de anunciación en ese niño. . . . Engendrado por el estupro, estaba allí sin embargo para testimoniar la inocencia, la incorruptible pureza de la raza humana, puesto que en él todo el tiempo recomenzaba desde el principio' (p.163). The message is one of hope against hope: the struggle will go on even if it must be renewed afresh with each generation.

What should be becoming clear by this stage is that the new novel was not just a reaction against the telluric fiction of the early twentieth century, but actually grew out of it as it developed and changed. But this alone was not enough, for alongside the increasing sophistication of rural-based narratives, there was emerging a new brand of urban fiction that helped radicalise the Latin American novel even further. Economic change shifted attention away from the interior towards the city, and the city is a key factor in the modernisation of the subcontinent's writing. The influence was a double-edged one: on the one hand, a rapidly changing technological environment promoted an awareness of new possibilities, a consciousness of the simultaneity of differing phenomena, and a desire to experiment, which resulted in the beginnings of new narrative forms; at the same time, that same shifting technological society caused an erosion of traditional values, generating instability,

13

uncertainty and, ultimately, a sense of social and even metaphysical disorientation. In this basic dualism lie the roots of much major Latin American writing of today.

In 1948 the Argentinian novelist Leopoldo Marechal (1900–70) published *Adán Buenosayres*,[18] an indication perhaps that the city at the centre of this economic and literary upheaval is Buenos Aires. This was a cosmopolitan city in a country transformed by massive European immigration and economic modernisation from the late nineteenth century onwards. But, despite the stimulating effects of change, as the pampa declined and the city grew larger, the latter experienced all the problems of dislocation, population growth, overcrowding and economic slumps. The very modernity of this situation promoted artistic activity and experimentation as literary traditions were destabilised alongside societal ones, but the downside of that modernity moulded the preoccupations of much of the literary production of the region – loss of roots, alienation, loneliness, frustration and failure. And here can be found the seeds of the novel's evolution away from the local, specifically Latin American milieu towards the wider, universal context of existential and metaphysical malaise. According to Shaw, in his indispensable study of the new narrative, a basic characteristic of modern Latin American literature is 'la desaparición de la novela "comprometida" y la emergencia de la novela "metafísica"'.[19] While it would be an exaggeration to talk of the erasure of one form by another, it is nonetheless plain that, as the twentieth century developed, social and existential themes went hand in hand, with the former often serving merely as a spring-board for the latter and with the certainties of rational social analysis being replaced by the uncertainty and scepticism of existential confusion. The genesis of Vargas Llosa's famous utterance that 'la novela deja de ser "latinoamericana", se libera de esa servidumbre'[20] lies here with the ebb in old-style *criollismo* and the birth of urban fiction.

Of the various authors from the River Plate area relevant to this development one of the most important early figures is the Argentine Roberto Arlt (1900–42) who – though not particularly well-known outside the Spanish-speaking world – was later to become something of a cult figure amongst novelists of the Boom such as Cortázar. Though there were other urban novelists around in Argentina and elsewhere, Arlt's work is significant in that it marks a break with simplistic social realism, being full of ambiguities and often

14

subordinating social elements to metaphysical concerns. His principal works, according to most critics, are *Los siete locos* (1929) and *Los lanzallamas* (1931), two linked novels revolving around Erdosain and his associate, the Astrólogo, in which the dehumanising effects of a mechanical society are mercilessly exposed. However, the scheme to overthrow capitalism cooked up by the two friends is so ideologically unsound and so downright whacky (involving the use of secret sects, deadly rays and noxious gases) that this almost seems to be a parody of committed literature. The deeper significance of the social criticism is its existential dimension: the grotesque vision of modern life (reflected in the distorted characters and the disjointed structure) links the inhumanity of industrial society to the more profound dilemmas of isolation, incommunication and lack of fulfilment in general.

But more familiar to most than either of these two works is Arlt's less mature first novel, *El juguete rabioso* (1926), which merits a brief consideration. Oddly enough it came out in the same year as *Don Segundo Sombra*, demonstrating that the urban novel did not replace the rural novel as such but developed alongside it (though with increasing importance). But in any case, *Don Segundo Sombra* was, in part, an elegy for a *bygone* age and witness to the industrialisation and Europeanisation of Argentina. Arlt's novel was therefore a timely counterpart. Though it contains many social realist elements, there is again an existential or metaphysical dimension. The original title, *La vida puerca*, refers not just to the injustices of Buenos Aires society but to the very nature of life itself. This explains the novel's persistent exaggeration of the element of filth and degradation. There is a variety of unsightly low-life characters, all of whom seem to inhabit a 'cuchitril': for example, Dío Fetente's house is an 'infierno'[21] while he is reduced to animal status, a 'tortuga' (p.51) in whose 'ojos lastimeros brillaba una perfecta desesperación canina' (p.62). Meanwhile the protagonist Silvio (a forerunner of Erdosain) is made to undergo a series of humiliating trials (jobs like the cleaning-out of an unspeakably dirty lavatory) until he too feels like a dog (p.95), 'tan pequeño frente a la vida, que yo no atinaba a escoger una esperanza' (p.96). Silvio's position is reflected in his attitude to sexuality, about which he fantasises in sado-masochistic terms (pp.52–3). He defines the sexual act (normally symbolic of the quest for fulfilment) as: 'congojosa sequedad del espíritu, peregrina voluptuosidad áspera y mandadora' (p.52). The perversion of sexuality, like the novel's inversion of the family unit, implies a degraded reality devoid of meaningful values.

Having said all this, the text, as befits its status as a precursor of the new novel, does contain ambiguities. Some have seen positive elements in Silvio's situation. He is, after all, a 'juguete rabioso' – not just society's plaything but a fighter, hitting back. Symptomatic of this are his two outbursts of arson. But though his attempt to burn the lower-middle-class bookshop might be seen as a rudimentary swipe at a certain social class, his later attempt to set fire to an old tramp – even if prompted by outrage at his own social inferiority – is an absurd and futile gesture betraying his basic impotence. Moreover, both his fire-raising efforts fail. More problematic, meanwhile, is his gratuitous betrayal of Rengo out of sheer jealousy (foreshadowing Erdosain's botched plan to murder Barsut). This search for fulfilment via self-degradation is a kind of pre-existentialist affirmation of independence from oppressive social and religious laws, giving Silvio the air of an early absurd hero. It is an idea which will recur in the work of other Latin American authors, but which does not ultimately seem to lead anywhere. Thus, Arlt ironically has Silvio feel 'llamas ardientes de esperanza y de ensueño' as he walks through 'las chatas calles del arrabal, miserables y sucias, . . . con cajones de basura a las puertas, con mujeres ventrudas, despeinadas y escuálidas hablando en los umbrales y llamando a sus perros o a sus hijos. . .' (pp.105–6), and the renewed optimism of the final lines is mocked by his tripping over a chair. As Flint has shown, anguish alone is the inevitable result of 'the contradiction between . . . man's aspirations and his base condition'.[22]

This is also a central theme in the work of the Uruguayan, Juan Carlos Onetti (b.1909) who, in literary terms, is a direct descendant of Arlt. Like Arlt, his work pre-dates the Boom; indeed many writers and critics regard his short 1939 novel *El pozo* as the breach that opened up the path to the new novel. Not only does this work mark a clear switch from external to internal reality with its first-person presentation of the mind of its protagonist Linacero, it also shows a clear link between the social and the metaphysical. What seems the case of a misfit in an alienating bourgeois system soon reveals itself to be an instance of existential crisis following loss of faith in any meaning to life. Even Linacero's escapes into fantasy (again hinting at things to come in the new novel) do not liberate him but only underline the emptiness of reality.

But *El pozo* is only one of many novels by Onetti who, unlike
Arlt, has lived to see the Boom and write through it. However, he is
not 'typical' of the Boom and did not really become popular until the
early 1980s. This is possibly because he has never had a major best-
seller, building up a reputation by accretion instead. In fact, he is
most famous for the fact that his novels form a series, 'la saga de
Santa María'. In *La vida breve* (1950), the hero Brausen flees from
Buenos Aires to the imaginary town of Santa María which was to
become a setting for almost all of Onetti's subsequent novels. The
unreality of the town (foreshadowing perhaps the very different
worlds of Rulfo's Comala, García Márquez's Macondo or Puig's
Coronel Vallejos) suggests that life there is unreal – in the sense that
it is false and inauthentic. But linked to this anti-bourgeois theme is
an Arltian pattern of self-degradation (Brausen, for example,
attempts to evade his own mediocre existence by taking up with the
next best thing to a prostitute and getting mixed up with her small-
time gangster lover), implying a view of life as squalid, futile and
fundamentally absurd. Hence the author, appearing to intervene in
one of the novels, tells us that despite his detailed documentation of
life in Santa María, 'no puedo descubrir un sentido indudable para
todo esto',[23] an attitude of detached, amused indifference which is
reflected also in the outlook of Díaz Grey, the town doctor, who has
been seen as a kind of Onettian alter ego: 'todos . . . son pobres
hombres y pobres mujeres. Ya no puedo ser empujado por los
móviles de ellos, me parecen cómicas todas las convicciones, todas
las clases de fe de esta gente lamentable y condenada a muerte'
(p.89).

Yet there is considerable ambiguity in all of this, for Díaz Grey is
not as transparent as he would like to present himself, and there is a
certain nobility about those who struggle and fail when set against
the smugness, narrow-mindedness and stupidity of the local
community. An important character in this respect is Larsen,
protagonist of *Juntacadáveres* (1964) and its sequel (though written
earlier) *El astillero* (1961). Larsen's scheme to open a brothel in the
first of the two novels mentioned is a welcome affront to Santa
María's petty bourgeois morality, but the scheme itself is cruelly
satirised. It is portrayed as Larsen's ideal in life, his vocation (words
like 'fe', 'convicciones', 'vocación' are used frequently). But this is
clearly an ironic, inverted ideal which is in any case contradicted by
Larsen's pathetic lack of resources and the inevitability of local

17

resistance. Though defeated partly by social hypocrisy, Larsen's failure is also symbolic of man's frustrated quest for purpose and direction in life. This dual motif of inverted values and the fruitless pursuit of ideals is a constant throughout the new novel (Rulfo's *Pedro Páramo* (1955) and Donoso's *El lugar sin límites* (1966) are cases in point), bridging the gap between traditional social concerns and the metaphysics of modernist fiction.

However, Larsen, driven out at the end of *Juntacadáveres*, returns to Santa María in *El astillero* (usually reckoned to be Onetti's most significant novel). His 'comeback' could be read in a positive light: he is determined to achieve success, impose his identity on the town and strike a blow of vengeance against this dreary bourgeois backwater. His plan is to become the manager of the local shipyard and marry the owner's daughter: eventually he will, he hopes, inherit the yard and become an important figure in the community. Moreover, this plan elevates Larsen to an heroic level in that it constitutes a challenge to mortality, as Turton explains: 'Larsen representa al hombre situado en el borde del invierno de la vida, y la puesta en funcionamiento del astillero equivale a un desafío a la muerte.'[24] Unfortunately for Larsen, though, all his schemes are doomed to failure. The novel hinges around the tension between his faith and the reality that the shipyard is bankrupt and in a state of ruin. Larsen's administrative activities are therefore symbols of the futility of action in life, rather like Colonel Aureliano Buendía's cyclic melting of the same gold to fabricate pointless ornamental fish in García Márquez's *Cien años de soledad* (1967). On top of this the woman he hopes to marry, Angélica Inés, is a half-crazy adolescent virgin who wants nothing to do with Larsen and is repelled by the sexual act. The inevitable destruction of Larsen's faith or hope is finally indicated by his own eventual madness and death. Thus Larsen both merits respect for being a fighter and a nonconformist, yet inspires repulsion and pity given his sordidness and foolishness. This ambivalence, compounded by his ambiguous presentation via an often uncertain narrative voice and together with the mixture of social rebelliousness and ultimate existential hopelessness, makes Larsen a kind of emblematic character of the Latin American new novel.

Moving on from Onetti, perhaps the most important of the River Plate existential novelists writing before the Boom is Argentina's Ernesto Sabato (formerly known as Sábato, with an accent) (b.1911). His 1948 novel, *El túnel*, is (due partly to its length and relative accessibility) one of the most widely studied modern Latin American texts. Though not as experimental as his later work, it is nonetheless an important forerunner of the new novel in that it marks a clear shift from external to internal reality. The setting is plainly the robotic, impersonal world of the big city Buenos Aires. But the emphasis is squarely on the position of the individual within that environment. Indeed, the novel is very much a presentation, ·from the inside, of the workings of the disturbed, twisted mind of a social misfit, Juan Pablo Castel, who suffers from isolation, loneliness and a sense of persecution. His murder of María Iribarne (the woman with whom he had hoped to establish a meaningful relationship) and his subsequent imprisonment in an asylum are indicators of the futile quest for communication and solidarity in an anonymous and alienating modern world.

Obviously, this socio-psychological investigation is a step forward from documentary social realism. But *El túnel* goes further still, introducing (more strongly than Arlt and even Onetti) an overriding metaphysical dimension. Castel's madness does not make him untypical of humanity. As with Andrés of Donoso's *Coronación* (1957), the madman is closer to the human condition in that his insanity parallels the chaos of the universe and his torment the consequent sense of existential anguish. A feature of Castel's mental imbalance is his perfectionism, his obsession with reason and logic, reflecting an inability to come to terms with loose ends or human inconsistencies: yet this is really suggestive of modern man's shared nostalgia for order and coherence in an age of scepticism and doubt. What happens with Castel is that, unable to find order in an orderless world, he succumbs to the more 'authentic' state of madness – that is, metaphysical awareness. Hence, he describes the transition in his painting from a classical, harmonious style to the mutilated, infernal images of his current work, which is 'como un museo de pesadillas petrificadas, como un Museo de la Desesperanza':[25] a transition, in effect, from aspiration for order to realisation of chaos.

This transition is dramatised most tellingly in Castel's relationship with María. When he sees her eyeing his painting in an apparently understanding manner, he thinks he has spotted a kindred spirit who will bring meaning to his life. The title of the painting, *Maternidad*, together with a string of other maternal references, add a Freudian dimension, hinting that Castel sees her also as a substitute mother figure. But this desire to return to infancy or the womb is equally symbolic of man's yearning to return to the childhood values of certainty and security. This is an impossible quest and, significantly, when Castel kills María, he stabs her in the belly (womb) and breasts (source of infant nourishment), thereby acknowledging the hopelessness of his desires. A similar implication lies behind their sexual dissatisfaction. Sexual activity, with its inevitable disappointments here as in many other Latin American novels, also represents the doomed quest for fulfilment in life: but the desperate attempts to achieve communication or 'fusión' via sexuality merely confirm 'la imposibilidad de prolongarla o consolidarla mediante un acto material' (p.67). Far from bringing communication and therefore meaning to life, the relationship with María accentuates Castel's loneliness and fuels his instability. Hence his comment, 'Tengo que matarte, María. Me has dejado solo' (p.134).

The whole problem is summed up in the image of the tunnel which gives the novel its title. He had hoped that he and María were living in converging tunnels which would eventually unite harmoniously. This, he now accepts, was an 'estúpida ilusión' (p.130). He realises that he is alone and anguished in his tunnel, while those who live outside the tunnel enjoy normal, everyday lives. The point is that life inside the tunnel is based on an awareness of the pettiness and absurdity of life. But insight of this nature is usually suppressed, resulting in the isolation of individuals with such an anti-social outlook. The symbolism of madness therefore implies that in locking away the madman we are burying our true intuition of the real nature of existence.

The basic obsessions of *El túnel* are developed in Sabato's other two novels, *Sobre héroes y tumbas* (1961) and *Abaddón el exterminador* (1974). The more famous former novel, for example, contains a notorious third section entitled *Informe sobre ciegos* in which Fernando Olmos – whose paranoid fear of the blind, like Castel's, is a symbolic fear of evil, chaos, the unknown – undergoes a process of self-destruction as he confronts the dark side of life represented by the hellish, subterranean world inhabited by the fiendish sect of blind people. His act of copulation with the blind woman is a symbolic recognition of his own propensity for vileness and evil, in itself a recognition of the negative nature of life. The idea of a world dominated by evil is an inversion of the orthodox view of an ordered universe watched over by a benign deity. Salvador Bacarisse takes this even further by identifying the two later novels with 'the Gnostic belief that the world is evil, since it was not God that made it, but the Devil'.[26] This connects Sabato's work with other major Latin American novels which exploit the implications of the notion of a mad or evil God: Asturias's *El señor presidente* (1940), and the already mentioned *Pedro Páramo* and *El lugar sin límites*, among others. Moreover, all this is tied in with the question of incest. Fernando is killed by the daughter with whom he had committed incest, while she takes her own life in order to rid herself of her incestuous inclinations; meanwhile, Bacarisse's article on *Abaddón* also identifies an incestuous element in that novel.[27] This links up with the incest theme of *Pedro Páramo* and *Cien años de soledad*. Once again, incest implies a fall from grace, an inversion of values, a world in which traditional beliefs have been turned upside down.

An idea of the importance of Sabato's influence on the new novel can be gleaned from the foregoing comparisons, His role in the reassessment of conventional world views is crucial, but so is his development of compatible techniques. Donoso, for instance, has written of the effect of reading Sabato on his own *El obsceno pájaro de la noche* (1970): '*Sobre héroes y tumbas* también me pareció una novela dirigida directamente contra mis tabúes, más que nada porque me hizo darme cuenta que intentar darle una forma racional a algo que yo mismo estaba viviendo como una obsesión, era un error no sólo de comportamiento, sino literario.'[28] In other words, Sabato's later novels transmit a distorted vision by means of narrative distortion through procedures such as chronological inversion, the use of multiple viewpoints, or the introduction of fantastic episodes. While *El túnel* foreshadowed some of the thematic concerns of the new novel, *Sobre héroes y tumbas* stands (along with other novels) at the gateway of the technical revolution which was to become so apparent in the 1960s. The appearance of *Abaddón* nearly a decade and a half later shows that, as well as being one of those who helped inspire the Boom, Sabato is also one of those who has survived it.

Sabato's 'survival' is not dissimilar to that of Onetti. As well as influencing the new novel they were in turn influenced by it (hence Sabato's appearance as a character in *Abaddón* and his transformation into a bat and Larsen's appearance with a page from a different Onetti novel in *Dejemos hablar al viento* (1979)). However, the experimental elements of that later work were also present in their earlier writing (consider the interior presentation of reality in

El túnel or Brausen's escape from a real city to an unreal town in
La vida breve). Equally Arlt's later work is far from close to
traditional realism. The point is that all of these novelists are linked
to another line of River Plate or Buenos Aires writing more
concerned with metaphysics, philosophical abstraction and ludic
formal games.

A key name here is that of Macedonio Fernández (1874–1952).
Although hardly studied at university level, Macedonio's work
represents one of the most complete breaks with traditional realism
in the history of Latin American letters, for whereas the fiction
examined so far questions the realist novel, Macedonio's rejects it
outright. His greatest work, *Museo de la Novela de la Eterna*,
exemplifies this perfectly. Published posthumously at the height of
the Boom in 1967, the novel (though written many years earlier) was
therefore not 'influential' in the conventional sense of the term, but
was nonetheless an extraordinary precursor of things to come.
Anticipating Borges, it concerned itself only with metaphysics rather
than the social themes of earlier literature. In particular, Macedonio
was concerned with attacking usually held notions of the self and
reality. His view (an extreme form of Idealism) was that there was
no self and no object of the self's attention, but merely a series of
states of perception. Using the novel as a surrogate for reality, he
hoped to shake the reader's sense of internal coherence by
shattering the text's novelistic coherence. Thus the idea of a given
self and a given reality was subverted by the obliteration of
traditional characters and traditional narrative forms, which were
replaced by a new artistic approach – 'belarte'. A typical character
of 'belarte' is the depthless Quizagenio (*Perhaps*-a-genius) whose very
name brings out his uncertain, equivocal nature. As for structure,
the reader's urge for order is frustrated by the novel's fifty-six
prologues and open ending, where another prologue encourages
future readers to edit or rewrite the text. These techniques encourage
the reader himself to enter the text to sort out the mess but fail to
provide the means to do so, and thus the reader's literary
disorientation becomes an equivalent for ontological disorientation,
provoking 'la conmoción de la certeza de ser' or 'el mareo de su
certidumbre de ser'.[29] This is, of course, exactly what much of the
nueva narrativa would later attempt to do. Indeed, the challenge to
common perceptions of reality via philosophical speculation, inversion
of logic, chronological disruption, circular narrative puts Macedonio

in the same league as the writers associated with Boom, while his authorial interventions and foregrounding of the fictional process actually link him to what was to become known as the post-Boom. But the main point is that in the early part of the twentieth century Macedonio Fernández was pushing the novel away from its traditional *criollista* roots towards a new era of problematic and experimental fiction.[30]

The writer who most obviously took up Macedonio's mantle was his friend and fellow Argentinian, Jorge Luis Borges (1899–1986). Though he differed from Macedonio in some respects, Borges was also to become renowned (indeed much more so) for his complex and demanding writing, his philosophical probings, his metaphysical games, his awareness of the pervasive ambiguity of reality, and his desire to move beyond the traditional concerns of literary fiction. It is this questioning of reality which is at the heart of the new narrative as a whole, and hence it is with the spectacularly influential Borges that the main body of this study begins. The following chapter on Asturias, meanwhile, brings Borges together with the other principal precursor of the Boom: *El señor presidente's* surrealistic and universalising presentation of standard Latin American themes marks a watershed in the development of the novel in the region. The process is then taken a stage further with an analysis of Rulfo's *Pedro Páramo* which, written on the threshold of the Boom, is a vital illustration of the techniques of the new novel and its use of the local context for universal, existential explorations. All of which paves the way for a consideration of the Boom proper, and so the next group of chapters deals with the so-called 'big four' of the Boom: Fuentes, Cortázar, García Márquez and Vargas Llosa. Here four of the most important novels of the 1960s are examined. Fuentes's Mexican contexts lead on from Rulfo, while Cortázar's text represents the anti-novel *par excellence*. Meanwhile, the García Márquez novel of the later 1960s switches the emphasis from structural fragmentation to subversion through fantasy. Vargas Llosa, however, is kept to the last, since his work differs from the other three in that, rather than challenging reality, he seeks more to express its complexity via the modernisation of the techniques of realism. The last two chapters are dedicated to a turning point in the story of the new narrative. Donoso's novel marks the culmination of the Boom, while Puig's, written round about the same time, sets off in a new direction, ushering in another stage which is now widely referred to as the post-Boom. This new stage will be the subject of the conclusion and final chapter.

NOTES

1 The civilisation-versus-barbarism polemic stems from the book by Argentina's Domingo Faustino Sarmiento (1811–88) called *Facundo. Civilización y barbarie* (1845). Though Sarmiento's book dealt specifically with the struggle between Unitarians and Federalists in the context of the Rosas dictatorship in Argentina, his views came to be applied to post-independence Latin America as a whole. The notion was that the blame for the brutality and backwardness of Latin America was the 'barbarism' of the people (especially in the interior) who needed to be tamed and 'civilised' by those with more sophisticated European-style values (usually from the cities).

2 Peter R. Beardsell, *'Don Segundo Sombra* and *machismo'*, *Forum for Modern Language Studies*, vol. XVII (1981), pp.302–11.

3 There are several other important Regionalist texts which could have been mentioned here, e.g.: *La vorágine* (1924) by José Eustasio Rivera (Colombia, 1888–1928); *Huasipungo* (1934) by Jorge Icaza (Ecuador, 1906–78); *El mundo es ancho y ajeno* (1941) by Ciro Alegría (Peru, 1909–67).

4 *Modernismo* is too vast and complex to be dealt with here. Effectively launched by the Nicaraguan poet, Rubén Darío (1867–1916), it was innovative in form and language and – though later more Americanist in content – more concerned with art and exoticism than social themes. There were a number of *modernista* novels of influence, like, for example, *Sangre patricia* (1902) by Manuel Díaz Rodríguez (Venezuela, 1868–1927) and *La gloria de don Ramiro* (1908) by Enrique Larreta (Argentina, 1875–1961), which paved the way for more adventurous works such as *Alsino* (1920) by Pedro Prado (Chile, 1886–1952) and the avant-garde *El hombre que parecía un caballo* (1915) by Rafael Arévalo Martínez (Guatemala, 1884–1975). Moreover, *modernismo* was probably a factor in encouraging the psychological dimension of the works of certain essentially realist writers like Horacio Quiroga (Uruguay, 1878–1937) and Eduardo Barrios (Chile, 1884–1963).

5 See, for example, Donald L. Shaw, *Alejo Carpentier* (Twayne, Boston, 1985), p.46.

6 See Roberto González Echevarría, *Alejo Carpentier: The Pilgrim at Home* (Cornell University Press, Ithaca and London, 1977), p.54 ff.

7 Alejo Carpentier, *Los pasos perdidos* (Bruguera, Barcelona, 1979), p.179. All subsequent references will be to this edition and will be included in the text.

8 González Echevarría, *Alejo Carpentier*, p.160.

9 See Donald L. Shaw, *Nueva narrativa hispanoamericana* (Cátedra, Madrid, 1981), pp.86–7.

10 Alejo Carpentier, *El siglo de las luces* (Seix Barral, Barcelona, 1979), p.7.

11 See Julio Ortega, *Poetics of Change. The New Spanish-American Narrative* (University of Texas Press, Austin, 1984), pp.142–5.
12 See González Echevarría, *Alejo Carpentier*, pp.229–33.
13 See ibid., pp.127–8.
14 William Rowe, *Mito e ideología en la obra de José María Arguedas* (Instituto Nacional de Cultura, Lima, 1979), pp.88–114.
15 Rowe, ibid., discusses these episodes on p.79 and p.119 ff.
16 Roa Bastos's next major novel *Yo el Supremo* was not published until 1974 and, though there is obvious continuity, differs sharply from *Hijo de hombre* in several important respects. It seems more appropriate to discuss it in the conclusion in the context of the post-Boom.
17 See Augusto Roa Bastos, *Hijo de hombre* (Losada, Buenos Aires, 1976), p.196. All subsequent references will be to this edition and will be included in the text.
18 Marechal, though important in literary terms, differs from other River Plate authors like Arlt, Onetti, Sabato (considered here) and Eduardo Mallea (Argentina, 1903–82) in that his work is profoundly coloured by his own Catholicism.
19 Shaw, *Nueva narrativa*, p.218.
20 Quoted by Jean Franco in *Spanish American Literature since Independence* (Ernest Benn, London, 1973), p.219.
21 Roberto Arlt, *El juguete rabioso* (Losada, Buenos Aires, 1973), p.52. All subsequent references will be to this edition and will be included in the text.
22 Jack M. Flint, *The Prose Works of Roberto Arlt: A Thematic Approach*, Durham Modern Languages Series HM4 (University of Durham, 1985), p.19.
23 Juan Carlos Onetti, *Juntacadáveres* (Seix Barral, Barcelona, 1983), p.171 All subsequent references will be to this edition and will be included in the text.
24 Peter Turton, 'Para una interpretación de *El astillero* de Juan Carlos Onetti', *Reflexión*, vols III–IV (1974–5), p.290.
25 Ernesto Sabato, *El túnel* (Seix Barral, Barcelona, 1983), p.127.
26 Salvador Bacarisse, '*Abaddón el exterminador*: Sabato's Gnostic eschatology', in *Contemporary Latin American Fiction* (Scottish Academic Press, Edinburgh, 1980), p.92. See also, by the same author, 'Poncho celeste, banda punzó: la dualidad histórica argentina. Una interpretación de *Sobre héroes y tumbas* de Ernesto Sabato', *Cuadernos Hispanoamericanos*, nos. 391–3 (1983), pp.438–54.
27 Bacarisse, '*Abaddón*', p.104.
28 José Donoso, *Historia personal del 'boom'* (Seix Barral, Barcelona, 1983), p.68.
29 See Macedonio Fernández, *Papeles de Recienvenido. Continuación de la nada* (Losada, Buenos Aires, 1944), p.128 and 'Doctrina estética de la novela', *Revista de las Indias*, July 1940, p.417 (published by Germán Arciniegas).
30 It should be noted that Macedonio differs in some respects from those who followed him, most notably in terms of his faith in immortality.

Unlike say, Borges, he is very much a mystic rather than a sceptic. For an excellent fuller analysis, see Jo Anne Engelbert, *Macedonio Fernández and the Spanish American Novel* (New York University Press, New York, 1978).

2

JORGE LUIS BORGES: *FICCIONES*

DONALD LESLIE SHAW

Jorge Luis Borges (1899–1986) was born in Buenos Aires into an old-established middle-class Argentine family with English connections. His education, begun in Argentina, was completed in Geneva during World War I with a Swiss baccalaureate; he never attended a university. Moving with his family to Spain, he began publishing avant-garde poetry in 1919 and, after his return to Buenos Aires in 1921, he was soon recognised as one of the leading young poets. His first eight books, from *Fervor de Buenos Aires* in 1923 to *Discusión* in 1932, were collections of poetry and essays. It was not until 1928 that he began to experiment with imaginative prose. In 1935 he published *Historia universal de la infamia*, a set of odd and freakish tales which constitute the prehistory of his fictional work. One of them, however, 'Hombre de la esquina rosada' has become famous as his first mature tale. It was followed by others, chiefly published in *Sur*, Argentina's most prestigious literary magazine. In 1942 these became *El jardín de senderos que se bifurcan*, incorporated into *Ficciones* two years later. From 1938 to 1946 Borges was employed in a municipal library in the suburbs of Buenos Aires but was dismissed for hostility to the Perón regime and for supporting the Allies during World War II. Thereafter he earned his living chiefly by lecturing and teaching. More collections of short stories followed *Ficciones*: *El Aleph* (1949), *El informe de Brodie* (1970), *El libro de arena* (1975). In the 1950s and 1960s there had been more essays, poetry, criticism and collaborations, notably with another major Argentine writer, Adolfo Bioy Casares (b.1914).

From 1953 to 1973 Borges was Director of the National Library of Argentina and also taught (principally Old English literature) in the University of Buenos Aires. In 1961 he shared with Samuel Beckett the Formentor Prize, the beginning of his real international fame.

After 1955 he was almost totally blind. During the 1960s he once more began to write poetry consistently and published several new collections of verse with great success. By now he was universally recognised as the 'grand old man' of Spanish American letters. More than a score of full-scale critical works and thousands of articles had been written about his work. He had received numerous other prizes and many honorary degrees while lecturing in many parts of the world. Sadly, and inexplicably, he never received the Nobel Prize.

Brought up to be bilingual in Spanish and English, he also spoke French, German and Italian. Before blindness overtook him he had steeped himself in all the major areas of Western literature. He published books on English, North American and Argentine literature, on Dante and on Old Germanic literature, with special reference to the ancient Icelandic sagas, which fascinated him for most of his adult life. He was deeply influenced by Schopenhauer, loved *The Arabian Nights* and constantly reread Stevenson, Chesterton, Kipling, Poe, Henry James and Hawthorne. A sceptic, he was fascinated with religious and metaphysical beliefs and ideas. These have always underpinned his writings and provide the best basis for an approach to his work.

The first eight stories of what was to be *Ficciones* were published as *El jardin de senderos que se bifurcan* in 1942. Two years later they were followed by six more, making up the first (1944) edition. Three more ('El fin', 'La secta del Fénix' and 'El Sur') were added in the second edition (1956).

To understand why the appearance of these tales was a turning point in the history of modern Spanish American fiction, we need to glance at the evolution of the novel in Spanish America earlier in the twentieth century.[1] A key date was 1908, when Argentina's Enrique Larreta published *La gloria de don Ramiro*, the last major novel of the previous creative cycle, that of *modernismo*. Written in coruscating prose, it was a self-consciously artistic evocation of the grand old military and religious tradition of the Golden Age of Spain. Somewhat paradoxically, it inaugurated the period we now associate with the six important novels whose popularity for the first time put Spanish American fiction on the map. The other five were: *Los de abajo* (1915) by Mexico's Mariano Azuela, *El hermano asno* (1922) by Chile's Eduardo Barrios, *La vorágine* (1924) by Colombia's José Eustasio Rivera, *Don Segundo Sombra* (1926) by Argentina's Ricardo Güiraldes and *Doña Bárbara* (1929) by Venezuela's Rómulo Gallegos.

The last five writers of the 'famous six' faced a double imperative. On the one hand they sought to incorporate into their work some of the changes in fictional technique which had been appearing in the European novel. On the other hand they aspired to break away from the imitation of the subject matter of European fiction, especially from imitation of the French realist pattern. They wished to deal instead with specifically Spanish American problems, life-styles and values. For this reason Rivera, Güiraldes and Gallegos turned away from urban environments or those of an idealised countryside and set their novels on the great plains or in the jungles of the vast, empty interior. They thus became the foremost representatives of 'nativist' fiction. In the 1940s the 'famous six' were still the established novelists of Spanish America. It was not simply that some of them were still writing; Gallegos published *El forastero* in 1948, while Barrios scored a major hit with *Gran Señor y rajadiablos* as late as 1949. But equally important is the fact that the decade of the 1930s in Spanish American fiction had been an undistinguished one. Its novelists failed to surpass the achievements of their older contemporaries. They really only extended the thematic range of Spanish American fiction so that it now began to include an interest in the ways of life and outlook of the indigenous Indian population, for example, or in the impact of North American economic imperialism. Without actually marking time, the novel had lost its earlier impetus.

Borges was of course exaggerating when in 1972 he said:

Pensemos que en casi toda la América Latina la literatura no es otra cosa que un alegato político, un pasatiempo folklórico o una descripción de las circunstancias económicas de tal o cual clase de población y que aquí en Buenos Aires ya estamos inventando y soñando con plena libertad.[2]

But the thrust of his assertion is clear. His attitude had long been shared by other major novelists. Cuba's Alejo Carpentier, for example, had already written in the 1960s:

Pensé, desde que empecé a tener conciencia cabal de lo que quería hacer, que el escritor latinoamericano tenía el deber de 'revelar' realidades inéditas. Y sobre todo salir del 'nativismo', del 'tipicismo', de la estampa pintoresca para 'desprovincializar' su literatura, elevándola a la categoría de valores universales.[3]

The diagnosis was the same. Mainstream Spanish American fiction had become stuck in the 1930s in an obsolete creative pattern which was too 'documental', too close to the reality it described.

How was a renovation to be achieved? The prevailing manner of writing was still broadly realistic. With a few honourable exceptions, novelists had been largely content to go on in one way or another reporting reality rather than questioning it. Here was where the change would come about. In part, its roots lay in Surrealism. The Nobel Prizewinner Miguel Ángel Asturias later recognised, like Carpentier, that the European movement, with which both were closely connected in Paris, had opened their eyes to the possibility of exploiting a new dimension of Spanish American reality. For convenience, we can call it Magical Realism. It was based on the astonishment which certain aspects of reality, both historical and contemporary, in the subcontinent can still produce, as well as on the magico-mythical outlook of its indigenous and black inhabitants.

But the true causes of the change lay deeper, in the collapse of confidence in the West of man's ability to perceive 'reality' at all. In a famous affirmation in the twenty-sixth chapter of his masterpiece *El Señor Presidente* (1946) Asturias declared that 'entre la realidad y el sueño la diferencia es puramente mecánica', undermining at one blow our comfortable certainties about our power to understand either ourselves or the world outside ourselves in terms of a one-to-one relationship with 'real' reality. His attitude was increasingly shared by other writers. The leading figure was Borges. He more than anyone else shattered the complacent acceptance by his fellow writers that there was any simple correlation between their sense-impressions and the apparential world outside. That is why *Ficciones* marks a watershed. After its lessons had been digested, it was no longer possible to go on taking 'reality', social, psychological or of any other kind, for granted. What Borges proposed went far beyond what the now somewhat discredited magical realists proclaimed. Among his more important pronouncements are these from *Otras inquisiciones*: reality is 'inasible' ('Nathaniel Hawthorne'); 'No sabemos qué cosa es el universo' ('El idioma analítico de John Wilkins'); 'Es dudoso que el mundo tenga sentido' ('El espejo de los enigmas'); and 'Los hombres gozan de poca información acerca de los móviles profundos de su conducta' ('Anotación al 23 de agosto de 1944'). Time, he reminds us, is a mystery; our sense of ourselves as individuals is perhaps an illusion; if the 'really real' exists, it is questionable whether human language can express it.

In a world no longer seen as governed by a benevolent Providence, in which no reliable absolutes exist, 'toda estrafalaria cosa es posible' (*Discusión*: 'La duración del infierno'). This is the idea of things, the view of life – as bewildering, but interesting – against which Borges's stories are set. But what of us, mankind, the readers? It has been persuasively argued by Alazraki[4] that, in Borges's view, man's characteristic response to his situation is to select from the flux of sense-impressions those which it is comfortable to live with, screening out, as far as possible, the rest. Thus man creates a mental habitat, a construct of reality in which to take refuge from a chaotic universe. For this last, Borges's favourite metaphor is the labyrinth. Why a labyrinth? And what kind of labyrinth? Seen from above, a maze can be perceived to combine order and chaos. Tidily symmetrical in appearance, its walks appear to lead progressively to the centre and allow a return to the outside. But once inside, direction is rapidly lost; the turnings, though regular, bear no relation to the objective. In addition, a Borgesian labyrinth must be thought of as circular, with no outlet. We are born already inside it. At its centre is death; or, in a few privileged cases, an epiphany, or perhaps the discovery of who we really are. What matters is less the centre, which few consciously reach, but the maze itself, the symbol of existence. It has an appearance of predictable regularity, which then turns out to be baffling; or, seen from the other perspective, it presents us with a series of baffling experiences which nevertheless contain teasing hints of design. Recognition of this duality is important: Borges is no mere vulgar sceptic, but one who is prepared to doubt even his own scepticism. There may possibly be an order governing what we think of as reality. So he writes in 'In Memoriam A.R.' (*El hacedor*) of

> El vago azar o las precisas leyes
> Que rigen este sueño, el universo.

But even if 'precise laws' exist to provide explanations, we may have forgotten how to interpret them, or perhaps may never have been programmed to comprehend them.

Borges's best tales, then, are in the nature of fables or parables designed to subvert, often with gentle humour, our comforting presuppositions about ourselves, our place in the universe, or the intelligibility of the universe itself if it is, in fact, more than a dream. In 1965, in a rare moment of revelation – for much of what he has said about his writings is playfully misleading – Borges remarked:

> dans tous mes contes, il y a une partie intelectuelle et une autre
> partie – plus importante je pense – le sentiment de la solitude, de
> l'angoisse, de l'inutilité du caractère mistérieux de l'univers, du
> temps, ce qui est plus important: de nous mêmes, je dirai: de moi-
> même.[5]

Before attempting to illustrate this view of *Ficciones*, one, that is,
which seeks to locate the collection's importance as a landmark in
Spanish American fiction in its subversion of received notions about
reality and about the writer's ability to express it, it is worth
mentioning an alternative interpretation. Sturrock, Del Río and
MacAdam,[6] among others, tend to suggest that Borges's stories are
not about the enigmatic nature of the 'real' at all, but essentially
about the act of writing. We cannot overlook this approach. It is a
possible way of reading the stories. But it is at best reductive, since it
imposes a narrow range of themes on them. At worst, it is
misguided, since it tends to produce interpretations of individual
tales which are unpersuasive. However, it does focus our attention
on the fact that, with *Ficciones*, Spanish American imaginative
writing suddenly becomes more aware of its fictive nature, more
ready to foreground and display its own devices. It thus compels the
reader to recognise what is being read as what it is: fiction. To this
extent *Ficciones* helped to open the way to forms of literature which
allude to their own limitations or parody themselves. In fiction we
think of Puig, the later Donoso and Cuba's Severo Sarduy. A notable
example is Vargas Llosa's *La tía Julia y el escribidor* (1977). Nor can
we afford to overlook the contribution of *Ficciones* to a renewed sense
of the importance of language in fiction, of works of fiction as *hazañas
verbales*, which played such an important role in producing the Boom
novelists' *salto de calidad*.

Cognate with the above-mentioned approach is that associated
with Isaacs and Dauster,[7] for instance, which suggests that it is art
which provides the answer to the chaos of reality, that art imposes
order and meaning, and that this is the ultimate metaphor
underlying Borges's writings. This too is a tenable position. It
appears to resolve the central contradiction of Borges's art: the fact
that he uses meticulously structured forms, in prose or verse, to
express the possibility that the world is mere blind flux. At first sight
it seems undeniable that Borges is privileging the artistic vision. But

it seems hardly in character for him to subvert reality in order to exalt art. Many of his statements poke gentle fun at the role of the creative writer and insist on the limitations of language. For him, art is not an absolute, much less *the* absolute. It seems more likely to be just another construct. Borges does not deny the need for constructs; all he asks is that we should be aware of them for what they are.

Even if the creation of satisfying artistic forms is not an adequate answer to existential chaos and the lack of providential design, Borges's formal achievements, which first became apparent in *Ficciones*, are critically important in another sense. It has sometimes been suggested (by Vargas Llosa[8] among others) that the famous six writers of the early part of this century were in fact 'primitive' in their fictional techniques. This is not strictly true. It is based on the fact that, preoccupied as they were with the discovery and expression of a genuinely Spanish American reality, they tended to see that reality as *unambiguous*, accepting in the realist tradition that what they observed around them on the *llano*, the Pampa, the battlefields of the Mexican Revolution or in the Amazonian jungle was really real. They adjusted their techniques accordingly. Form in literature and art is a metaphor. The characteristic realist novel form, in which an omniscient narrator recounts events and human reactions to them as if the events themselves formed a comprehensible causal sequence, and as if the reactions of the characters were by and large rationally explicable, makes up a reassuring metaphor of an intelligible world.

Borges's world is not such a world. What he had to discover were forms which provided metaphors that are the opposite of reassuring, which do not suggest a predictable world and which in consequence are sometimes less immediately accessible to the reader who is accustomed to passive acceptance of the fictional texts he reads. If reality is an enigma, then the figuring-forth of that enigma must in turn reflect it, not just in terms of theme, but also in terms of form. New wine cannot be put into old bottles: a new, disturbing vision of life cannot be adequately expressed in the old reassuring ways. To take an example: 'El acercamiento a Almotásim' is plainly a work of fiction. But what is its form? It is that of a book review, a conventionally non-fictive form. Similarly, in the postscript to 'Tlön, Uqbar, Orbis Tertius', the narrator refers to the story as an article. 'Tres versiones de Judas' is also cast in the form of an article and 'Funes el memorioso' in the form of a contribution to a symposium of essays. The meaning is self-evident: since we cannot know the really real, there is no difference between fiction and fact; 'created' reality is as real as observed reality and vice versa; any attempt on our part to describe reality is bound to be a fiction.

The world inhabited by the realist novelists is thus radically called into question. The idea of presenting a world in a way which the reader is called upon to recognise as reflecting more or less faithfully a pre-existing reality against which the behaviour of the characters and the truth of the episodes can somehow be checked, and which is somehow more authoritative than the copy, is undermined. The process extends to the reality of ourselves. In a famous passage in 'Magias parciales del Quijote' (*Otras inquisiciones*), Borges writes:

> ¿Por qué nos inquieta que Don Quijote sea lector del *Quijote*, y Hamlet, espectador de *Hamlet?* Creo haber dado con la causa: tales inversiones sugieren que si los caracteres de una ficción pueden ser lectores o espectadores, nosotros, sus lectores o espectadores, podemos ser ficticios.

When Gabriel García Márquez in *Cien años de soledad* speaks of a place near Macondo where 'hasta las cosas tangibles eran irreales' and makes the village priest – the representative of a God-ordained pattern of reality – say to the last Aureliano: 'Ay hijo. . . . A mí me bastaría con estar seguro de que tú y yo existimos en este momento', he is echoing Borges. Similarly, when Brausen in *La vida breve* (1950), by Uruguay's Juan Carlos Onetti, and one of the first important Boom novels, steps out of reality into his private dream of an imaginary city, Santa María, we are conscious of the presence of Borges in the background.

Such a mode of writing often demands a different reader-response. We enjoy the fiction of the nativist writers chiefly through self-identification with the episodes and characters. But we can hardly identify ourselves with Yu Tsun or Funes or the Indian student of 'El acercamiento a Almotásim', they have too little interior life. How then do Borges's stories appeal? The analogy is with the pleasure we get from detective stories or even crossword puzzles, that is, from problem solving. Many of Borges's best stories are puzzling and teasingly demand to be 'cracked'. At the end of a first reading we tend to want to 'unpack' the stories, to understand them more fully, to figure out a deeper meaning and check it by rereading. The result is an increase in reader-satisfaction, especially if, as is often the case, we come to recognise several levels of meaning coexisting in the same tale.

This need to collaborate with the author, to involve oneself more deeply with the text, to read more alertly, has been recognised as of major importance in the approach to the new novel,[9] which has followed Borges's lead. To take an example: in the middle of Rulfo's *Pedro Páramo* there briefly appears a curious, incestuous, Adam-and-Eve-like couple, in whose hut the narrator dies. The episode is pivotal to the novel as a whole. But it is left to the reader to work out, if he can, the meaning. Critics like Ortega and Freeman[10] have shown that it is one of the keys to the novel's mythical dimension. Once we grasp its importance our reception of the novel changes and our response to it is heightened. It would, of course, be false to assert that Borges alone was responsible for encouraging what Julio Cortázar has called the shift from the 'lector-hembra' to the 'lector-macho'. But if we wished to identify the point at which the shift began to occur, we should have to locate it close to the date of publication of *Ficciones*.

Rejection of old-style realism carries with it, as an obvious consequence, the liberation of fantasy. This too is part of what makes *Ficciones* an important landmark. Fantasy, thereafter, blossoms in Spanish American fiction, either in the form of magical realism or in the less self-consciously American form which it takes, for instance, in Cortázar. But we are not dealing with 'pure' fantasy of the kind which we might perhaps associate with Tolkien or with some kinds of science fiction; that is, fantasy for its own sake. The importance of fantasy in Borges, and by extension in Cortázar, García Márquez or more recently Chile's Isabel Allende, is its relation to what we take to be reality. 'Tlön, Uqbar, Orbis Tertius' is a case in point. Like so many of Borges's best tales it changes direction before the end. Most of the story is concerned with a fantastic world which functions as though philosophic idealism, the doctrine that to be is to be perceived, that the mind creates reality, were an accurate description of the way things work. But the ending is different: Tlön is revealed to be a mere verbal creation. All seems well. But then the fantasy begins to invade the 'real' world, a purely verbal construct begins to modify people's lives. Our sense of a secure, predictable universe begins to be undercut.

How does Borges respond? Behind his serene public stance it is not hard to detect hints of despair. But they are offset by an unalterable attachment to the value of human dignity, often expressed in his work in terms of disinterested physical courage, and also by a whimsical humour which is not the least important attribute of *Ficciones* as a landmark text. Spanish American literature before Borges was, with a few notable exceptions, remarkably unfunny. A solemn sense of the writer's responsibility was the rule. But Borges's work, however sobering its implications, does not exclude a sense of fun. 'La Secta del Fénix', which presents universal human sexual behaviour in terms of the activities of a secret society, is an outstanding example. More characteristic is the put-down of the pretensions of those who assert their ability to decipher some of the contents of the books in the Biblioteca de Babel, that is, to be able to reveal some meaning in human experience. Their conclusion is described as the discovery of a Baltic dialect of Guaraní – the language of the natives in Paraguay – with inflections borrowed from classical Arabic! The ultimate unintelligibility of things is greeted with no tragic outcry, but with an amused smile at those who cannot accept it with a measure of detachment.

We may now turn to the stories themselves. Although it has been suggested that there is a paradigmatic Borges story form, a kind of Borgesian 'ur-text', it is in fact difficult to reduce the stories to any such model. However, in the case of *Ficciones*, we can begin by recognising that the motif of the journey or quest links together 'El acercamiento a Almotásim', 'La Biblioteca de Babel', 'El jardín de senderos que se bifurcan', 'La muerte y la brújula', and 'El Sur'. In these stories it functions as a metaphor of man's conscious or unconscious desire to reach a deeper level of knowledge or understanding, a desire which Borges treats rather ironically. The knowledge is either not attained, or if attained is not a source of life-affirming values.

'El acercamiento a Almotásim', the earliest of the stories in *Ficciones*, originally published in 1936, sets the pattern. In contrast to 'Hombre de la esquina rosada', Borges's first widely acclaimed tale, which purported to deal in a broadly realistic way with slum hoodlums, it dispenses at once with anything which might seem to have to do with observation of life. The form of the tale, a pseudo-review of a novel, tells us that the story is a fiction based on a fiction. Next we learn that the 'novel' in question is an altered version of an earlier work of which the original is out of reach. We intuit that there is no such original. Thus we are already at several removes from reality. The formal 'frame' for the story portends the conclusion, for it leads us directly to the notion that nothing exists outside the mind. Inside the frame the story is that of a non-believing Indian student, who is led by a series of seemingly chance events to embark on a pilgrimage in search of the divine. Symbolically the search is circular (portended by the circular tower from which it begins) and merely brings the student back to himself. A footnote complements the earlier implication, that it is the mind which creates 'reality', with the more pantheistic notion that all is in all, that the microcosm includes the macrocosm. But a third idea is also intercalated: that the student's circular quest for the divine is merely the human equivalent of an endless or circular quest for a higher divinity on the part of God himself. The postulation of such a possibility naturally tends to devalue utterly the student's mystical pilgrimage. His aspiration is mocked by God's. All that is left is an infinite spiral.

The quest of the librarian in 'La Biblioteca de Babel' is essentially the same as that of the student. Each seeks an attribute of the divine: the student, goodness; the librarian, truth: an ultimate explanation of things. The difference lies in the more sophisticated setting. The student's India is mere undifferentiated chaos. But the library has the appearance of orderly, predictable and hence reassuring regularity. The implication is obvious: the design implies a designer. But when the books are opened, their contents are unintelligible, albeit they all teasingly use the same alphabet. The library is a clear example of the Borgesian labyrinth: order enfolding chaos. The arrangement of the opening paragraphs is significant. The first emphasises order; the third disorder, via the lack of connection between the letters on the spines of the books and their 'formless and chaotic' contents. But, in between, the librarian has begun his quest. This symbolises man's instinctive aspiration to find an explanation of his existence, in this case the 'master catalogue' of the library, the key to the meaning of the universe. The librarian's comments on the quest expose the delusions to which men fall prey when they seek to reconcile the incomprehensibility of the library's contents, the books (that is, the pure flux of existence), with some over-arching pattern. The fact that the books contain permutations of twenty-five signs implies that man can filter mentally his experiences or sense-impressions into pre-ordained categories. But this does not of itself render them more explicable. Only when we select and rearrange the result arbitrarily, according to our needs, do we make an intelligible book (a habitable construct of reality). We note that the librarian's 'explanations', which culminate in the contradictory postulate that the library (reality) is both infinite and cyclic at the same time, reveal that he is as deluded as the rest of mankind, his fellow librarians.

Close thematically to 'La Biblioteca de Babel' is 'La lotería en Babilonia'. As the library combines regularity with incomprehensibility, so any kind of lottery combines organisation with blind chance. Both the library and the lottery are therefore variants of the labyrinth as metaphors of existence. Borges's problem in the tale is how to convert the familiar idea of a lottery by gradual stages into such a metaphor. Much of the pleasure of reading the story comes from identifying these stages. We notice that as each modification takes place the lottery becomes not only more like life, but also more logical. The first reform imposes symmetry: as there are winners who receive more cash than they paid, so there are losers who lose more than the cost of the ticket. At the same time money ceases to be the only stake. A second reform renders participation secret, free and obligatory: now Babylonians are born into the lottery as they are born into existence. The identification life = lottery seems already total. But a further reform is still necessary: to subject the workings of the lottery itself to chance and to render it all-embracing. At this point the metaphor is complete; all is 'un infinito juego de azares'. It is, in fact, a double metaphor, for it is the product of the devotion of the Babylonians to logic and symmetry. Borges seems to be implying not only that life is governed by pure chance, but that the more we try to regulate it, the more chaotic it becomes. Man's mental processes serve only to complicate further what is already sufficiently unknowable.

Even before all the reforms have been described, Borges has already begun to shift the emphasis from the lottery itself to the Babylonians and their outlook: that is, from the way life is to the way we look at it. The Babylonians, subjected to a life dominated by blind chance, submerged in total chaos, nevertheless prefer to envisage existence as governed by 'las operaciones de la Compañía'. Like the librarian of Babel, they cannot give up the idea of an ultimate guiding hand. As he sees the unintelligibility of the books as less significant than the regular construction of the library, so they see the workings of chance as a mere interpolation of the unpredictable into the 'orden del mundo'. Borges is plainly satirising man's determination to postulate a divine pattern behind events. The history of 'la Compañía' (which, he reminds us, is shot through with fiction) is the history of the Church and its teachings about a God who moves in bafflingly mysterious ways.

A second group of tales ('El jardín de senderos que se bifurcan', 'La muerte y la brújula' and 'El Sur') show us men who, unlike the student in 'El acercamiento. . .' and the librarian of Babel, actually reach the centre of their private labyrinths. But only to find unhappy consequences. 'El jardín de senderos que se bifurcan' is in appearance an ingenious World War I spy story, in which the protagonist, Yu Tsun, finds an unexpected way to alert his German paymasters to the danger of a British offensive. But once we arrive at the core of the tale, the interview between Yu Tsun and his victim Albert, we realise that the story has acquired a new and profound theme: that of time, the foremost of all Borges's preoccupations. The directions Yu Tsun receives for finding Albert's house suggest to him those for moving through a labyrinth. This in turn reminds him of a baffling novel written by one of his ancestors and mysteriously associated with a labyrinth. The first part of his interview with Albert dispels the mystery: the novel was the labyrinth. By a tragic irony Yu Tsun finds himself compelled to kill the man who has solved a long-standing family puzzle. If the murder had taken place at this point, the spy story would merely have framed a familiar concept, that of the spatial world as a labyrinth, with a cruel irony at its centre. But the recognition vouchsafed to Yu Tsun is different. What really gives us the illusion of understanding reality is not just being able to perceive it spatially. It is our tendency to perceive it in reassuring terms of cause and effect. But such terms are temporal: cause precedes effect. We impose a time scheme, that is, an order, by organising our perceptions chronologically, and thus grant them a seeming intelligibility. But what if our time scheme were based on a false or imperfect premise? Suppose our idea of time were dictated by the need to create a habitable construct of reality and bore no relation to, or were a childish simplification of, time as it equally well might be: not linear and progressive at all, but labyrinthine, with lines of time crisscrossing each other in all directions, only one of them being perceptible to us? Not content with offering us a spatial labyrinth as a symbol of the world, Borges grafts on to it a temporal labyrinth. Prepared for this by the amount of insight he had enjoyed on his way to Albert's house, Yu Tsun becomes aware of a myriad of time dimensions in which both might exist. As in other Borges tales, what had begun as a mere physical adventure has turned into an intellectual one. But as the awareness is granted, Yu Tsun's pursuer arrives and he is compelled to carry out his murderous plan. The killing of Albert ingeniously solves a concrete problem for his murderer. But what had seemed to Yu Tsun worth the sacrifice of his own life is rendered utterly insignificant by his discovery, and that discovery he owes to his victim. Insight, for Borges, is nearly always insight into the chaos and horror of reality.

But he did not wish, unlike some modern writers, to mirror that chaos in the form of his stories. Asked in 1976 why he enjoyed detective stories, he replied: 'frente a una literatura caótica, la novela policial me atraía porque era un modo de defender el orden, de buscar formas clásicas, de valorizar la forma'.[11] Interesting as the remark is, it is not the whole story. If Borges enjoyed the careful plotting and the intellectually satisfying design of successful detective stories, he also knew from the example of Chesterton that they could readily be adapted to serve as metaphors of search in a puzzling universe. This is why a number of his stories loosely follow the model of a detective story, with an initial problem, an exploration or discussion of possible solutions and a final explanation. The problem of the detective story as a metaphor is that it implies the possibility of arriving at a solution through rational enquiry; this is certainly not Borges's standpoint. Hence his best-known detective story is a deliberate parody of the genre.

'La muerte y la brújula' is in fact a detective story turned inside out. The first indication of this is that the pedestrian, Watson-like Treviranus is right all along in his interpretation of events, while the Holmes figure, Lönnrot, eventually becomes the criminal's victim. Part of the reason for this inversion of roles is given at the end of the first paragraph with the notation: 'Lönnrot se creía un puro razonador.' His dismissal of Treviranus's commonsense suggestions and his resolve to see in two murders and the scenario for a third an intellectual riddle to be solved by rigorously rational means leads him directly and uncritically to his death. So we are entitled to see in the tale an anti-rationalist parable, a warning against trying to force a rationally acceptable interpretation on to the events of experience, which will often refuse to fit the pattern. Once more Borges is preoccupied with man's inveterate tendency to grasp at whatever offers the hope of imposing an order on the chaos of life. 'Bastaba', he writes in 'Tlön, Uqbar, Orbis Tertius', 'cualquier simetría con apariencia de orden – el materialismo dialéctico, el antisemitismo, el nazismo – para embelesar a los hombres.'

So far, so good. But what about Scharlach? Critics from Gallagher to Fama[12] have recognised that in addition to containing an implicit critique of nationalism, the tale can also be seen to have an 'undercurrent místico' like 'El acercamiento a Almotásim'. Lönnrot's quest becomes 'un camino místico'.[13] There are too many references to God (The tetragrammaton (= JHVH), the 'Nombre' (always capitalised), the Trinity (Ginzberg, Ginsburg, Gryphius)) for this to escape notice. Gallagher's view that perhaps 'the criminal is God, and there emerges the image of a God who deliberately plants false clues, who deliberately goads man's intellectual vanity into the belief that he is arriving at a solution only to laugh in his face at the end by killing him'[14] seems to indicate the direction in which the story is pointing. As Borges inverts the pattern of the traditional detective story so that it is the criminal who hunts the detective, so he inverts the traditional Christian image of a benevolent God. This is another feature of *Ficciones* which was to become commonplace in subsequent Spanish American fiction.[15]

In 'El Sur' we once more see the interweaving of two themes. The first is concerned with reaching the centre of one's own private labyrinth. Earlier Borges had written in the tenth chapter of *Evaristo Carriego*: 'Yo he sospechado alguna vez que cualquier vida humana, por intricada y populosa que sea, consta en realidad de un momento: el momento en que el hombre sabe para siempre quien es.' The magical moment may be a moment of betrayal as in 'Biografía de Tadeo Isidoro Cruz' in *El Aleph*, or of discovery of the non-existence of the individual personality as in 'El fin'. In each case there comes a flash of insight. Here what Dahlmann suddenly discovers, in the face of death, is his fundamental Argentine-ness, foreshadowed in the opening paragraph. He chooses to die in a knife fight, that most traditionally Argentine of deaths. We notice that this traditionalist theme is inserted into a wider cultural context, that of the code of honour of the Hispanic race as a whole, since it is this which impels Dahlmann to accept the challenge to fight. Both the national and the racial traditions are implicit in the figure of the old gaucho who throws him the weapon he needs. Since Dahlmann is suspiciously like Borges himself, who was also a librarian and suffered a similar illness, this theme seems also to include a wish-fulfilment fantasy by a writer who envied the courage of his military ancestors and who freely admitted that much of his fiction was autobiographical. Nor does this exclude the possibility of recognising in Dahlmann's experience a universal significance, since revelatory test experiences come to us all.

The other theme of 'El Sur' brings us back to the subversion of reality. As the tale proceeds, a series of hints are dropped that all may not be as it seems. Borges himself gave the clue by remarking to Irby[16] that possibly everything after the onset of Dahlmann's illness might be a mere hallucination caused by the illness itself. Some critics, notably Phillips and Gertel,[17] regard this as the only way to read the tale. Others, including Alazraki and Hall,[18] insist on the ambiguity of Borges's procedure. How are we to interpret the fact that the owner of the store or snack bar knows Dahlmann's name, the presence of the old gaucho (in 1939!) and the reference back to the clinic in the last sentence of the story, unless Dahlmann is dreaming? Be the answer as it may, the implications remain: the world of wakefulness and that of dreaming are not separate worlds; we cannot readily tell them apart. But if that is so, Dahlmann's discovery of his essential Argentine-ness, his sense of honour and his act of courage are all perhaps part of a hallucination.

There is clearly not only scepticism here, but also a certain irony. Irony implies a measure of detached awareness in the ironist of the way things tend not to turn out as we hope or expect and hence to mock our aspirations. The greater the discrepancy between anticipation and reality, the more bitter the irony. But only if, in the case of fiction, the characters suffer enough to involve us, the readers. In Borges this is rarely the case, for, as we have seen, his characters tend to have little or no emotional life. Where emotions appear, they tend to be 'told' not 'shown', as when we read the detached description of Dahlmann's hellish pain while he is suffering from septicaemia. Consequently, Borgesian irony tends to be resigned and unobtrusive situational irony, suggested, but not insisted upon. The characters accept it with dignity (Lönnrot), remorse (Yu Tsun), even, in the case of the wizard in 'Las ruinas circulares', with initial relief. Irony in literature is a warning not to expect life to conform tidily to our plans. Thus, in 'Las ruinas circulares', 'Funes el memorioso' and 'El milagro secreto', the protagonists are granted, like Lönnrot, a kind of boon, only to find that it mocks the recipient.

The mockery in 'Las ruinas circulares' begins with the adjective in the title. Nothing in a Borges story is ever there by chance, whether it is a reference to a mask factory in 'La lotería en Babilonia' or to the statues (including one of Hermes, with twin faces) in the garden at Triste-le-Roy. There are even certain call-signs such as the word *vértigo*, which always signals the approach of the critical moment, or the number 1001, which implies unreality. Colours, especially grey, yellow and red, are commonly symbolic. In the same way, references to circularity and to circular objects (the moon, the gramophone record, the circle of light of the lamp, the clock face in 'El jardín de senderos que se bifurcan', the circular tower and circular quest in 'El acercamiento a Almotásim') are always highly significant. Circularity implies futility: in this case the circular ruins prefigure the circular destiny of the wizard.

The boon granted to him is that of creating something 'real' out of a mere dream. This can be interpreted in more than one way. Perhaps it signifies that what seems to be the product of individual creativity is created not *by* the artist or writer in question but *through* him by the collective mind or the mind of God. In that case the story would be an allegory of the production of art. On the other hand, if we shift the emphasis from what is created to the creator, we see that by adding something to reality, he gives proof of his own autonomous existence. These two interpretations can be made into one, as they were by the Spanish author Unamuno in *Amor y pedagogía* (1902), where the proof of existence is the addition of something by the individual to God's pre-ordained plan, as an actor may add an ad lib to a script. What underlies the stories both of Unamuno and Borges is the question of ultimate human reality. For Unamuno there was still a remnant of hope that this was guaranteed by the existence of God. Not so for Borges. His story uses interior reduplication to suggest that the wizard is as unreal as his 'son'. By extension, we too may be unreal. For as we saw in the earlier quotation from 'Magias parciales del Quijote', this undermining of the reality of the self is precisely the effect produced by interior reduplication. The circularity can be extended to include a God who dreams the God who dreams the wizard, by analogy with the God who seeks a God just as the student of 'El acercamiento a Almotásim' in turn seeks him; particularly in view of Borges's poem 'Ajedrez II' (*El hacedor*) which contains the key question:

¿Qué Dios detrás de Dios la trama empieza
De polvo, y tiempo y sueño y agonías?

However we finally interpret it, 'Las ruinas circulares' is concerned with illusion. So, too, is 'Funes el Memorioso'. One of our intellectual illusions is that greater conscious awareness is always life-enhancing. Both in 'Funes', 'La escritura del Dios' and 'El Aleph' Borges ridicules this supposition, remarking thankfully in the last, after receiving a vision of the totality of the universe: 'felizmente, al cabo de unas noches de insomnio, me trabajó otra vez el olvido'. Earlier in 'La postulación de la realidad' (*Discusión*) he had explained that if we were unable to screen out most of reality, selecting only what we are able to cope with, life would be impossible. The very nature of perception itself is selective. It follows that adaptation to life means learning what to forget. The ironic 'boons' that Funes receives are precisely those of heightened perception and of remembering the totality of what he perceives. This is a Midas story. Which of us has not wished that our perceptions were clearer and our memories more tenacious? As Midas was granted the golden touch so Funes is granted ultra-sharp awareness combined with perfect recollection. The consequence, instead of being enriching, is crushing. Funes becomes a freak, so overwhelmed with perceptions that he is unable to think synthetically, to categorise. He sees the world for what it is: pure chaotic flux.

Hladík in 'El milagro secreto' is also granted his heart's desire: to complete a work of art. Like Dahlmann, Hladík has much in common with Borges, including a sense that art is the secret justification of his existence. In 'Mateo, XXV, 30' (*El otro, el mismo*) Borges reproaches himself:

Has gastado los años y te han gastado
y todavía no has escrito el poema.

So too Hladík, facing the prospect of the firing squad, longs to finish his drama and is miraculously granted his aspiration. At first it seems that the story is in a different category from 'Las ruinas circulares'. But irony rapidly supervenes. What happens is virtually a parody of a miracle; for a secret miracle is worthless. The function of miracles is to reveal the intervention of a benevolent deity in the workings of the world. Hladík's miracle dies with him; it reveals nothing, and the story of it is a 'fiction'. A further irony arises from the fact that the drama which is miraculously completed itself subverts the notion of a coherent and meaningful world, since its themes are delirium and circularity. The miracle is once again a mockery. But the story is interesting also from a different point of view. Like 'El jardín de senderos que se bifurcan' it has at its centre the mystery of time. Time as we usually conceive it is for the sceptical Borges probably no less an illusion than space or matter. 'Negados el espíritu y la materia, que son continuidades', he writes in 'Nueva refutación del tiempo' (*Otras inquisiciones*), 'negado también el espacio, no sé qué derecho tenemos a esa continuidad que es el tiempo.' Time is ultimately discontinuous: an endless succession of discrete, though infinitely fleeting, individual instants. Each of these instants is autonomous and each constitutes time's only reality. The cat in 'El Sur' lives in the eternity of the instant. It is this that is granted to Hladík.

In regard to all the stories so far discussed we perceive the need on the reader's part to distinguish between the actual events of the tales and their deeper implications. 'Pierre Menard, autor del Quijote' and 'Examen de la obra de Herbert Quain', which are specifically about literary creation, serve to illustrate the contention that this is in fact the way to read Borges's stories. In one sense the theme of 'Pierre Menard...' is close to that of 'Las ruinas circulares'. Menard, like the wizard, is trying by means of the imagination to perform an impossible task: to rewrite *Don Quixote* in the same words that were used by Cervantes, but as an original work. The idea that books are written out of books and not out of observation of life is a clear inference. But it is not the only one. Nor is it enough to notice that words alter their meanings and associations as time goes on, so that no book written in the past can be read today as it once was read. There is more: for Menard to be able to achieve his object there would not only have to be something in the nature of 'eternal return' present in reality, but more particularly a kind of recurrent determinism, since we cannot conceive of the act of creation separately from all that which contributes to the formation of the writer's mind. Herbert Quain's works in their turn remind us of the book/labyrinth of Ts'ui Pên in 'El jardín de senderos que se bifurcan', which attempted to include all possible endings. Quain's *April March* attempts to include an arbitrary number of beginnings. In both cases we are not far from the world of Tlön in which novels habitually 'abarcan un solo argumento con todas las permutaciones imaginables'. The repetition of the idea is partially motivated by Borges's desire to satirise the artificiality of much realist fiction in which episodes are presented in a linear chronological way. But at a deeper level, to which the reference to 'los demiurgos y los dioses' in 'Examen. . .' directs our attention, Borges is reminding us once more of our ingrained tendency to select from reality and experience in order to make our construct. The form of *April March* symbolises our desire to order events causally. Its plots operate in reverse because we cannot impose predictability on the future. But the result is no less artificial. Man tries to simplify; the 'higher powers', meanwhile, continue to shuffle infinite and infinitely interconnected series of causes and effects, whose complexity fiction cannot even begin to reflect.

We remain with three stories of treachery, guilt and betrayal: 'La forma de la espada', 'Tema del traidor y del héroe' and 'Tres versiones de Judas', together with 'El fin'. The way in which the meeting of a character with one who is in some sense his 'double' (Moon and his comrade, Lönnrot and Scharlach) tends to end in death has been plausibly traced to Stevenson's influence on Borges.[19] But we can still discern that of Chesterton in 'Tema. . .' where, as in 'The man who was Thursday', an unaccountable series of events turns out to have been the work of an individual, Nolan. Nolan succeeds single-handedly in imposing his will on reality. Once more the implications have to do with order and chaos. Nolan imposes an order on historical events, certainly; but what kind of order? On the one hand it is vaguely repetitive, its circularity again suggesting futility. But more importantly it is merely a human construct, partly borrowed from art. By an act of imagination Nolan not only patterns his present, but conditions the behaviour of Ryan in the future. His achievement is grandiose, but it undermines all confidence in our ability to understand the past.

One of Borges's most disconcerting concepts is that which links him to some forms of the Theatre of the Absurd (Beckett, Stoppard): the non-existence of human individuality. Not content with questioning our confidence in the 'real' outside ourselves, he questions too what we hold most dear: our own unique selfhood. Thus in 'La forma de la espada' the originality of the narrative strategy lies in the way Moon, the traitor, tells his story from the standpoint of the victim, only revealing his true identity in the trick ending. Borges hints at the meaning when Moon remarks: 'acaso Schopenhauer tiene razón; yo soy los otros, cualquier hombre es todos los hombres.' We sense that, as in the case of Lönnrot and Scharlach, there is a deliberate attempt to blur the difference between the betrayer and the betrayed. So that if, at one level, this is a crime-and-punishment story in which Moon's expiation of his treachery is his compulsion to seek the contempt of others by the particular way in which he tells his story, this is only the outer level. The inner level is not moral but metaphysical.

This is confirmed by 'El fin'. Here the apparent theme is not treachery but vengeance. The story evokes, with additions and embellishments, two episodes from José Hernández's (1834–86) nineteenth-century narrative poem *Martín Fierro* (1872 and 1879). These are Martín's successful knife fight with a negro and a singing contest later in the poem. Martín's killer after the contest turns out to be the brother of his earlier victim. Again the story has a trick ending in that the identities of the two antagonists are not revealed until the penultimate paragraph, just as Moon's is not revealed until the end of 'La forma de la espada'. This seems to be the point of the tale; but it is not. The climactic closing line returns to the inner theme of the earlier story; '. . .ahora no era nadie. Mejor dicho era el otro.' Recognition of the fact that there may be no continuity of the personality except through memory, which is fallible, or through ongoing dispositions or traits, which are unreliable, opens the door in this case to the idea that the repetition of an action identifies the agent with whoever committed the act previously. As the negro kills Martín he repeats Martín's action in killing his brother. By the same token, he inherits the weariness, the sense of guilt and the sense of futility which had haunted Martín thereafter, and thus, in a way, 'becomes' Martín.

'Tres versiones de Judas' represents the culmination of the idea. Here Borges applies the concept of the oneness of betrayer and betrayed to the archetypal examples: Christ and Judas. Borges gradually induces us to consider the possibility of inverting the positions in which we usually place Christ and Judas so that the true redeeming sacrifice is made by the God, not as Christ but as Judas. If previously he had tried to subvert our comfortable presuppositions about how the universe works, or about our own individuality, here he slyly questions one of our central spiritual assumptions. *Tout se tient.*

To conclude: *Ficciones* was not a completely isolated phenomenon of the 1940s, since the process of superseding old-style realism had already begun in Europe before the end of the nineteenth century and in Hispanic letters took a great stride forward early in this century with Unamuno's development of the *nivola*. There were important predecessors of Borges in Spanish America, notably Macedonio Fernández. But the importance of *Ficciones* as a foundation building-block of the new novel in Spanish America is indisputable. Fuentes has placed Borges along with Asturias as the two founding fathers of the Boom.[20] Donoso described himself as 'deslumbrado' by his first reading of Borges and as having rushed to imitate him.[21] The list could easily be extended. Borges was followed by a phalanx of new novelists who shared at least some of his ideas about reality and who were no less resolved to find new narrative strategies to express them. Only in some areas of the post-Boom has confidence in observed reality begun falteringly to revive. But it is still too soon to doubt Cabrera Infante's assertion that: 'No hay un solo escritor hispanoamericano que escriba ahora y que pueda echar a un lado la influencia de Borges.'[22]

NOTES

1 Much of what follows over the next few pages is discussed at greater length in Ch. 1.
2 Cited in Fernando Sorrentino, *Siete conversaciones con Jorge Luis Borges* (Pardo, Buenos Aires, 1974), p. 120.
3 Alejo Carpentier, in Salvador Arias (ed.), *Recopilación de textos sobre Alejo Carpentier* (Casa de las Américas, Havana, 1977), p. 19.
4 Jaime Alazraki, 'Tlön y Asterión: metáforas epistemológicas', *Nueva Narrativa Hispanoamericana*, vol. I, no. 2 (1971), pp. 21–33.
5 Cited in Georges Charbonnier, *Entretiens avec Jorge Luis Borges* (Gallimard, Paris, 1967), p. 20.
6 See John Sturrock, *Paper Tigers* (Clarendon Press, Oxford, 1977); Alfred MacAdam, *Textual Confrontations* (Chicago University Press, Chicago, 1987); Carmen Del Río, *Jorge Luis Borges y la ficción* (Universal, Miami, 1983).
7 Frank Dauster, 'Notes on Borges's labyrinths', *Hispanic Review*, vol. 30 (1962), pp. 142–8; N.D. Isaacs, 'The labyrinth of art in four *Ficciones* of Jorge Luis Borges', *Studies in Short Fiction*, vol. 6 (1969), pp. 383–94.
8 Mario Vargas Llosa, 'Primitives and creators', *Times Literary Supplement*, no. 3481, 14 Nov. 1968, pp. 1287–8.
9 Gustav Siebenmann, 'Técnica narrativa y éxito literario', *Iberoromania*, vol. 7 (1978), pp. 50–66.
10 George Ronald Freeman, *Paradise and Fall in Rulfo's Pedro Páramo*

(CIDOC, Cuernavaca, Mexico, 1970); the gist is more easily available in Spanish as 'La caída de la gracia' in Joseph Sommers (ed.), *La narrativa de Juan Rulfo* (Sepsetentas, Mexico City, 1974), pp. 67–75. Julio Ortega, '*Pedro Páramo*', in *La contemplación y la fiesta* (Monte Ávila, Caracas, 1969), pp. 17–30; in English in his *Poetics of Change* (University of Texas Press, Austin, 1984), pp. 33–41.

11 Cited in Andrés Avellaneda, *El habla de la ideología* (Sudamericana, Buenos Aires, 1983), p. 43.

12 D.P. Gallagher, *Modern Latin American Literature* (Oxford University Press, Oxford, 1973), p. 102; Antonio Fama, 'Análisis de "La muerte y la brújula" de Jorge Luis Borges', *Bulletin Hispanique*, vol. 85 (1983), pp. 161–73.

13 Fama, 'Análisis de "La muerte. . ." ', p. 171.

14 Gallagher, *Modern Latin American Literature*, p. 103.

15 See my 'Inverted Christian imagery and symbolism in modern Spanish American fiction', *Romance Studies*, no. 10 (1987), pp. 71–82.

16 James Irby, 'Encuentro con Borges', *Universidad de México*, vol. 16, no. 10 (1962), p. 8. Also in book form: *Encuentro con Borges* (Galerna, Buenos Aires, 1968), p. 34.

17 Allen Phillips, ' "El Sur" de Borges', *Revista Hispánica Moderna*, vol. 29, no. 2 (1963), pp. 27–45; Zunilda Gertel, ' "El Sur" de Borges', *Nueva Narrativa Hispanoamericana*, vol. 1, no. 2 (1971), pp. 35–55.

18 Jaime Alazraki, *Versiones, Inversiones, Reversiones* (Gredos, Madrid, 1977), pp. 27–45; J.B. Hall, 'Borges' "El Sur": A "Jardín de senderos que se bifurcan" ', *Iberoromania*, vol. 3 (1975), pp. 71–7.

19 Daniel Balderston, *El precursor velado: R.L. Stevenson en la obra de Borges* (Sudamericana, Buenos Aires, 1985), pp. 95–102.

20 Cited in Helmy F. Giacoman, *Homenaje a Carlos Fuentes* (Las Américas, New York, 1971), p. 60.

21 José Donoso, *Historia personal del boom*, 2nd edn (Seix Barral, Barcelona, 1983), p. 33.

22 Guillermo Cabrera Infante, interview with Rita Guibert, *Revista Iberoamericana*, vol. 37 (1971), p. 552.

3

MIGUEL ÁNGEL ASTURIAS: *EL SEÑOR PRESIDENTE*

GERALD MARTIN

Miguel Ángel Asturias was born in Guatemala City in October 1899, one year after Manuel Estrada Cabrera became president of the Guatemalan Republic, a position he occupied as dictator until his overthrow, in which Asturias participated, in 1920. Asturias's father was a lawyer by profession, like Estrada Cabrera himself, and was forced to quit his post as judge due to political difficulties with the dictator. Had it not been for Asturias, Estrada Cabrera would by now have fallen into relative oblivion as just one of many ruthless Latin American dictators, but *El Señor Presidente* (1946) has ensured that this tyrant's notoriety will live on as long as Latin American fiction is read. The novel's central themes, inextricably woven together, are oppression, evil, distortion, terror and imprisonment, and – less obviously but unmistakably – their opposites. Asturias's treatment of these motifs affords a classic example of the way in which lived experience is converted into art, which then itself becomes part of history.[1]

The Asturias family fled from the terrors of the capital city to the small provincial town of Salamá in 1903, and it was there that the young Miguel Ángel first experienced the Guatemalan interior and the native Indian inhabitants which were to be so influential in his later life and work. This period of his life is recaptured in the magical prose of *El Alhajadito* (1961). In 1907 the family returned to the capital and the boy began his formal education in church primary schools. Although his mother was a teacher, his parents now set up a general store in La Parroquia, the oldest and most traditional part of the city, in order to make ends meet, given the loss of the ex-judge's professional income. The business at this time was mainly directed to supplying provisions to Indians and Ladinos from out of town,[2] though the mother would later run a smaller general grocery store for the rest of her life.

In 1912 the young Asturias, elder of two sons, began his secondary education in the Instituto Nacional de Varones, and later enrolled, first in the Medical Faculty, and then, in 1917, in the Law Faculty, in the University of San Carlos. By this time Estrada Cabrera had been in power for almost two decades, but 1917 marks the beginning of a decisive movement against him, and Asturias always maintained that the great earthquake of that year, which destroyed much of the city and forced the inhabitants to camp out in the streets and squares together, made a significant practical and symbolic contribution to the tyrant's overthrow. When in 1919 Cabrera attempted to have himself re-elected once more, a movement of opposition parties, workers and students combined to overthrow him and in 1920 the dictator was captured and arrested. Asturias, who had been active in the student movement and had himself been briefly jailed by Cabrera, interviewed the ex-dictator in prison and was secretary to the tribunal which tried and sentenced him.

In 1922 Asturias graduated, but practised law only briefly. In that year he wrote 'Los mendigos políticos', a short story which in time would become the first chapter of *El Señor Presidente*. In 1923 his undergraduate thesis 'El problema social del indio', was published, the first work of its kind to appear in Guatemala. Between them, these two works gave an early indication of the directions – politics and indigenism – in which his artistic development would go.

By this time, however, the novice writer was in personal danger again, having agreed to defend a soldier accused of murdering a superior. When a close friend was beaten and crippled by the military, Asturias's father bought him a one-way ticket to Liverpool (the episode is fictionalised in *Viernes de Dolores* (1978)), and the young ex-lawyer spent the next ten years in Europe. The plan was for him to study economics at the University of London but after five months the lure of Paris in the *années folles* proved too strong and Asturias moved there in 1924, to study ethnology at the Sorbonne under Georges Raynaud, work as a correspondent for the new Guatemalan newspaper *El Imparcial*, but above all to carry out research in the university of life and become a writer. During the next ten years he travelled most of the Old World, made a return trip to Guatemala in 1928, visiting Cuba on the way, and met many of the leading Latin Americans of his generation, as well as international celebrities from Unamuno and Blasco Ibáñez to Joyce, Valéry and Picasso, from Conan Doyle and Krishnamurti to

Mussolini. During this period of intense experience the young writer also worked hard: by the time he returned to Guatemala in 1933, when the fall in coffee prices following the slump had made it impossible for Guatemalans to sustain themselves abroad, Asturias had translated Raynaud's versions of the *Popol Vuh* and the *Anales de los xahil* into Spanish, and had written more than 500 newspaper articles, scores of poems, numerous short stories, the dazzling *Leyendas de Guatemala* (1930), the first draft of *El Alhajadito* and, with the exception of a few pages added later, *El Señor Presidente*, his most famous novel, completed by 1933 but not finally published until 1946.

The reason for the delay was that on his reluctant return to Guatemala in 1933 the country was in the grip of another ferocious dictatorship, that of the fascist-inclined colonel, Jorge Ubico, in power from 1931 to 1944. There can be little doubt that had Asturias tried to publish the novel he would have paid for it with his life. Thus it was that a young writer who seemed in 1930 to have the world at his feet, with the newly published *Leyendas* acclaimed by no less an authority than Paul Valéry, now had to endure twelve years of silence, humiliation and even self-betrayal, years which coincided with the rise of Hitler and Mussolini, the Stalinist purges, the defeat of the Republicans in the Spanish Civil War and the horrors of World War II, one of the darkest periods in history. Asturias published almost nothing during this period, turned to drink, embarked upon a disastrous marriage which produced two sons and much tortured poetry, and by the time of the Guatemalan Revolution of 1944 seemed to have lost his way in life, both artistically and politically.

Nevertheless, the new president, Juan José Arévalo, was an old friend and sent the ageing bohemian off as cultural attaché to Mexico City and then Buenos Aires, undoubtedly the two most vibrant centres of Spanish American culture this century. In the former Asturias widened his acquaintance with Amerindian culture and history, and in the latter married Blanca Mora y Araujo, who was writing a thesis on him and had the strength of character necessary to sort out his problems and manage his career. The publication of *El Señor Presidente* in Mexico in 1946 had been at Asturias's own expense, in an edition hardly anyone had read. In 1948 it was republished in Buenos Aires and became an overnight sensation. The appearance of the even more audacious *Hombres de maíz* in 1949 confirmed that in Asturias Latin America had discovered one of its greatest novelists. At this point however Asturias changed direction and his writing took on a more overtly political turn. Between 1950 and 1960 he wrote his famous *Trilogía bananera* (*Viento fuerte* (1950); *El papa verde* (1954); *Los ojos de los enterrados* (1960)), about the exploitation of Guatemalan land and labour by the US United Fruit Company, a series which made him Latin America's best known 'committed' writer in an age heavily influenced by Sartre's existentialism, on the one hand, and Soviet socialist realism on the other. In 1954 the basic truth of Asturias's analysis was exemplified by the overthrow, with the connivance of the United States, of the Guatemalan Revolution's second government led by the radical nationalist President Árbenz. Asturias, who was Guatemalan Ambassador in El Salvador at the time, went into exile, where most leading Guatemalan intellectuals have remained ever since, and wrote the furiously anti-imperialist stories of *Weekend en Guatemala* (1954).

For the next twelve years the writer and his wife lived mainly in Buenos Aires, until in 1962 his support for the Cuban Revolution led to a brief period of imprisonment, following which, ever poorer, they resided in Italy until 1966, when Asturias was awarded the Lenin Peace Prize. That same year Julio César Méndez Montenegro, the first civilian president for many years, offered the exiled writer the Guatemalan ambassadorship in Paris, and Asturias accepted, hoping to contribute to the peace process in Guatemala. As things turned out, this period saw the intensification of guerrilla struggle in the country (Asturias's elder son Rodrigo has been a leading figure in these campaigns over the last twenty-five years) and the beginnings of US-planned counter-insurgency campaigns everywhere in the continent, and especially in Guatemala. In 1967, at the height of the Boom of the Latin American novel, and in the year that García Márquez's *Cien años de soledad* was published and Che Guevara was killed, Asturias became the first Latin American novelist to win the Nobel Prize and was able at last to anticipate an old age without financial and political problems. Ironically enough, his refusal to resign from his diplomatic post despite the increasing militarisation of the Méndez regime – an agonising decision for a 'revolutionary' writer, who had no need of the money or the prestige but believed that staying on was the best way of serving his country – meant that he became a controversial figure in his declining years and made it easy for sometimes unscrupulous critics to consign him prematurely to the past. He died in Madrid in 1974.

During his later years the novelist had continued to write intensively. In 1963 the extravagant *Mulata de tal* had appeared, followed in 1969 by *Malandrón* and, posthumously, by *Tres de cuatro soles* (1977) and *Viernes de Dolores* (1978). All were remarkable achievements for a man past 60 but none has the importance of *Leyendas de Guatemala*, *El Señor Presidente* and *Hombres de maíz*. These are works which will remain as Latin American classics when most of this century's writing is forgotten. Asturias will be remembered as one of the crucial literary figures – the others would be the Brazilian Mário de Andrade, with *Macunaíma* (1928), the Cuban Alejo Carpentier, with *Ecué-Yamba-O* (1933), and the Argentinian Borges, with his incomparable *Ficciones* – who in the 1920s contrived both to explore and define Latin American identity whilst at the same time helping to integrate the continent's culture into the mainstream of Western history. By so doing. they initiated a process which for some critics began only in the 1960s, though the most superficial review of the matter reveals this view to be false.[3] On the contrary, the 1960s was the moment at which the process of literary modernism (in the Anglo-American sense) became generally visible and available to a wide range of Latin American writers. But in that sense the Boom is the climax and consummation of a process, not its beginning, and no one made a more significant contribution to that process than Miguel Ángel Asturias, a writer who managed to be poetic, political and mythological at one and the same time, and with a degree of synthesis rarely achieved then or since.

Although one should never forget that their corollaries are the guerrilla, the freedom fighter and the liberator, it must be admitted that the dictator and the military caudillo are figures invariably associated with Latin America in the often stereotyped vision of the Western imagination. Famous books like *Facundo: civilización y barbarie* (1845) by Domingo Faustino Sarmiento, or the novel *Amalia* (1851) by another Argentine writer, José Mármol, had been reflecting the phenomenon since the early decades after independence, but there can be little disagreement that Asturias's *El Señor Presidente*, almost a century later, was the first work to explore dictatorship in both its political and psychological context. Indeed, Asturias was able to unravel what has historically been a stereotype in order to reveal a much more interesting and enduring archetype beneath, as the great Uruguayan critic Ángel Rama recognised in 1976:

> En esta línea, como en tantas otras, hay que conceder la primacía
> a Miguel Ángel Asturias. Por controversial que sea ya, para
> nosotros, su percepción del dictador centroamericano, es forzoso
> reconocer que la publicación de *El Señor Presidente* (1946) es un
> punto de partida de obligada mención, por lo que implica de
> intento de abordar la realidad latinoamericana presente a través
> de una figura clave que podría procurarnos la comprensión del
> conjunto social. En una conversación con Elena Poniatowska (en
> *Palabras cruzadas*), Alejo Carpentier subrayó que la razón que
> explicó en su momento el éxito de la novela de Asturias fue que se
> había atrevido a presentar 'un arquetipo latinoamericano'. O sea
> que había operado una literatura de reconocimiento, pero no al
> nivel de las manifestaciones externas de la sociedad sino de sus
> formas modelantes, de las energías inconscientes que adquirían
> forma y expresión a través de precisas imágenes, como en la
> proposición jungiana sobre los arquetipos.[4]

This, then, is a novel which examines a concrete political
phenomenon which has been particularly prevalent in the Hispanic
world, but at the same time universalises it to explore the roots of
social violence generally and their projection in the patriarchal
repression which Freudian and, more recently, feminist thought have
sought to unmask. In so doing, Asturias completely reverses the
signs of a novel like Gallegos's famous *Doña Bárbara* (1929), which
could itself be interpreted as a dictator novel aimed at the tyranny of
Juan Vicente Gómez in Venezuela, though merely by reasserting the
values of nineteenth-century liberalism. Since the 1930s, of course
(in fact, shortly after Asturias's death), a celebrated trio of novels on
the subject appeared: Alejo Carpentier's *El recurso del método* (1974),
Gabriel García Márquez's *El otoño del patriarca* (1975) and Augusto
Roa Bastos's *Yo el Supremo* (1975).[5]

The genesis of a novel is nearly always more complex a matter
than at first sight it appears. Estrada Cabrera's dictatorship
enveloped the future writer's entire childhood and youth, coming to
an end only in his twenty-first year. His own father's career was
ruined by the tyrant, and any faith the young Asturias might have
retained in the legal profession was destroyed by the knowledge that
Estrada Cabrera himself was a lawyer, like most Latin American
politicians then and since, in a continent of 'Generals and Doctors'

(the title of an influential novel written in 1920 by the Cuban Carlos Loveira). Thus *El Señor Presidente*, in which every action and every thought is circumscribed by the real dictator and his mythological aura, reflects in the most concrete way the horizons of Asturias's own childhood and adolescence. From that darkness, that imprisonment (not only the dictatorship, but also Hispanic traditionalism, colonial provincialism, Catholicism and the Family), Asturias travelled to Paris to undertake his cultural apprenticeship to the twentieth century, in a city which offered perhaps the most extraordinary confluence of ideas, schools and personalities assembled in one Western city since the Renaissance. Politically, it was the moment following the First World War and the Russian Revolution, events which for a young Latin American were complemented by the Mexican Revolution and the student movement which had begun in Córdoba, Argentina, and spread throughout the continent after 1918. Artistically, this was the era of the avant-garde, a moment in which the arts were changing more rapidly than at any time in the past and in which their interaction was closer and more intensely theorised than ever. Culturally, in terms of everyday experience, it was the moment when the American Way of Life, the new mass lifestyle of the capitalist West, was first established on a pattern that has not altered in its essentials down to the present time.[6] From the standpoint of the Guatemalan darkness and confinement from which Asturias had escaped, Paris must have seemed more than ever to embody its reputation as the 'City of Light'. The contrast between that light and the earlier darkness, perceived retrospectively and at first unconsciously, is perhaps the most important shaping phenomenon of the entire novel, and one which stems directly from the author's own experience.

Beyond this contrast of darkness and light, an elemental conception which endures throughout Asturias's oeuvre as an almost cosmic vision of the world, the young Guatemalan learned three major lessons in Paris. First, a simultaneous experience of revolutionary political thought and of psychoanalytical theory; secondly, an immersion in the Parisian avant-garde, above all the Surrealist movement (itself a synthesis of political and psychological revolution, and the essential antecedent for Latin American 'magical realism'), and an understanding of the relation between Surrealism and the new – 'seventh' – art, the cinema; and thirdly, an appreciation of the science of ethnology and its reflection in the vogue for primitivism and nativism in art, manifested in his own scholarly activity in translating the *Popol Vuh* into Spanish and his own artistic activity in writing the *Leyendas de Guatemala*. All this gave him a new understanding of his own national culture and a new means of communicating it. *El Señor Presidente* is, of course, a novel about Guatemala, but a Guatemala viewed through a lens 'made in Paris'. The moment one thinks about the problem, one sees that this is not only a novel which brings to bear on his small country a consciousness enlarged by his European experience, but also a novel that could not have been written without that experience. The eye is inseparable from the image in a work itself heavily influenced by the cinema. The synthesis achieved in this text – thanks to a truly revolutionary awareness of the nature and function of both language and myth – explains why Asturias is, perhaps more than any other single writer, the inaugurator of the new Latin American novel of the 1950s and 1960s.

El Señor Presidente, then, was born in Guatemala as 'Los mendigos políticos' in 1922, rewritten nine times in Paris between 1923 and 1932 as *Tohil* (the Maya-Quiche god of fire), and completed, with substantial changes only to Chapter 12, 'Camila', and minor amendments to the Epilogue, on his return to Guatemala.[7] Since the novel opens with darkness in Chapter 1, whose first version dates from 1922, and closes with darkness in the Epilogue, it is entirely appropriate that those two parts should have been written in the repressive environment of the Central American state. Yet there are a number of contradictions here, many of which are dramatised through the addition of Chapter 12, as we shall see. Guatemala is a 'young' country (the 'land of eternal springtime', moreover) in the 'New' World; yet history dictated that Asturias should find 'enlightenment' and 'liberation' in the Old (autumnal) world of Paris, where after all the celebrated lights were by then nocturnal. It was there, in the legendary avant-garde cafés, that Asturias and his Latin American friends sat reminiscing lugubriously about their own national tyrants and vying with one another in their narration of horrors and injustices. Both Alejo Carpentier, whose native Cuba was in the fearsome grip of Machado, and Arturo Uslar Pietri, from a Venezuela under the heel of Gómez, have recalled those meetings and in particular Asturias's incantatory verbal renderings of selections of his own novel about Guatemala and Estrada Cabrera. All were under the powerful influence of the

Surrealist movement, but no other Latin American writer of the era succeeded, as Asturias did, in applying the tenets of Surrealism and other such avant-garde movements to the requirements of a historically specific novel.

Until 1978 many critics hesitated to believe Asturias's consistent claim that the novel was complete when he returned to Guatemala in 1933, and took 1946 not only as the date of publication but also as the effective moment of composition. Clearly in terms of its effect on the rest of Latin American literature, 1946 is the relevant date; but if we speak genetically, in terms of the creative process of a novel conceived as a cultural construct, then *El Señor Presidente* must be restored to its true origin as a work largely written in the avant-garde Parisian 1920s and therefore contemporaneous with such 'Regionalist' novels as Gallegos's *Doña Bárbara* (1929) or Icaza's *Huasipungo* (1934). This has quite radical implications not only for our revision of Asturias but also for the emergence of the entire Latin American new novel, as noted above. Even in terms of Asturias's own inspiration, this redating has significant effects. For instance the American critic Jack Himelblau had already shown in a series of important articles published before 1978 that, far from being merely a nightmarish fantasy, a work of overblown exaggeration, *El Señor Presidente* is based overwhelmingly on historical fact and is, indeed, a *roman à clef*.[8] Needless to say, the events of the last twenty-five years in Central America have gone beyond anything Asturias recorded, and have thereby vindicated the novel's historical relevance. However, Himelblau went on from his proof of authenticity to infer that Asturias's novel had acquired most of its factual foundation from a famous historical work on Estrada Cabrera, *¡Ecce Pericles!*, by another notable Guatemalan novelist, Rafael Arévalo Martínez, completed in 1941 and published in 1945. On the contrary, the rediscovery in 1975 of Asturias's 1932 manuscript demonstrates beyond all doubt that the novel was complete at that time and had incorporated many of the incidents recorded by Arévalo more than a decade before him. (Most of them were in any case common knowledge in Guatemala, where the 'fantastic' and the 'grotesque' have been everyday events for large stretches of its history.)

The discovery of the 1932 manuscript has other implications relating particularly to the discovery that the only major change is the insertion of Camila's visit to the sea and to the cinema in Chapter 12. Although a number of critics have argued that this flashback is diversionary, and hence a structural weakness, it can also be argued that it is one of the most striking pieces of writing in the novel and has a quite considerable effect on the way we interpret it. I would argue that this insertion materialises Asturias's own renewed recognition, having returned to the darkness of Guatemala, of what his novel really signified. He came to understand the extent to which he was – as we all are – the product of his own experience, but in his case that experience had been especially dialectical and dramatic. Asturias was a human axis or bridge between two different worlds, the City of Darkness and the City of Light, oscillating between America and Europe, Guatemala and Paris, Underdevelopment and Modernity. Once again, critics who have called the novel 'hybrid' seem to me to have misunderstood the intentions of this most consciously 'mestizo' of writers, who refused always to choose between the two worlds, and sought synthesis through violent juxtaposition and contradiction (as, indeed, have so many other Hispanic artists from Quevedo through Goya to the present day).

In this conception of the work's construction, *El Señor Presidente* would become a novel whose intense linguistic vitality and sheer psychic energy materialise in the most dramatic manner the experience of a writer whose view of the world was changing constantly and progressively as he wrote it. Although Latin American fiction now has a wide number of original and unforgettable experiences for the reader, *El Señor Presidente* was at one time almost unique for the violent effect which a first reading exerted upon the consciousness, and for many readers this remains the case today. This intensity and immediacy is communicated in the most deliberate and transparent way in the Camila episode added after 1932, and, in a characteristic union of form and content, that episode is precisely about the intensity and immediacy of a youthful coming into the world. The addition of four elements in particular – the mirror, the family portraits, the sea and the moving pictures of the cinema – reveal Asturias's own realisation that his novel is not only about a Guatemalan dictator but about his own coming to consciousness, channelled partly through Cara de Ángel's moral transition but initially, and equally importantly, through Camila's sensual and perceptual awakening, after a dull (nineteenth-century) childhood in a house that is more like a museum:

Los domingos por la tarde se dormía o se aburría en la sala,

59

cansada de ver retratos antiguos en un álbum de familia, fuera de
los que pendían de las paredes tapizadas de rojo o se habían
distribuido en esquineras negras, mesas plateadas y consolas de
mármol, mientras su papá ronroneaba como mirando a la calle
desierta por una ventana, o correspondía a los adioses de los
vecinos y conocidos que le saludaban al pasar. Uno allá cada
año.[9]

Camila's first visit to the seaside teaches her to see the world anew
(as in Shklovsky's concept of 'defamiliarisation', one of the central
tenets of Modernist art), and awakens her sleeping sensuality,
reminding us that desire was the seed of revolution both for the
Surrealists and for the young radicals seeking social and sexual
revolution in the 1960s, when the Boom exploded on the world
literary scene and the 'New' or 'Modernist' Latin American Novel
entered its second phase:

> La inmensidad en movimiento. Ella en movimiento. Todo lo que
> en ella estaba inmóvil, en movimiento. Jugaron palabras de
> sorpresa en sus labios al ver el mar por primera vez, mas al
> preguntarle sus tíos qué le parecía el espectáculo, dijo con aire de
> huera importancia: '¡Me lo sabía de memoria en fotografía!'
>
> (p.73)

Soon after this the sea merges in her consciousness with her
anticipation of a first visit to the moving pictures, and previously
static 'retratos' leap into life:

> Todo en movimiento. Nada estable. Retratos y retratos
> confundiéndose, revolviéndose, saltando en pedazos para formar
> una visión fugaz a cada instante, en un estado que no era sólido,
> ni líquido, ni gaseoso, sino el estado en que la vida está en el mar.
> El estado luminoso. En las vistas y en el mar.
>   Con los dedos encogidos en los zapatos y la mirada en todas
> partes, siguió contemplando Camila lo que sus ojos no acababan
> de ver. Si en el primer instante sintió vaciarse sus pupilas para
> abarcar la inmensidad, ahora la inmensidad se las llenaba. Era el
> regreso de la marea hasta sus ojos.
>
> (p.74)

Nothing could illustrate more clearly Asturias's search for the
relation between form and content, nor the sense of interaction, as in

this last image, between human consciousness and the world. These foregrounded elements – mirror, images, movies, ocean – did not change the meaning of the novel in any fundamental way, but they did give it life and set it moving: they made its thematic complexity more visible and more coherent. Asturias was able to associate his own process of psychic development, exemplified through Camila (a much more complex creation than Gallegos's almost contemporary Marisela, and an anti-patriarchal one in contrast with Gallegos's reaffirmation of masculine authority), with that of his own young country, caught between tradition and the need for modernisation. This production of text from context, which close study can help to reconstruct, is then mirrored in the novel itself, as *consciousness* and *discourse* (the 'actions', the 'dialogue', both internal and external, of the 'characters') is produced from the *contextual field* (the 'background' or 'setting' of the novel).

Asturias was probably the first Spanish American novelist to understand the implications of what we would now call anthropology and structural linguistics for culture and for fiction, and to perceive that the novel was first and last 'una hazaña verbal'. Unlike some later novelists, however, he did not infer from this that language was a separate reality and somehow not contextual; on the contrary, he saw that the context is, precisely, reflected in our own individual consciousness. He therefore understood implicitly that language and culture were, however contradictorily, totalities, and set out, rather like James Joyce, and three decades before the Boom of the new novel, to produce fictions which would themselves be structured totalities, demonstrating how Rama's 'archetypes' infused everything in their surrounding semantic and social field with meaning. This is why the plot of *El Señor Presidente*, like that of his later *Hombres de maíz*, is both simple and highly complex: it can be seen as having the economy of the classical or the intricacy of the baroque, and there is no necessary contradiction between the two statements. It is as if the novel were feeding off itself, as if its foreground action were being carved out of the background, or as if the main characters were somehow superimposed on the supporting cast.

There are two main characters and two plot lines. The first character, whose absence from most of the action only emphasises his domination of everything and everyone, is the Dictator, 'El Señor Presidente', who embodies every form of authority, real and imagined, good and bad (except that for Asturias most forms of

61

authority are inherently evil), from Jehovah and Lucifer through the various forms and phases of the Latin American caudillo to the primal father figure who, according to Freud and Jung, haunts and terrorises all of us from his dwelling-place in the depths of our unconscious. The President is based directly and in detail upon Estrada Cabrera, but Asturias never mentions his name (nor that of Guatemala), in order to generalise his work's associations both on the temporal pattern already mentioned and spatially across the other republics of mestizo America. The second major character is Miguel Cara de Ángel, the President's 'favourite' and the man who does much of his dirty work. Asturias said that he was based in part on a historical figure, but given the similarity to the author's own name and what has been said of the novel's genesis in self-analysis, it would be surprising if he were not also a form of metaphorical self-criticism and a comment on those intellectuals and artists (like Darío, Chocano and Gómez Carrillo), and in general the parasitical middle sectors from which Asturias himself came, who supported Estrada Cabrera as they have so often supported governments of this kind, in Latin America as elsewhere.

The first plot line, then, is a dramatisation, through a series of interlocking incidents, of the nature and methods of the regime. The very first incident of the novel is the murder – in one sense arbitrary, in another sense entirely structural – of a high-ranking army officer, Colonel Parrales Sonriente, by a mentally retarded figure, the unforgettable *Pelele*, the man who is no one. The President, the man who is everything, uses this involuntary crime as a pretext to arrest, torture and ultimately murder two leading citizens who are deemed 'enemies of the regime', that is, who have dared to question, in however trivial a fashion, the President's right to be always in the right and on the right. These two victims, emblematically, are a soldier, General Canales, and a lawyer, Licenciado Carvajal, who represent professions and social groups historically indispensable to such regimes. Their experiences and those of their hapless relatives give us one chain of insights into the perverted nature of the system and unleash a series of further horrors on anyone 'suspected' (i.e. accused: truth is irrelevant) of associating with them.

The second plot is a bifurcation of the first, takes a separate but related path through the field of horrors, and eventually coincides exactly with it once more at the end of the novel. Cara de Ángel, 'bello y malo como Satán', is instructed to lead General Canales into a trap so that he may be executed under the '*ley fuga*'. The general escapes (later to be treacherously poisoned), Cara de Ángel becomes involved with his teenage daughter, having at first intended to rape her, and her predicament and his growing love gradually begin to distance him, then to alienate him morally from the President, and finally to turn him into an opponent, albeit a passive and unheroic one, of the regime. The logic of the novel, however – since one of its central messages is solidarity – requires that what has happened to others can happen to oneself. Like other privileged characters in the novel, Cara de Ángel discovers that not even he is above the 'Law' (in this case, that of the devil or the jungle), and after all the other victim figures have been eliminated he dies betrayed, symmetrically, by one of the first people he decides to help after becoming a partially reformed character. His frightful end, in a subterranean dungeon worthy of Dante, is made more agonising by his belief, adding mental to physical torture, that Camila, by now his wife, has become the President's mistress.

In addition to these and subsidiary characters such as Camila herself and Pelele, there are literally dozens of minor personages, innocent and guilty, victims and predators, all defined absolutely by their relationship to the President, his power structure and a spy system which seems a premonition of our own era of electronic surveillance:

> . . .el bosque monstruoso que separaba al Señor Presidente de sus enemigos, bosque de árboles de orejas que al menor eco se revolvían como agitadas por el huracán . . .Una red de hilos invisibles, más invisibles que los hilos del telégrafo, comunicaba cada hoja con el Señor Presidente, atento a lo que pasaba en las vísceras más secretas de los ciudadanos.
>
> (p.35)

This image is translated into a hundred separate incidents, as the regime's corruption of human relationships and exploitation of the lowest instincts is played out. The exhaustive logic of systematic incrimination, perversion and betrayal is one of the most persuasive and troubling aspects of the novel, and the expert constructive technique with which Asturias plots it has perhaps been insufficiently appreciated.[10]

The novel is in three parts. In the first, '21, 22 y 23 de abril' (the year is 1916, as a reference to the battle of Verdun in Chapter 32 reveals), a Goyesque or Buñuelesque world of Christianity, beggars and moral ambiguity is unveiled:

> . . .¡Alumbra, lumbre de alumbre, Luzbel de piedralumbre! Como zumbido de oídos persistía el rumor de las campanas a la oración, maldoblestar de la luz en la sombra, de la sombra en la luz. ¡Alumbra, lumbre de alumbre, Luzbel de piedralumbre, sobre la podredumbre! ¡Alumbra, lumbre de alumbre, sobre la podredumbre, Luzbel de piedralumbre! ¡Alumbre, alumbra, lumbre de alumbre. . ., alumbra. . ., alumbre. . ., alumbra, lumbre de alumbre. . ., alumbra, alumbre. . .! Los pordioseros se arrastraban por las cocinas del mercado, perdidos en la sombra de la Catedral helada, de paso hacia la Plaza de Armas, a lo largo de calles tan anchas como mares, en la ciudad que se iba quedando atrás íngrima y sola.

(p.7)

One recent critic has suggested that this opening of *El Señor Presidente* is also the first page of the 'new Latin American Novel', and it would be difficult to disagree.[11] The mortal darkness is punctuated by the murder of Parrales Sonriente when he taunts the orphaned Pelele with the word 'Mother!' (the symbolism is obvious, both in the universal sense as well as in the specific historical context of a Latin America robbed of its original Indian civilization and colonised by a violent patriarchal society). The beggars are interrogated, not to discover the truth but to torture them into false accusations against Canales and Carvajal, though one, the blind and legless Mosco, courageously tells the truth until the moment he dies. Then a secret policeman, Lucio Vásquez, is sent to murder Pelele, and takes along his horrified friend, Genaro Rodas, to see the fun. Vásquez shoots the beggar, watched by an unknown witness in the archbishop's palace, and Rodas has nightmares of remorse as he recalls the pitiless assassination. Meanwhile, Cara de Ángel is ordered by the President to facilitate Canales's escape from arrest so that he can be conveniently shot and eliminated, and he enlists Vásquez's assistance in creating a diversion. The plan succeeds, the house is ransacked and La Chabelona, Camila's nanny, is left fatally injured as a result of the invasion.

The second part '24, 25, 26 y 27 de abril' opens with the controversial flashback – the only one in this most concentrated of novels – which shows us Camila's lonely upbringing following the early death of her mother, and the awakening of her sexuality on a seaside outing. Thereafter the story resumes where it left off, as Cara de Ángel takes Camila into hiding in the seedy bar owned by *La Masacuata*, Vásquez's girl-friend. (La Masacuata, despite her evident promiscuity and low station, is one of the few decent characters in the novel; most of the others, like her, are female and working-class.) Meanwhile Fedina Rodas, wife of Genaro and a maid in Camila's house, is picked up by soldiers under the ruthless Auditor de Guerra, and taken away for interrogation. Her interrogation and torture and the death of her baby make up one of the most harrowing sequences in the novel, after which she is sold to a brothel and eventually ends up, deranged, working in a convent. Genaro himself is then subjected to similar treatment, followed by Licenciado Carvajal, who is arrested and thrown into a dungeon occupied by a student and a sacristan whom the reader has already met in Part I. After a bomb scare puts a farcical end to a day of national celebration and propaganda, Camila's relatives turn their backs on her and she is left completely destitute and in hiding. When she becomes ill, Cara de Ángel, who is falling in love with her, begins to undergo a moral crisis, and as a first step on the road to mending his ways decides to warn one Major Farfán that he has fallen out of favour with the President. This part ends with Canales crossing the frontier into exile, determined to return with a revolutionary army.

The title of the final part, 'Semanas, meses, años', reiterates what has been said above as to the way each incident comes out of an endless store of similarly structured possibility, and also suggests the way in which dictatorship suppresses not only freedom but the normal historical time implicitly associated with it. It opens with a dialogue of four voices in the darkness of a prison dungeon, including a student – no doubt the positive side of Asturias's self-representation – urging revolutionary consciousness upon his cellmates. Another of the prisoners, Carvajal, is subjected to a farcical trial, sentenced to death, and subsequently executed, despite his wife's desperate efforts to have him reprieved. Meanwhile Cara de Ángel, resorting to any superstitious ritual available, marries Camila, who is herself on the point of death, on the advice of a spiritualist. In Chapter 32, 'El Señor Presidente', the dictator shows his displeasure (she is the daughter of his enemy, and Cara de Ángel's first loyalty is owed to him), and the favourite's downfall is set in motion: Genaro Rodas is released from prison and set to spy on him. In Chapter 34

Camila recovers and Cara de Ángel takes her on a journey which is both a convalescence and a honeymoon in the countryside, where she begins to reciprocate his love (significantly for the novel as a whole, it is entitled 'Luz para ciegos'). On their return to the capital they are forced to attend a dinner engagement at the presidential palace in Chapter 35, entitled 'Canción de canciones', as the President symbolically excludes all the husbands and has his court poet read the Song of Songs to their wives, while Cara de Ángel, in hiding, spies on the scene. The oedipal inferences are obvious. In Chapter 36, whose title, 'La revolución', is as ironic as that of the novel itself, Canales dies and with him all hope of change.

Chapter 37, 'El baile de Tohil', sees Cara de Ángel make his last visit to the palace and the dictator informs him that he wishes him to make a diplomatic mission to Washington. Anticipating a trap Cara de Ángel tries to decline, but the President insists. Staring into space the ex-favourite sees a hallucinatory vision of primitive Indian tribesmen dancing around the totem of their bloodthirsty god of war:

> Un grito se untó a la oscuridad que trepaba a los árboles y se oyeron cerca y lejos las voces plañideras de las tribus que abandonadas en la selva, ciega de nacimiento, luchaban con sus tripas – animales del hambre –, con sus gargantas – pájaros de la sed – y su miedo, y sus bascas, y sus necesidades corporales, reclamando a Tohil, Dador del Fuego, que les devolviera el ocote encendido de la luz. Tohil llegó cabalgando un río hecho de pechos de paloma que se deslizaba como leche.
>
> (p.232)

Tohil demands human sacrifices if he is to protect the tribes, and the warriors agree, whereupon he declares: '¡Estoy contento! Sobre hombres cazadores de hombres puedo asentar mi gobierno. No habrá ni verdadera muerte ni verdadera vida' (p.232). Cara de Ángel is forced to leave Camila and is arrested at the port, just when he thinks he is out of harm's way, by none other than Farfán, who owes him his life, and Genaro Rodas. Cara de Ángel is thrown into a stinking dungeon and left to rot, until the day when he hears that Camila has become the President's mistress, when his heart breaks and he dies. She meanwhile has had a son, left the capital and gone to live in the country. Finally, the Epilogue shows the would-be revolutionary student, released from prison, returning to his home 'at the end of a cul-de-sac', where he finds his mother praying. The novel ends, as it began, with bells clamouring in the darkness: '¡Chiplongón!. . . Zambulléronse las campanadas de las ocho de la noche en el silencio. . . ¡Chiplongón!. . . ¡Chiplongón!. . .' (p.256). The last words are those of the mother's prayer: '*Kyrie eleison*'. The novel has come full circle, though of course the reader has had the opportunity to undergo the change in consciousness which came too late for the glamorous, self-centred Angel Face.

The onomatopoeia of the chiming bells reminds us of the 'boom-bloom' of the opening lines of the novel. Asturias and Arturo Uslar Pietri frequently recalled that in those same Parisian conversations where they exchanged stories about dictators, they also played at word games. It was the age of the verbal wizard James Joyce, of a Surrealist movement dredging the newly discovered unconscious for the lost magic of language, of the Dada-style *jitanjáfora* invented by the Cuban Mariano Brull and the Mexican Alfonso Reyes, and, not least, of a new concern with ethnology which emphasised the fact that for primitive culture, as for the Bible, in the beginning was the word. Only Asturias, as his drinking partners conceded, was able to put these experiments to functional use in his fiction. At its worst, as in his *Trilogía bananera*, this sometimes became an almost mechanical linguistic exercise, but at its best Asturias's sense of the potency of language, deriving from his work on the *Popol Vuh*, gave his writing an authentically mythological force and intensity unrivalled in Latin American fiction and, paradoxically, an almost classical certainty which at times recalls Cervantes, Góngora and the incomparable Quevedo. There are moments in *El Señor Presidente* when the writing achieves remarkable levels of integration, such as the episode where Cara de Ángel is escaping from the President, fearfully and guiltily, on his journey by train to the coast:

> Cara de Ángel abandonó la cabeza en el respaldo del asiento de junco. Seguía la tierra baja, plana, caliente, inalterable de la costa con los ojos perdidos de sueño y la sensación confusa de ir en el tren, de no ir en el tren, de irse quedando atrás del tren, cada vez más atrás del tren, más atrás del tren, más atrás del tren, más atrás del tren, cada vez más atrás, cada vez más atrás, cada vez más atrás, más y más cada vez, cada ver cada vez, cada ver cada vez, cada ver cada vez, cada ver cada vez, cada ver cada ver cada ver cada ver cada ver. . .

> De repente abría los ojos . . . y se encontraba en su asiento. . .
>
> (p.237)

Such word-play may not be to every reader's taste, but this is surely one of the most astonishing moments in Latin American literature, as Asturias reproduces the sound and motion of the train, the interweaving of time ('vez') and space ('ver'), Cara de Ángel's fear of being caught and sensation of being left behind ('cada vez más atrás'), and his unconscious terror of death (as 'cada vez' jolts into 'cada ver', 'corpse', like a ticking clock suddenly sounding doom or a beating heart stopping in death). It is what the Brazilians would later call 'concrete poetry', twenty years ahead of time, and fully integrated into the requirements of the text. Critics have frequently talked of Asturias's debt to Valle-Inclán's brilliant *Tirano Banderas* (1926), and there are undoubtedly influences, but these should not be exaggerated. The Spaniard's method of characterisation always immobilises caricatures and distances the reader, whereas Asturias's equally masterful use of language contrives to produce the opposite effect: dynamism, interiorisation and identification, so that the reader will be forced to take up a point of view – physical, emotional and moral – and thus internalise the suffering and the predicaments of the characters. Chapters 3 and 4 of Part I, 'La fuga del *Pelele*' and 'Cara de Ángel', merit special study for their functional use of impressionist, expressionist and surrealist imagery, and are unquestionably classic pages of avant-garde fiction in Spanish, commencing with the wretched beggar's desperate escape through the streets of the nightmare city:

> *El Pelele* huyó por las calles intestinales, estrechas y retorcidas de los suburbios de la ciudad, sin turbar con sus gritos desaforados la respiración del cielo ni el sueño de los habitantes, iguales en el espejo de la muerte, como desiguales en la lucha que reanudarían al salir el sol.
>
> (p.16)

The precision and economy are masterful. To call sleep and dreams the 'mirror of death', and to see the unconscious as that which unites all human beings is to adopt a Freudian perspective ('Entre la realidad y el sueño la diferencia es puramente mecánica' (p.159)); to stress social and economic inequality and to see daily life as a struggle is to adopt a socialist perspective (although Asturias's ideological position in this novel, taken as a whole, is transitional between liberalism and socialism). The persistent fusion of Freudian and Marxist systems of thought henceforth characterises Asturias's writing and explains why for some he is 'the greatest novelist of Revolution'.[12] Pelele flees on:

> Medio en la realidad, medio en el sueño, corría *el Pelele* perseguido por los perros y por los clavos de una lluvia fina. Corría sin rumbo fijo, despavorido, con la boca abierta, la lengua fuera, enflecada de mocos, la respiración acezosa y los brazos en alto. A sus costados pasaban puertas y puertas y puertas y ventanas y puertas y ventanas. . . De repente se paraba, con las manos sobre la cara, defendiéndose de los postes del telégrafo, pero al cerciorarse de que los palos eran inofensivos se carcajeaba y seguía adelante, como el que escapa de una prisión cuyos muros de niebla a más correr, más se alejan.
>
> (p.18)

The exhausted beggar sleeps on a rubbish dump, but is attacked and wounded by vultures, breaking his leg in his efforts to escape. His already warped mind is further wracked by fever, and the surrealist imagery is intensified:

> Las uñas aceradas de la fiebre le aserraban la frente. Disociación de ideas. Elasticidad del mundo en los espejos. Desproporción fantástica. Huracán delirante. Fuga vertiginosa, horizontal, vertical, oblicua, recién nacida y muerte en espiral.
>
> (p.19)

Obviously this distortion of perception, almost a Surrealist Manifesto, is intended to represent not only Pelele's torment but the deformation of moral reality in general in a world where everything is the opposite of what is proclaimed. As has been noted, the novel is based on a series of oppositions, in sequential chain, overlapping and superimposed. These have no real beginning or end, but consideration of all the evidence suggests strongly that the Paris-Guatemala contrast, experienced directly by Asturias himself, is the existential point of departure. Guatemala, land of newness, youth and springtime, has been turned into a land of nocturnal darkness and death; Paris, old and autumnal, has provided the enlightenment for which French culture is famous. Clearly these are reversible conceptions (and in *Hombres de maíz* Asturias would indeed reverse them) but in this novel Paris, or Europe (the point of view), is light and Guatemala, or America (the object of vision), is darkness, and it is this alternation which predominates from the very first lines; flowing from it come good and evil, truth and lie, life and death, freedom and imprisonment, the central themes of the novel. Not that the novel is simplistic: for the most part light is truth and knowledge, and darkness falsehood or ignorance, but at other times the darkness is the fertile and spontaneous realm of the unconscious, whilst Cara de Ángel, as we have seen, is, like Lucifer himself, both 'bello' and 'malo'. Asturias shows us that the truth is hard to find, at the best of times, but in a world of distortions and inversions most characters do their best to avoid it, acting like puppets in the hands of the dictator. It is typical that the author grants Pelele, deranged and haunted – the most completely introverted and the least perceptive character in the novel – a vision of the difficulties involved:

> ¡Soy la Manzana-Rosa del Ave del Paraíso, soy la vida, la mitad de mi cuerpo es mentira y la mitad es verdad; soy rosa y soy manzana, doy a todos un ojo de vidrio y un ojo de verdad: los que ven con mi ojo de vidrio ven porque sueñan, los que ven con mi ojo de verdad ven porque miran! ¡Soy la vida, la Manzana-Rosa del Ave del Paraíso; soy la mentira de todas las cosas reales, la realidad de todas las ficciones!

(p.22)

Needless to say, this is really a message for the reader, as Asturias returns us to the 'maldoblestar de la luz en la sombra' of the opening lines and begins to show us how to read the novel. Before we can 'raise our consciousness' and interpret reality morally or politically we have to recognise the difficulty of interpreting it sensorially and existentially. In other words we have to perceive that we perceive it, and to perceive ourselves perceiving it: the world is a labyrinth not a mirror, and it is this that art must 'reflect'. The 1920s avant-garde had come to realise that art in the contemporary world of mass transport and mass media involved both a speeding up and a fragmentation of experience, and that the interpretation of reality was in the first instance a question of vision. Numerous critics have likened this novel to a film, but without seeing the full implications of the analogy, which is hinted at in Chapter 12, 'Camila', as suggested above. In the cinema we sit in the darkness until the film starts, when a stream of images – themselves a mix of light and dark – are projected on to a screen, until the film ends and darkness returns. The parallel between this and the mythological experience of each human being – born from the womb and then living a stream of days and nights, before entering the darkness once more – is not difficult to perceive. Most of the characters in this novel see what they want to see, interpret the world according to their desires or their terrors, and find reality impossible to face. Some, like General Canales, see it through their professional role rather than their authentic humanity: '¿Cuál era la realidad? No haber pensado nunca con su cabeza, haber pensado siempre con el quepis' (p.169). Most of them only finally face up to reality, like Cara de Ángel himself, when they are confronting death, the final 'moment of truth'. Until that moment the overwhelming majority refuse to identify with their suffering fellow citizens and close their eyes to what is going on: 'Los presos seguían pasando. . . . Ser ellos y no ser los que a su paso se alegraban en el fondo de no ser ellos. . .' (p.255). Clearly this is a call both for solidarity and commitment, terms which apply equally to the Christianity in which Asturias was educated and to the socialism which he later espoused. Both require a revolution of conscience and consciousness.

In an earlier article the present writer was so concerned to demonstrate the cosmic, mythological or existential aspect of the novel, largely overlooked by critics, that he almost denied that the novel was in any meaningful sense 'political'. This now seems to me to have been a serious error: few novels are more political, because few novels establish such a radical relation between specific political situations, a moral position in relation to society, the mechanisms and imperatives of our everyday sense perceptions, and what one could call an anthropological perspective on human existence. Perhaps the most remarkable achievement of the work is that, through a sort of linguistic catharsis, on the one hand, and through a contrast between form and content, on the other, this gallery of grotesque and dreadful events, however distressing, is not ultimately pessimistic, despite its baleful ending. The characters may despair and suffer exemplary disaster, but the author's message is one of love, hope, solidarity and liberation. This paradox has never been better explained than in a review of the novel by Gabriel Venaissin in 1953:

Dudo que novela alguna haya logrado crear un ambiente de mayor asfixia. Pero lo milagroso en este libro está en haber partido de este universo para alcanzar otra cosa. Asturias inventa un lenguaje de libertad total. Partiendo de un mundo envenenado, no hay un solo instante en que no nos sintamos proyectados hacia el cielo y las estrellas, conducidos hacia el espacio, empujados hacia la libertad desde una realidad en que la libertad muere a cada instante.[13]

As one of the characters says of his predicament: '¡Vaya una ocurrencia..., hablar de la libertad en la cárcel!' (p.181). This, however, was Asturias's endeavour throughout his literary career. Steeped in Catholic doctrine and traditional Hispanic fatalism from childhood, he was only too well aware that the soul is the unwilling prisoner of the body and life is but a dream; or that each of us is a river flowing down to the sea of death, which is the trap or permanent dungeon into which we fall; but like his friend and fellow writer Augusto Roa Bastos, author of *Hijo de hombre* (1960), he also fervently believed that men and women were not irredeemably condemned during their time on earth to struggle for domination and the power to oppress and crucify one another. *El Señor Presidente* is not only an act of witness and an act of protest, but also a call for moral commitment and an act of faith in the possibility, despite everything, of a better world.

NOTES

1 For a treatment of the novel's overall design I refer the reader to my earlier '*El Señor Presidente* and how to read it', *Bulletin of Hispanic Studies*, vol. 47, no. 3 (1970), pp.223–43. Much of that article seems valid to me today, except for its insistence that the novel is not about 'politics' but about 'evil'. I no longer believe that these two aspects are mutually exclusive, and would refer the reader to my '*El Señor Presidente*: una lectura contextual', in M.A. Asturias, *El Señor Presidente*, critical edition, ed. R. Navas Ruiz (Klincksieck, Paris and Mexico, 1978), pp.lxxxiii–cxxxix. *El Señor Presidente* is available in English translation as *The President*, trans. F. Partridge (Gollancz, London, 1963; republished by Penguin, 1972).

2 Reminiscences of this period have contributed to the second half of *Hombres de maíz* (1949). See my critical edition of that novel, M.A. Asturias, *Hombres de maíz* (Fondo de Cultura Económica, Paris and Mexico, 1981).

3 D.L. Shaw, *Nueva narrativa hispanoamericana* (Cátedra, Madrid, 1981) gives the best overview of the process. See also my 'Boom, yes; "nueva" novela, no: further reflections on the optical illusions of the 1960s in Latin America', *Bulletin of Latin American Research*, vol. 3, no. 2 (1984), pp.53–63.

4 Ángel Rama, *Los dictadores latinoamericanos* (Fondo de Cultura Económica, Mexico, 1976), p.6.
5 When these three novels first appeared, they were normally studied together in comparative articles or books; now, with the perspective of history, it is more common to see them integrated in a foursome with *El Señor Presidente*. For an excellent recent example, see Julio Calviño, *Historia, ideología y mito en la narrativa hispanoamericana contemporánea* (Editorial Ayusa, Madrid, 1987).
6 See Marc Cheymol, *Miguel Ángel Asturias dans le Paris des années folles* (Presses Universitaires de Grenoble, Grenoble, 1987), for an outstanding study of Asturias in this period; also my 'The literature, music and art of Latin America from 1870 to 1930', in L. Bethel (ed.), *Cambridge History of Latin America*, vol. 4 (1986), pp.443–526.
7 See J.M. Saint-Lu, 'Apuntes para una lectura "semántica" de *El Señor Presidente*', in Navas Ruiz's critical edition, cited above, pp.xxxv–lxxxii.
8 See especially J. Himelblau, '*El Señor Presidente*: antecedents, sources and reality', in *Hispanic Review*, vol. 41 (1972), pp.43–78. On Estrada Cabrera in addition to Arévalo Martínez's *¡Ecce Pericles!*, see *El Autócrata* (1929) by another novelist, Carlos Wyld Ospina. Also by Himelblau, see 'Tohil and the President: the hunters and the hunted in the *Popol Vuh* and *El Señor Presidente*', *Kentucky Romance Quarterly*, vol. 31, no. 4 (1984), pp.437–50. R. Verzasconi, 'Apuntes sobre las diversas ediciones de *El Señor Presidente*', *Revista Iberoamericana*, vol. 46 (1980), pp.189–94, makes erroneous deductions, having not been aware of the 1932 manuscript.
9 Pp.72–3. All quotations from the text are taken from the Navas Ruiz critical edition cited above.
10 See J.C. Rodriguez Gómez, 'Miguel Ángel Asturias: una estructura del subdesarrollo', *La Estafeta Literaria*, no. 396 (Madrid, 18 May 1968), pp.4–8; and I. Verdugo, '*El Señor Presidente*: una lectura "estructuralista"', in Navas Ruiz's critical edition, pp.clvii–ccxiii.
11 See W.H. Gass, 'The first seven pages of the boom', *Latin American Literary Review*, no. 29 (1987), pp.33–56.
12 See '*Les yeux des enterrés*', *L'Express*, 17 Jan. 1963.
13 'M.A. Asturias: *M. le Président*', *Esprit*, vol. 21, no. 7 (July 1953), pp.153–8.

4

JUAN RULFO: *PEDRO PÁRAMO*

PETER BEARDSELL

It was during the 1960s that Juan Rulfo was tardily 'discovered'. Logically his impact should have come in the 1950s, with the publication of his short stories *El llano en llamas* (1953) and his short novel *Pedro Páramo* (1955). But the stories were largely ignored and the novel – though quite favourably reviewed in Mexico soon after its publication – failed for a while to break through the barrier of public uneasiness and incomprehension. Only a decade later were his innovative narrative methods more fully appreciated, and his blend of Mexican and universal themes more profoundly understood.

Rulfo's background was partly that of a family of landowners and lawyers in the state of Jalisco. He was born in 1918 as Juan Nepomuceno Carlos Pérez Rulfo Vizcaíno, and spent his childhood in Apulco and San Gabriel (within the district of Sayula). In this region his family were ruined during the 1926–9 civil war (the *Guerra de los Cristeros*). Rulfo's father met a violent death in 1925, as did his uncle and grandfather during the civil war. His mother died in 1927. Brought up by his grandmother in San Gabriel, and then in an orphanage in Guadalajara, Rulfo developed feelings of depression and solitude that he later found difficult to overcome. He earned a living with a variety of jobs. From 1935 he worked for ten years in the archives of Mexico's Immigration Department. His next job was with the Goodrich tyre company as a travelling sales representative from 1947 to 1954. Then he became part of the Comisión de Papaloapan, an irrigation project in the Veracruz region. In Mexico City, from 1956, he began to write film scripts, and in Guadalajara in 1959 he worked for television. Finally, in 1962, he joined the Instituto Indigenista, which concerned itself with the relationship between the state and the primitive, marginalised Indian communities.

Writing, he always maintained, was not his profession but his

74

hobby ('escribo cuando me viene la afición, si no, no. . .').[1] It was in 1940 and 1942 that he wrote his first novel and his first short story, pieces that he subsequently found weak and unworthy of publication (though the story and an excerpt from the novel were in fact printed). More short stories began to appear from 1945 in magazines like *Pan* in Guadalajara and *América* in Mexico City (published by the 'Tribuna de la Democracia', a group whose members included Rulfo himself). These stories were collected with several new ones in 1953 in a volume of fifteen entitled *El llano en llamas*. One of the memorable impressions derived from reading these stories is of their setting in open country or small towns or villages in Jalisco. Besides giving a local identity, the landscape acts as a backcloth, enhances moods, heightens ideas, and even precipitates and determines human behaviour. A historical context is sometimes indicated: the years of the Revolution, the aftermath, the Guerra de los Cristeros. Even the language reflects local idiom in carefully modified form. But the enduring value of the collection lies in its depiction of universal human experience intensified and warped by the extreme local circumstances. Poverty, hardship and suffering dominate the human condition in an apparently hostile environment. It is a world of violence, cruelty, anarchy, incest, prostitution and religious hypocrisy. Thieves and murderers are found in abundance. Revenge is one recurrent theme, and guilt another. In most of these stories Rulfo fascinates us with the psychological implications of events. At times he gives an insight into a character's mind, but more frequently he creates a strange dissonance between the tone of the narrative and the nature of the events described. His first-person narrators are particularly effective in this respect when their neutrality or indifference runs counter to our own moral or emotional standpoint. Indeed our active collaboration as readers is required to compensate for Rulfo's deliberate avoidance of analysis and explanation. But we are willing collaborators, for Rulfo easily holds our interest with a masterful versatility of techniques, such as the unexpected changes of narrative standpoint, the delayed presentation of vital facts and the extensive use of foreshadowing. Many of these techniques were to reappear in *Pedro Páramo*, as were the themes and the overall atmosphere.

Rulfo later recalled his sense of frustration at the low sales of this book of stories, which the Fondo de Cultura Económica published in its series 'Letras Mexicanas' in editions of between 2,000 and 4,000 copies. However, a grant from the Rockefeller Foundation gave him the time and opportunity to write intensively for a few months in 1953 and 1954. Two fragments of a new work appeared separately: 'Un cuento' described at the time as being part of a novel entitled *Una estrella junto a la luna*, and a piece purporting to belong to a novel called *Los murmullos*. Both proved to be excerpts from *Pedro Páramo*, which was published in 1955 by the Fondo de Cultura Económica.

After this, Rulfo's literary career was essentially a question of growing prestige and stagnating creativity. It is worth recalling his work on film scripts[2] and mentioning his role as adviser to the Centro de Escritores Mexicanos (responsible for distributing grants to young writers). It is also important for us to notice how he became associated with the process of liberation in Latin America and the Third World through a kind of cultural militancy. This was the purpose in Mexico of the magazine *Cambio*, which he co-edited with writers like Julio Cortázar and José Revueltas. In recognition of his international prestige the Mexican state awarded him its Premio Nacional de Literatura in 1970, although in fact his creative writing had been virtually at a standstill for fifteen years. He kept the public guessing about prospects for any subsequent work. There was a good deal of conjecture about a novel supposedly entitled *La cordillera* and reputedly almost ready for publication in 1969 (possibly along with two other novels). But by 1977 Rulfo was talking only of a nameless work which he might some day publish as a 'noveleta' together with a few stories. When he died, in 1986, the public was still waiting.

When *Pedro Páramo* is considered in perspective we are able to perceive themes such as the Mexican socio-political phenomenon known as *caciquismo*, or the universal preoccupation with death and eschatology expressed through a profoundly Mexican culture. But when the novel is being approached for the first time we have no opportunity to achieve such a perspective – at least until the half-way point – and our mind is fully engaged in coping with the paradoxes and enigmas, the surprises and disclosures. It is at first a novel of mystery and discovery. In perspective Pedro Páramo himself would be recognised as the dominant character, but on a first reading his son, Juan Preciado, captures the attention from the moment he begins to narrate, and it is not until the second half of the novel that he fades into the background. (As we shall see later, the best mythical interpretations of the novel also focus on Juan's journey, encounters and experiences.)

The opening word of the novel ('Vine') establishes a relationship between Juan and the reader: that of the story-teller and his audience.[3] (Only much later is the theoretical falseness of that relationship revealed, when Dorotea is discovered to be his audience.) By the end of the first fragment we know that the narrator has begun a quest, and our interest is aroused in his motivation and his progress. Rulfo has begun with a rapid and disarmingly clear presentation of material, identifying the quest's location (Comala), stating its reason ('porque acá vivía mi padre'), indicating the son's estrangement from his father ('un tal Pedro Páramo') and closeness to his mother ('Mi madre me lo dijo'), and explaining the journey as fulfilment of a promise to his dying mother. Within half a page some uncertainty has been introduced. Juan's mother has urged him to seek what his father owes him by right, and we wonder what kind of past conflicts may have caused her bitterness. And temporarily Juan's attitude becomes less clear. There is no expression of emotion about his mother's death, and he repeatedly admits that his promises were made merely to placate her. However, by the end of the first fragment Rulfo pretends to restore the impression of simplicity. Juan candidly recalls that his search was motivated by dreams, wishful thinking and hope, and emphatically declares: 'Por eso vine a Comala'. In an important respect this opening fragment typifies the development of the novel. It sets up an opposition between reader expectation and actual fictional reality. (The expectation is that Juan's love for his mother and promises to her will prove to be the cause of his quest.) At the same time it tardily reveals information which, running counter to expectation, disturbs, disappoints or shocks the reader.

Juan's arrival in Comala, narrated in the second fragment, continues the process. According to his mother's description Comala would lie on a green and fertile plain, but Juan remembers his first visual impression in sharply contrasting terms: heat, transparency, greyness and emptiness. He is guided to the town by a passing stranger who reveals three facts about Pedro Páramo, each revelation being highlighted by technical devices. The first, 'Yo también soy hijo de Pedro Páramo' (p.67), is accompanied by the mocking caws of a flock of crows; the second, that Pedro Páramo is 'un rencor vivo', comes reinforced by a crack of the muleteer's whip; the third, 'Pedro Páramo murió hace muchos años', closes the fragment, leaving us with a pause in which to absorb the negative impact of the three revelations. Above all, Juan's quest now appears void. But within a few pages a new kind of mystery has been developed, arousing Juan's curiosity, uneasiness and fear. We readers participate in the narrator's own struggle to comprehend the nature of this town, with its eerie emptiness and with inhabitants whose reality becomes increasingly doubtful. Rulfo gradually introduces the elements of uncertainty. A woman comes into sight, disappears, reappears and speaks, and we sense that if Juan needs to reassure himself that 'sus ojos eran como todos los ojos de la gente que vive sobre la tierra' (p.71) there are reasons for him (and us) to be thinking of something phantasmal. This is Eduviges Dyada, whose claim that she has been informed of Juan's visit by his mother becomes not merely surprising but positively unreal when she ascribes the faintness of his mother's voice to the fact that she is dead. Like Juan, we repeatedly search for the touchstone that would confirm our grasp of reality, such as the relatively comforting notion that Eduviges is mad. But like Juan we find each touchstone successively removed. When Eduviges's corporal existence is discounted, Damiana Cisneros seems to offer a relatively 'normal' viewpoint. But she too proves immaterial, and her disappearance in the middle of a conversation (p.109) dramatically exposes the stark notion that Juan is (was) the sole occupant of a ghost town.

In one important respect the reader's discoveries differ from those of Juan. While Juan is in conversation with Eduviges (or possibly asleep) three fragments of third-person narrative intervene (pp.75–9). It is necessary for us to cope, therefore, with an additional subversion of our desire for comprehension and logic. Rulfo delays the moment of clarification until the end of the second of these fragments, when he identifies the new character and enables us to recognise these as scenes from Pedro Páramo's childhood. For the moment there is no obvious link between them and Juan's arrival in Comala, but within a few more pages the connection begins to appear. Eduviges recalls the time of Miguel Páramo's death (pp.86–8); almost immediately we encounter scenes narrated in the third person which deal with the same period. Juxtaposed with these is a fragment concerning the death of Pedro's father (pp.88–9). The chronology is profoundly obscure to us at this point, but we have the sense of glimpsing scenes and hearing conversations from earlier epochs. When Rulfo returns us to Juan's first-person narrative we wonder whether Juan too has perceived these scenes and conversations, for he refers to shouts and screams and Damiana offers the explanation: 'Tal vez sea algún eco que está aquí encerrado' (p.98). After another cluster of scenes from earlier epochs Damiana enlarges on the idea: 'Este pueblo está lleno de ecos' (p.107). And four fragments later, as though to confirm this, Rulfo writes: 'Ruidos. Voces. Rumores. Canciones lejanas' (p.113). Whatever the explanation that subsequent analysis makes possible, there can be no denying the impression that Rulfo appears to have been seeking for the first-time reader: that the novel concerns Juan Preciado's experiences and discoveries, and that the scenes from earlier periods are phantasmal re-enactments, the interminable echoes of moments of trauma, crisis, wistfulness and torment, which help Juan and the reader to assemble a picture of Pedro Páramo and Comala.

The encounter with Donis and his sister is a final illusion of Juan's contact with reality, until the woman's body decomposes in the heat and Juan goes into the street in search of air to breathe. Although this could be seen, in retrospect, as hallucinations pointing to Juan's death, it hardly prepares us for that on a first reading. The last words of the fragment – 'Fue lo último que vi' (p.125) – remind us that Juan is still narrating and therefore promise an account of his survival. Rulfo's greatest surprise occurs here, at the centre of the novel, in the paradoxical sentence that begins the next fragment: '¿Quieres hacerme creer que te mató el ahogo, Juan Preciado?' (p.126). The first-person narrative form has deceived us into believing that Juan has a tangible link with our own world. It is now revealed as an illusion. Juan's narrative has been the words of a dead man, part of a dialogue with a dead woman, Dorotea, who shares his tomb. Juan's quest has led him to an awareness of his father's life but also to an encounter with his own death. From this point in the novel our difficulties diminish, for although the second half continues to pose questions many of the mysteries introduced previously are steadily resolved. With Juan now confined to a minor and passive role, our attention focuses on the development of Pedro Páramo's career, with occasional glimpses of Susana San Juan.

At this point it will be useful to step back from the narrative in which we have willingly become absorbed, and to achieve some perspective on the overall course of events. Chronologically the events belong to six phases. (1) Pedro Páramo is seen during childhood years in a relatively poor family. He does chores for his mother and grandmother, holds an apprenticeship in the telegraph office, and dreams of Susana (who has left Comala). His father, Lucas Páramo, suffers a violent death. (2) The beginning of Pedro's rise to power is exposed, as he uses a combination of astuteness and ruthless force to gain control of most of the local land. Through his administrator, Fulgor Sedano, he arranges to marry Dolores Preciado in order to resolve his debt and acquire her property. Sedano settles a boundary dispute with Toribio Aldrete by eliminating the man. Pedro Páramo has become the local *cacique*. (3) The third phase concerns events before and after Miguel Páramo's death. One of Pedro's illegitimate sons, baby Miguel, is brought to the cacique by the priest, Padre Rentería. As a young man Miguel gains a reputation for unrestrained wantonness. Among his misdemeanours are murder (Rentería's brother) and rape (Rentería's niece). Miguel is killed when thrown from his horse, and soon afterwards Eduviges Dyada commits suicide. This is the period when Padre Rentería is seen tormented by guilt for his lack of resistance to Pedro Páramo's power and influence. (4) The Revolution reaches Comala. But with tactics that are wary, cunning and hypocritical Pedro avoids any loss of land. It is during these years that Susana San Juan returns to Comala with her father, Bartolomé. Pedro arranges for the death of Bartolomé in the mines and marries his daughter, but by now Susana is mentally unbalanced and slipping towards death. When Comala fails to mourn her death, Pedro swears to allow the town and district to fall into decay. (5) The fourth fragment from the end of the novel, covering the last years of the Revolution and the period of the Guerra de los Cristeros (i.e. a decade in all) acts as a transition to the time of Pedro's death. (6) Some years later Dolores Preciado dies and her son, Juan, travels to Comala in search of his father.

This simplified plan of events is a useful aid to our analysis of *Pedro Páramo* for a perverse reason. We naturally feel more at ease with the material when we can recognise it in familiar terms: a chronological sequence with perceptible causes and effects, carefully organised by a God-like author or narrator. Our plan therefore illustrates our dependence on the very things that Rulfo set out to undermine by arranging this novel as a collection of narrative fragments, juxtaposing episodes from different periods in time and defying the traditional assumptions about the text, the narrator and the author. His bold and inventive technique led some of the early critical reviews to complain of an unjustified randomness in the novel, but it was this technique that soon led him to be recognised as a forerunner of the Boom.

The narrative is presented from three standpoints. One is that of Juan Preciado, who tells in the first person what happened to him just before and after his arrival in Comala (including his memory of his mother's words and his recollection of stories told by Eduviges, Damiana and Donis's sister). Another – although far less important – is that of Susana San Juan, whose few first-person meditations unexpectedly intervene two-thirds of the way through the novel ('Estoy acostada. . .' (p.144)). Finally there is the standpoint from which events are narrated in the third person. Some critics call it the omniscient author's point of view, but the term is less than ideal in this case for there is a marked lack of omniscience in many of the fragments. Some are dialogues unaccompanied by narrative, others convey images or sounds at a superficial level, while several do actually present characters' thoughts as well as their words, deeds and appearance. What Rulfo appears to have sought is a medium that is almost as cinematographic as it is literary. The author acts like an instrument that picks up sounds, sights, feelings, thoughts and so on, in Comala. Among the sounds that are picked up are, of course, the voices of Juan Preciado and Susana San Juan (in the first-person narrative fragments). The author (instrument) does not edit, restructure or explain, but only transmits and displays signals.

That is in fact an exaggeration of the technique, for Rulfo has obviously imposed his artistic will on the novel's form. Despite superficial appearances, the order of fragments is not haphazard.[4] For example, the four consecutive fragments from '¿Qué es lo que pasa, doña Eduviges?' (p.85) juxtapose the deaths of Pedro's son and father and interconnect them through their psychological effect on the central character. If we work outwards from these four fragments, we notice that they form part of a larger series with thematic cohesion created by Eduviges's conversation with Juan, Eduviges's contact with Miguel Páramo, the effect of Miguel's death on Padre Rentería, and the effect of Eduviges's suicide on Padre Rentería. Several other clusters of fragments might similarly be shown to have interdependency and cohesion, notably the six between the appearance and disappearance of Damiana (all focused on Fulgor Sedano's role in Pedro's early business affairs) and the ten that begin with Susana's 'Estoy acostada' (all focused on Susana or on Pedro's obsession with her). There is even a tendency towards a chronological arrangement of episodes within each cluster. (In fact there is almost a chronological structure throughout the second half of the novel.) We may also perceive an artistic design underlying the frequent cases of contrastive juxtaposing. Juan's sweet memory of his mother's words, for example, is sometimes contrasted with a more bitter reality: the descriptions of Comala (p.66), the meanings of the word 'murmullo' (p.127). The most frequently used contrast is that between the arid emptiness of Juan's Comala and the moist fertility of earlier epochs. In fact, mention of rainfall serves almost as a motif to help the reader to recognise and respond to fragments that deal with Pedro Páramo's lifetime. The self-consciousness of Rulfo's striving for artistic effect is often visible in the repetition of words. Sometimes such repetition links fragments that are obviously interrelated ('Más te vale' ends and begins two interrupted parts of the conversation between Eduviges and Juan (pp.88 and 97)). But at times the verbal linkage operates as a device to draw attention to underlying connections (Dorotea asks Juan in the confinement of their tomb, '¿No sientes el golpear de la lluvia?' and the next fragment, in which Dorotea's role in the lives of Pedro and Miguel is obliquely shown, begins with the words 'Al amanecer, gruesas gotas de lluvia cayeron sobre la tierra' (p.130)).

Rulfo admitted to having changed the structure of *Pedro Páramo* to cut out 'divagaciones, intromisiones y explicaciones aberrantes'.[5] Any remaining impression of randomness is therefore deliberately sought. Three different types of explanation have been given by Rulfo himself. One is to engage the reader's participation in the re-creation of the novel, 'teniendo en cuenta al lector como coautor' ('Con Rulfo. . .', p.5) – a characteristic of the typical Boom novels of the 1960s. The greatest advantage of this method is not merely to mystify or to entertain the reader but to enable us to learn something about the nature of reality as we construct the substitute reality of the text. In another of his explanations Rulfo likened a fragmentary, non-chronological structure to life itself: 'La vida es caótica. No tiene una secuencia lógica'.[6] But this comment is more appropriate to the technique in *El llano en llamas* than to its use in *Pedro Páramo*, where the lives that are presented to us are those of the dead. Whatever the reasons for *other* novelists adopting this kind of narrative method, Rulfo's best justification is surely that 'los muertos no viven en el espacio ni en el tiempo'.[7] In other words, to use a chronological arrangement would mean subjecting the characters of a dead town to the control of linear time. The fragmentary structure therefore works as a suitable medium for suggesting an atemporal way of perceiving an alternative reality.

The complexities of narrative technique do not ultimately obscure the novel's social realism. Rulfo himself recalled that 'Yo, en principio, quise presentar un cacique que es una cosa característica de México. . . predomina en cierta región de México' ('Con Rulfo. . .', p.4) before the novel managed to separate itself from the author's control. Although it does not belong, as one critic has claimed, 'en la categoría de ficción neo-realista',[8] we must surely recognise its geographical, historical and social basis before going any further.

In the third fragment of the novel Juan Preciado mentions that the day before arriving in Comala he had left the town of Sayula. According to Donis's sister one of the many roads from Comala leads to Contla. The novel is located, therefore, within reach of these towns in the state of Jalisco about fifty to eighty miles south of the city of Guadalajara – the area where, it will be recalled, Rulfo was born and brought up. Further south, some forty miles from the Pacific coast, lies a town with the name Comala. However, Rulfo has always insisted that his fictional town is based not on the real Comala but on San Gabriel, which had been a fertile and prosperous town of seven or eight thousand inhabitants but became an isolated and run-down place of one hundred and fifty (*Autobiografía armada*, p.61). Thousands of acres of formerly productive land became eroded, leading to the abandonment of local towns ('Con Rulfo. . .', p.4). After thirty years' absence from San Gabriel, Rulfo returned and spent a night there with the wind howling through the bushes, and this created the final stimulus for the novel that he had been planning for a decade. He chose the name Comala for its symbolic value, the word *comal* being used in Mexico to denote an earthenware pot for cooking tortillas, which leads to the idea of Comala's own scorched situation – 'lugar sobre las brasas' (*Autobiografía armada*, p.61). It is worth noting that recent travel guides to Jalisco offer attractive descriptions of the state's towns, landscape and climate, and that Rulfo himself admitted the real Comala to be fertile and developing. This implies that for the purpose of his work of fiction he has focused on one part of the region, selectively, in order to highlight his fundamentally negative attitude towards Mexican small-town life and values and towards the problems faced by human beings on this earth.

Rulfo has been fairly reluctant to admit a historical context: 'Sí, hay ciertos hechos allí. . .' but 'nunca se menciona una fecha' (*Autobiografía armada*, pp.64–5). However, the pages on the Revolution towards the end of the book serve as a point of reference from which approximate dates for other parts of the action may be calculated. The Revolution is briefly alluded to in the fragment where Pedro remembers Susana being brought back to Comala; at that time 'había gente levantada en armas' (p.152). It fully enters the novel when 'un hombre al que decían *el Tartamudo*' brings news that Fulgor Sedano has been killed (p.163). Everything suggests the year 1910 or 1911, during Madero's revolution against Díaz. A few pages later, fragments that mention the *Villistas* from the north are presumably set in 1913 or 1914, when Pancho Villa was commander of the Army of the North in its advance towards Mexico City during the revolution against Victoriano Huerta. Finally, the fragment that begins: '*El Tilcuate* siguió viniendo' (p.187) condenses four conversations from four different periods. Names or references act as approximate keys to the dating: *El Tilcuate's* men would become *carrancistas* around 1914 or 1915, during the period of Villa's defeat by Venustiano Carranza; they would join Obregón at about the time of Carranza's removal from Mexico City in 1920; they would be released from duty ('andamos sueltos') during the next few years (by 1923 the army was only 60 per cent of its former strength); and Padre Rentería would resort to arms around the beginning of the Guerra de los Cristeros in 1926. If Susana's return is in 1910, and Pedro had waited thirty years for her – as his voice says at the beginning of one fragment (p.151) – then it may be seen that the scenes concerning his adolescence and early manhood are situated during the 1870s and 1880s. Those dealing with his death belong somewhere between 1926 and 1929, during the Guerra de los Cristeros.[9]

Having established the historical period of the action, we may now consider what bearing this information has on the development of themes. Rulfo repeatedly informed interviewers that his earliest objective was to present a *cacique*. Local Indian governors (*tlatoque*) of ancient Mexico were the predecessors of modern *caciques*. In the course of time most large property owners became known by the term, being recognised informally by the state and central governments as the regional political bosses. Rulfo evidently saw one advantage in the system: 'la estabilidad política del país tiene mucho que ver con el caciquismo, pues cada cacique domina cierta región que el Estado deja en sus manos' ('Con Rulfo. . .', p.4). But the novel conveys an exceedingly negative impression overall. Pedro rises to power during the years of Porfirio Díaz's government (1876–80; 1884–1910), which was notorious for facilitating the expansion of large estates. He shows a *cacique* to be autocratic, self-interested, ruthless, above the law, and capable of murder. And the economic dependency of a region on one individual is shown to be potentially disastrous. Once Pedro vows to exact his revenge on the community Comala begins to decay: '–Me cruzaré de brazos y Comala se morirá de hambre. Y así lo hizo' (p.187).

The state of Jalisco was the scene of violent conflict during the period of the Revolution: battles between Federal and rebel armies; the seizure of *haciendas* by groups of peasant revolutionaries; the sacking of towns and villages. It is notable that *Pedro Páramo* offers only a handful of brief, elliptical and partial glimpses of this activity: peasant groups who took up arms because others had done the same were unclear about their ideological purpose, were joined by hordes of opportunists, were susceptible to bribery by landowners, and shifted their allegiance according to the prevailing tide of fortune. There is none of the emphasis on social injustice that we find in his short story 'La tierra que nos han dado'. The focal point continues to be the *cacique's* retention of supreme power over his property and the neighbourhood, by means of astuteness, hypocrisy and bribery to steer the revolutionaries and opportunist groups away from Media Luna. In effect Pedro pays for protection by ensuring that the dominant local guerrilla band is under his control. When the area falls into decay, it is not the result of any social revolution, only the consequence of Pedro's fatigue and revenge.

To an extent, therefore, *Pedro Páramo* does fulfil Rulfo's original plan to illustrate Mexico's *caciquismo*. The geographical location and historical settings, though imprecise, could not be considered as merely coincidental. The eponymous protagonist's life represents the formation of a *cacique* and his impact on a region. We see in his activities one manner in which *caciquismo* survived the Revolution. On the other hand so diffuse is the author's interest that the novel never assumes the characteristics of a political commentary. More important is the overall impression of Pedro as an individual, with his combination of universal and Mexican psychological traits.

To the people of Comala the adult Pedro Páramo reveals himself as haughty, unscrupulous and violent, and the image that he leaves after his death is of 'un rencor vivo' (p.68). But the reader is given an insight into Pedro's yearning for the love of Susana San Juan. It may not help us to like the character any more (particularly when we realise that to obtain Susana he arranges the death of her father) but it does help us to understand him more fully and to see him as an individual. Even Pedro, despite his material power, remains unfulfilled and dies disillusioned with his life. This inner world of the protagonist – which he shields from other characters – is exposed in fragments from his childhood whose tenderness contrasts with the harshness of his adult behaviour. He is introduced to us as a nostalgic dreamer, longing for his childhood sweetheart. Susana – pure and unattainable – seems to epitomise his remote aspirations. It is not an excessively simplistic contrast, however, for the fragments of his childhood and adolescence also show him with an eye for making money and an unwillingness to submit. One fragment in particular offers a clue to his development: the scene when news of his father's death is brought (pp.88–9). At first his mother's weeping prompts his natural concern: '¿Por qué lloras, mamá?' But the narrative follows Pedro's train of thought. The greyness of the sky and the presence of his grieving mother in the doorway both constitute obstacles to the arrival of the sun and the dawn. The grief itself becomes a hindrance to him. He creates an emotional distance between himself and his mother – 'aquella mujer' – and when he speaks again to her the intimate word 'mamá' has been replaced: 'Y a ti quién te mató, madre?' It is a fairly clear indication that Pedro's egocentric outlook is developing. The only death that matters is one's own. Pedro seems to be hardening himself in order to become impervious to external influences on his life.[10] The love for Susana is one aspect of vulnerability that Pedro never manages to control or suppress. But the people of Comala are not permitted to see this as a sign of weakness in the man. Indeed one of the main purposes in allowing us as readers to perceive some of the vulnerability of Pedro appears to be that of demonstrating the superficiality of his external image. He is therefore typical of the macho type described by Octavio Paz in his essays analysing the Mexican national character. 'Entre la realidad y la persona', writes Paz, 'establece [el mexicano] una muralla...de impasibilidad y lejanía... Para nosotros, contrariamente a lo que ocurre con otros pueblos, abrirse es una debilidad o una traición. El hermetismo es un recurso de nuestro recelo y desconfianza.'[11]

The peculiarly Mexican qualities of the novel are equally present in the treatment of religious attitudes and death. Many fragments suggest a powerful influence of the Roman Catholic Church over a community. But Rulfo offers a picture of spiritual imperfection and unattainable standards, of human nature remorselessly leading people in behaviour that the Church forbids, and of a Church steeped in doctrine, perplexed yet inflexible. In these fragments Padre Rentería acts as the insecure and anguished representative of the Church. He is aware of living by double standards. In his fear of offending Pedro Páramo, whose money supports him, he has permitted – he believes – all the evil in Comala. He seeks absolution from his superior in Comala, but this is denied. All he receives from this priest is a cynical view of Providence and of human nature. Everything comes into the world by the grace of God but in bitter form: 'Estamos condenados a eso' (p.141). In Comala numerous characters appear to have been condemned never to reach Heaven. When Dorotea is told that her sins are too great she gives up hope (p.135). But she complains at the priest's injustice in thus removing life's greatest motivating force. Injustice seems also to be at the heart of Eduviges's failure to receive Rentería's blessing, since Rulfo presents it as a consequence of the inflexible application of doctrine. In Rentería's own words: '¡Tantos bienes acumulados para su salvación, y perderlos así de pronto!' (p.96). Rentería's torment is increased by doubts about his right to grant or refuse pardon: 'No podrás ir más al cielo. Pero que Dios te perdone. . . . Yo también te perdono en nombre de él' (p.143). There is no conviction in his response to Dorotea's confession, only tiredness, desperation and a desire to be freed of her. The same hopeless and evasive impulse leads him to dispatch the queue of people awaiting confession with his back turned to them.

To complete our impression of Padre Rentería we must take into account his decision to resort to arms in the Guerra de los Cristeros (p.187). This civil war, concentrated in the state of Jalisco and the western mountains, was caused partly by anti-clerical measures introduced by the Revolutionary government and partly by anti-revolutionary activity using the defence of the Church as a banner and the cry 'Cristo Rey' as their slogan. Priests had only two options: to go into hiding or to take up arms. Rentería's choice of the latter course suggests an attempt to resolve his inner anguish and a lifetime's indecision by means of simple, firm action in defence of the

Church. In the final analysis, however, there are no grounds for inferring any approval on the author's part. Rulfo's family suffered enormous tragedy and deprivation in this conflict, and the safest assumption is that Rentería's decision represents only a despairing commitment to a destructive course of action in a general context whose implications for spiritual values were thoroughly negative.

Although in these respects *Pedro Páramo* expresses Rulfo's view of the Catholic Church's impact in a small town and its vicinity, certain features clearly lift the novel to a more transcendental level. The Comala thronging with people belongs to only parts of the book. The town to which Juan Preciado travels is inhabited by the dead. The novel is 'un diálogo de muertos' ('Con Rulfo. . .', p.4). A first distinction may be noted between the dead above the ground and those in the tombs below. In Comala Juan Preciado meets several apparently real people: Abundio, Eduviges, Damiana, Donis and his sister. From time to time the voices of others can be heard. These apparently real people are referred to by some of the characters themselves as souls in torment. According to Donis's sister, 'esto está lleno de ánimas; un puro vagabundear de gente que murió sin perdón y que no lo conseguirá de ningún modo' (p.120). Damiana says of Eduviges: 'Debe de estar penando todavía' (p.99). In one of her most explicit passages Dorotea recalls the separation of her soul from her body as if it were an event with a physical dimension: 'Y abrí la boca para que se fuera. Y se fue. Sentí cuando cayó en mis manos el hilito de sangre con que estaba amarrada a mi corazón' (p.135). Dorotea assumes that her soul is 'vagando por la tierra como tantas otras; buscando vivos que recen por ella' (p.135). Clearly Rulfo has given a physical dimension to religious beliefs. The Roman Catholic concept of Purgatory appears to be their basis, with the characters referred to undergoing the cathartic pains which purge them and cleanse their souls of sin. But there is a problem if we are looking for a strict interpretation according to orthodox terms, for Rulfo's characters (or souls) appear to be offered no hope of eventual admission to Heaven. Another Catholic concept, Hell, may be involved here. It is worth noting that Abundio refers (humorously) to Hell as a place other than Comala ('muchos de los que allí se mueren, al llegar al infierno regresan por su cobija' (p.68)). But below the ground in the graves and tombs the characters, aware of their confinement and behaving like living entities rather than lifeless skeletons, could be undergoing a kind of

Hell in which they are condemned incessantly to remember their past lives, full of frustration and guilt.[12] If this is the case, we cannot fail to notice the absence of any apparent suffering or torment, which means that again the orthodox image has been amended. The reason, of course, is that in Mexico Roman Catholicism is but one of the religious ingredients. As Rulfo pointed out, 'el indígena metió su paganismo, su superstición, su forma de imaginar, de pensar las cosas' ('Con Rulfo. . .', p.4). A full explanation of *Pedro Páramo* therefore must take into account the syncretism caused by the racial and cultural mix.

One of the remarkable features of the novel is the extent to which it is about deaths or Death. Following the death of his mother, Juan Preciado travels to a dead town in which he meets his own death. Various fragments narrate the deaths of Comala's inhabitants, several of them violent (Lucas Páramo, Toribio Aldrete, Miguel Páramo, Fulgor Sedano, Bartolomé San Juan, Damiana Cisneros, and possibly Pedro himself),[13] a few of them moving (Susana San Juan, Abundio's wife). Some of the characters (such as Susana) speak with an unusual detachment about death. The whole book is based on a potentially macabre situation: a dialogue of the dead. But instead of a morbid or gruesome atmosphere we have a combination of mystery, fear, naturalness and humour. The dead themselves have a similarity to the living that is at once disconcerting and reassuring. Can death be terrible if the dead can joke like Dorotea with Juan? Unsure of his companion's name or gender, Juan makes an elementary blunder: '¿Dices que te llamas Doroteo?' (p.126). Her reply contains magnificent irony. She sets the record straight and courteously puts him at his ease in a manner fully compliant with the etiquette of the living, while simultaneously drawing attention to the ultimate absurdity of their being concerned with such trivial worldly details: 'Da lo mismo. Aunque mi nombre sea Dorotea. Pero da lo mismo' (p.126). Later she refers to their future with amusing understatement: 'Ya déjate de miedos. Nadie te puede dar ya miedo. Haz por pensar en cosas agradables porque vamos a estar mucho tiempo enterrados' (p.130). Rulfo's own explanation of the treatment of death in *Pedro Páramo* was that 'en México se le teme a la muerte, pero al mismo tiempo, el pueblo se burla de ella', and he pointed to traditions on All Saints Day as an illustration of the national attitude: 'El día de los muertos se hacen calaveras de azúcar y la gente se las come' ('Con Rulfo. . .', p.4).

The prominence of death is one of a number of fundamental ingredients of *Pedro Páramo* that turns our minds to universal themes, Another of them is the journey that forms a structural basis. If we connect Juan's journey to Comala with his encounter with death, we recognise that his experiences constitute a kind of metaphysical quest, such as those known throughout the world in myths. Many critics have drawn attention to the underlying mythical content of the novel.[14] The most convincing mythical interpretations are those concerning Juan's experiences (rather than Pedro's life). In making a journey from his mother's bedside to his father's town – i.e. from his home back to his place of origin – Juan makes an archetypal journey. In particular it is consistent with the universal myth of Eternal Return (according to which no event is unique, and the course of human history is a sequence of cycles). Moreover there is a specifically *náhuatl* version of the myth in which Mother Earth orders her children to leave in search of the appointed place, as Dolores Preciado virtually orders her son to depart on his quest. At the core of the Myth of Eternal Return is a place (usually a temple or sacred city) at which heaven, earth and hell meet: a Cosmic Centre or *Axis Mundi*. In Mesoamerican mythology this Axis Mundi is fundamental. Our discussion of religion and death above clearly indicates that Comala fits this model. Though not exactly contiguous to heaven, it could certainly be seen as a meeting-point of Church, earth and hell.

In the course of his journey Juan follows the model of the archetypal hero. After leaving home he travels to 'the threshold of adventure'[15] where a 'shadow presence. . .guards the passage' (his encounter with Abundio on the road to Comala). Like a mythological hero he enters 'a world of unfamiliar yet strangely intimate forces'. He then undergoes 'tests' and receives 'magical aid'. Juan 'arrives at the nadir of the mythological round' after sleeping with the sister of Donis. The archetypal hero's triumph is marked by 'sexual union with the goddess mother of the world', 'recognition by the father-creator', 'his own divinization', or 'theft of the boon he came to gain'. Here we notice Rulfo's ironical use of and divergence from the archetype: Juan's sexual union with the incestuous sister; his discovery of facts about his father; his death and survival in a subterranean existence; his failure to obtain the object of his quest. The next stage of the archetypal hero's journey – his return – is of course not a part of Rulfo's book. Juan's fate is more in keeping with that of the hero in *mexica* mythology. In the latter the conquest of the archetypal place required the sacrifice of the man-god.[16] Incidentally, Juan's descent beneath the ground is capable of being seen as an equivalent of the subterranean journey in Aztec mythology.

A further aspect of the mythical dimension of Juan's journey concerns the dominant role played in it by feminine characters. The son's quest is spurred by the Mother, and the return to his origins leads to a re-encounter with her. According to this interpretation the various women in Juan's journey – Dolores, Eduviges, Damiana, the sister and Dorotea – represent different forms of the mother figure. The mythological *Magna Mater* has a benevolent function as a goddess of fertility and health. But she has a malignant function as goddess of natural cataclysms; goddess of moon, water and night; and goddess of the earth to which the dead return (goddess of infertility).[17] In Aztec mythology the malignant goddess or Terrible Mother is represented by Coatlicue. It is possible to read *Pedro Páramo* in terms of this archetype. Dolores sends her son on a quest that leads to his death. On the journey Juan encounters a series of transformations of the Great Mother, one of whom is the sister of Donis (Adonis is the Greek god of beauty loved by Aphrodite). The Biblical Adam and Eve are one point of reference for this couple, and the Fall from Grace is represented by their incest. In the Biblical context Juan's implied sexual union with the woman leads to his own Fall. But universal mythology – and particularly Mesoamerican mythology – underlie the Biblical. In this aspect the woman is Juan's mother (Eve is the mother of all human beings), so that the Great Mother has seduced her son. Rulfo emphasises the sister's transformation into earth ('El cuerpo de aquella mujer hecho de tierra, envuelto en costras de tierra, se desbarataba como si estuviera derritiéndose en un charco de lodo' (p.125)), making her consistent with the *náhuatl* mythical concept of the Great Mother as Mother Earth (besides referring to the Biblical idea of returning to dust). After his death Juan is entombed with Dorotea, as though he were united with the last of the transformations of the mother figure (Álvarez, pp.37–61).

The question arises, of course, whether Rulfo consciously sought to give his novel such mythical dimensions.[18] There is no doubt that some of the links between the text and myths are rather tenuous. For example, the myth of Oedipus is represented by one son (Abundio) killing the father (Pedro) while another son (Juan) has intimate relations with the mother (Donis's sister). The myth of Andromeda (suggested by the name of Bartolomé's mine) is enacted because Susana is a victim whom the father relinquishes to the monster (Pedro Páramo) in order to save Comala from destruction. But problems arise only when precise parallels are sought. There are too many obvious hints at allegorical meanings (such as the names of characters and places) for everything to be accidental, and the transcendental level of the novel is undeniable. In the final analysis it can be seen that Rulfo departs from the main myths before their completion, especially in the case of the Myth of Eternal Return, which the negative outcome of *Pedro Páramo* seems to contradict.[19]

This discussion of *Pedro Páramo* has led us through the mysteries of an unsophisticated first reading, the social realist theme of *caciquismo*, the portrayal of Mexican psychological traits, the eschatological preoccupations derived from cultural syncretism, and the myths which give the book its most transcendental dimension. It would be inappropriate to make any attempt to isolate one or other of these perspectives as the essence of the novel. Rulfo himself acknowledged that the process of writing created a momentum that carried his work beyond the limited original plans: 'Fue una cosa intuitiva y producto puramente de la imaginación. Adquirió vida propia hasta que logró separarse del autor y tomar su propio camino' ('Con Rulfo. . .', p.4) Moreover, the simultaneous presence of several layers of meaning is a feature that we ultimately acknowledge as being inherent not only in the work as a whole but in its constituent parts. A lasting ambiguity has been introduced into the manner in which several events and situations are presented.[20] At times the identity of characters speaking or spoken to is obscure. A notable cluster of such cases occurs after Damiana Cisneros fades out, leaving the echo of Juan's voice calling her name. The four fragments that follow (pp.110–13) appear to introduce us obliquely to facets of life in Comala during Pedro's time, particularly his rapacious appetite for women and for land. But it would be little more than supposition to identify the anonymous voice coaxing 'Chona' (p.112) as that of Pedro. Another problem inherent in these and several other fragments is that of locating their temporal position. It is impossible to find the exact slot for each of the four fragments in the overall train of events. In this case ambiguity arises inevitably from the need to create an impression of endlessly reverberating phantasmal echoes.

A different kind of ambiguity occurs, however, when we cannot be sure what actually *happens*. Perhaps the most important instance is the presentation of Pedro's death in the last two fragments. What impedes our full cognisance of the facts here is a combination of factors, particularly the elision of details, the shifting focus of attention, the choice of material, and the dual significance of certain key sentences. Abundio must look a threatening figure as – knife in hand – he demands money to bury his wife because Pedro 'se escondió debajo de las cobijas' and Damiana shouts '¡Están matando a don Pedro!' (p.192). But at the vital moment Rulfo diverts the narrative's focus from an account of what happens to an insight into Abundio's thoughts. Abundio is incompletely aware of things: grief over his wife's death, irritation caused by Damiana's shouting. The narrative then elides events that we ourselves would consider crucial and, following Abundio's range of awareness, mentions the approaching men and the fallen figure of Damiana, whose open mouth is now silent. The men seem to associate the bloody knife with Damiana's body, since they readily accept Pedro's indication that he is unharmed. It is only in the last fragment that we realise that Pedro could have been fatally wounded, when he is unable to raise his hands and slowly falls to the ground. But again the narrative adopts an interior point of view. There is no mention of pain, only of weakness, nostalgia, awareness that he is dying, and absence of the will to survive. He is guided into death (presumably) with the phantasmal assistance of Damiana.

Rulfo did not intend us to be able to say that Pedro is killed by Abundio. This is a possible inference; but the text leaves open an alternative: that Pedro dies because he lacks the will to continue living. We might perceive one or two specific reasons for this avoidance of clear statement. To a dead man it is of no significance whether he was murdered or died of natural causes; in a dialogue of the dead the scale of values is different from those in the world of the living. But this deliberate ambiguity surrounding a crucial event in a conspicuous position in the novel is surely Rulfo's careful indication to us that his text as a whole should not be read on one level alone. *Pedro Páramo* is not gratuitously obscure. The ambiguities of the narrative are contrived to lift the meaning beyond the level of conventional fiction and superficial reality in order to help the reader to experience the nature of Comala's reality.

PETER BEARDSELL

NOTES

1 *Los narradores ante el público* (Joaquín Mortiz, Mexico, 1966), p.24.
2 See *El gallo de oro y otros textos para cine* (Era/Alianza, Madrid, 1982).
3 Juan Rulfo, *Pedro Páramo* (Edición de José Carlos González Boixo, Cátedra, Madrid, 1984), p.63. All page references are to this edition, and are given within brackets in the text of this chapter.
4 For a detailed analysis see José González Boixo, *Claves narrativas de Juan Rulfo* (Colegio Universitario de León, 1980), p.192 ff.
5 'Con Rulfo desde Madrid'. Interview with Juan E. González in *Sábado*, suplemento de *Uno más Uno*, 29 Sept. 1979, p.5. All subsequent references to this interview are given in the text after the abbreviated title 'Con Rulfo. . .'.
6 Quoted by M. Coddou in H. Giacoman (ed.), *Homenaje a Juan Rulfo* (Las Américas, New York, 1974), pp.66–7.
7 Reina Roffé, *Juan Rulfo. Autobiografía armada* (Corregidor, Buenos Aires, 1973), p.63.
8 Samuel O'Neill, in *Homenaje. . .*, p.286.
9 A more ambitious but excessively precise chronology is offered by Narciso Costa Ros in 'El mundo novelesco de Pedro Páramo', *Revista Chilena de Literatura*, no. 11 (abril, 1978), p.36 (quoted in José Riveiro Espasandín, *Pedro Páramo* (Guías Laia de Literatura, Barcelona, 1984), pp.46–7). 1858 is given as the date of Pedro's birth, 1864 as that of Susana's birth, and 1874–9 as the period when Pedro's grandfather, grandmother, father and mother die.
10 In his edition of *Pedro Páramo* J.C. González Boixo suggests (p.89) that the final words belong to a far later period in time than the rest of the fragment. It does not seem necessary to resort to such an explanation.
11 Octavio Paz, 'Máscaras mexicanas', in *El laberinto de la soledad* (Fondo de Cultura Económica, Mexico, 1973), p.27.
12 See Hugo Rodríguez Alcalá, *El arte de Juan Rulfo* (INBA, Mexico, 1965) and George R. Freeman, *Paradise and Fall in Rulfo's 'Pedro Páramo'. Archetype and Structural Unity* (CIDOC, Cuaderno 47, Cuernavaca, Mexico, 1970).
13 González Boixo and a majority of critics argue that in the last two fragments Abundio kills both Pedro and Damiana. But the textual evidence is inconclusive, leaving open other inferences which – as we shall see – are important for an understanding of the book.
14 In the space available here it is impossible to do full justice to the mythical interpretations of *Pedro Páramo*. Readers are recommended to consult Nicolás Emilio Álvarez, *Análisis arquetípico, mítico y simbológico de Pedro Páramo* (Ediciones Universal, Miami, 1983) and Violeta Peralta and Liliana Befumo Boschi, *Rulfo: la soledad creadora* (Fernando García Cambeiro, Buenos Aires, 1975). My own selective account is particularly indebted to the former.
15 Joseph Campbell, *The Hero with a Thousand Faces*, 2nd edn (Princeton University Press, Princeton, NJ), p.245. Quoted in Álvarez, *Análisis arquetípico*, p.62.

94

16 Alfredo López Austin, *Hombre-dios: religión y política en el mundo náhuatl* (UNAM, Mexico, 1973), p.127. Quoted in Álvarez, *Análisis arquetípico*, p.64.

17 Erich Neumann, *The Great Mother: an Analysis of the Archetype*, translated by R. Manheim, 2nd edn (Princeton University Press, Princeton, NJ, 1974). Quoted in Álvarez, *Análisis arquetípico*, p.42.

18 Anthony Stanton, wary of critics' insistence on universal or Greco-Roman archetypes, makes a strong case for placing the anthropological material within Mexican culture. See 'Estructuras antropológicas en *Pedro Páramo*', *Nueva Revista de Filología Hispánica*, vol. 36 (1988).

19 Gerald R. Freeman in *Homenaje. . .*, pp.257–81.

20 On this subject see in particular Steven Boldy, 'The use of ambiguity and the death(s) of Bartolomé San Juan in Rulfo's *Pedro Páramo*', *Forum for Modern Language Studies*, vol. 19, no. 3 (1983), pp.224–35.

5

CARLOS FUENTES:
LA MUERTE DE ARTEMIO CRUZ

ROBIN FIDDIAN

Carlos Fuentes is Mexico's most prolific, versatile and commercially successful living writer, and the recipient of numerous literary prizes which testify both to the constancy of his creative powers over a period spanning more than thirty years, and to the prestige which he enjoys throughout the Spanish-speaking world. The Biblioteca Breve prize of 1967 for *Cambio de piel* – the fourth in a total of more than a dozen novels or novellas that have been published to date – was followed a decade later by the Rómulo Gallegos prize for *Terra nostra* and then in 1987 by the equally prestigious Premio Cervantes which, all but coinciding with the publication of *Cristóbal Nonato*, set the seal on a career which has been notable as much for its tireless self-renewal as for its author's assiduously cultivated public profile and international projection. For Fuentes, like García Márquez and Vargas Llosa, is rarely out of the public eye, whether in Latin America, where he lived as a child – in Panama City, Quito, Montevideo and Rio de Janeiro between 1928 and 1934 and in Santiago and Buenos Aires from 1941 to 1943 – the United States of America, where his father served as counsellor of the Mexican Embassy from 1934 to 1940 and where Fuentes has held a series of academic positions at Harvard, Princeton and other universities, or in Europe, where he has lived in London and Paris and held a professorship at the University of Cambridge in 1986–7.

A former ambassador of his country under the presidency of Luis Echeverría (1970–6), Fuentes has regularly represented the political and cultural interests of Spanish America in the world at large, assuming a continental persona which was already apparent in the early 1960s. According to José Donoso, when Fuentes attended a congress of intellectuals at the University of Concepción in 1962 his articulate enthusiasm for the nascent values of the Cuban Revolution served as a catalyst for a wider response: 'Su entusiasmo por la figura de Fidel Castro en esa primera etapa, su fe en la revolución, enardeció a todo el Congreso de Intelectuales, que a raíz de su presencia quedó fuertemente politizado'. The impact of the Cuban Revolution throughout Latin America, its liberating and agglutinative effect on political opinion, are well-known facts of mid-twentieth-century history. Equally important for an understanding of the literary currents of the period is an acknowledgement of the role of individuals like Carlos Fuentes who through their public demeanour and professional example helped to create an *esprit de corps* among those who would shortly find themselves in the vanguard of the so-called Boom of Latin American fiction. 'No sólo por el estímulo literario de sus primeras novelas, sino también por su generosidad en forma de admiración y de ayuda', Donoso wrote, 'Carlos Fuentes ha sido uno de los factores precipitantes del *boom*.' Exploiting his considerable diplomatic and promotional skills, Fuentes became 'el primer agente activo y consciente de la internacionalización de la novela hispanoamericana de la década de los años sesenta'.[1]

Over the course of that heady and expansive decade which saw the publication of future classics like *Rayuela* (1960), *La ciudad y los perros* (1963), *La casa verde* (1966) and *Cien años de soledad* (1967), Fuentes himself produced no fewer than five novels or novellas: *La muerte de Artemio Cruz* and *Aura* (both in 1962), *Cambio de piel* and *Zona sagrada* (1967) and *Cumpleaños* (1969), as well as an important essay, *La nueva novela hispanoamericana* (1969), which surveyed the literary trends of an entire continent from the communal perspective – clearly defined in the opening pages of the text – of 'nosotros, los hispanoamericanos'. Through the 1970s in interviews like the one with Herman Doezema, and into the 1980s when he addresses audiences at UCLA, California, and Cambridge, England, Fuentes continues to speak for a continental body of opinion whose shared concerns include the threat posed to national sovereignty by North American espionage and military intervention, the prospects of the Southern nations for peace and prosperity in a world moving from a bipolar to a multipolar order, and the pressure on national governments constantly to reassess social, political, economic and cultural imperatives in an age of unequalled and unequal technological progress.[2]

The function of the writer in such circumstances, Fuentes believes, is to contest officially sponsored systems of thought and organisation of reality, to unsettle and subvert orthodox perceptions of the world. Searching for a literary form suited to that purpose, the writer discovers a powerful and versatile tool in the novel: from Cervantes, through Sterne, Balzac, Flaubert and Dostoevsky, down to Joyce, Kafka and present-day writing, the novel has served consistently to call the world into question ('pone en duda el mundo'), successfully resisting fixity and closure, '(la) pretendida autosuficiencia y. . . (la) segura reducción'.[3] In 1980 Fuentes declared, 'Yo creo mucho en la vitalidad de la novela, en su misión, en su función, su vigencia',[4] reaffirming a long-held belief in the novel's capacity to accommodate tragedy, dialectic and dissent, to confront society with evidence of its own alienation and to expose the vulnerability of liberal democratic ideals in a dehumanised world:

> Something we are seeing every day, it is mass communications, it is the atom bomb, it is AIDS, it is a million things that destroy the formal, formative bearings of the individual that is so precious a creation of Western civilization. The novel has always jumped ahead and shown its concern for this central problem.[5]

In Latin America, where writing and politics go hand in hand, ideological protest has often been accompanied by linguistic iconoclasm in the novel. Works by the Cuban Lezama Lima and also Roa Bastos, Cortázar and Fuentes, among others, exemplify a search for new norms of literary expression which are intended to deconstruct 'una larga historia de mentiras, silencios, retóricas y complicidades académicas'. If, as Fuentes suggests, 'Todo es lenguaje en América Latina: el poder y la libertad, la dominación y la esperanza', it follows that a creative departure from accepted standards of verbal decorum constitutes a revolutionary act: 'Nuestra literatura', Fuentes affirms, 'es verdaderamente revolucionaria en cuanto le niega al orden establecido el léxico que éste quisiera y le opone el lenguaje de la alarma, la renovación, el desorden y el humor. El lenguaje, en suma, de la ambigüedad'.[6] Fuentes's own experiments with the forms and language of fiction match this blue-print very closely. Originally misinterpreted as gratuitous exercises in self-indulgence and the 'puerile' imitation of alien (European Modernist) models,[7] the narrative fragmentation, syntactic disruption and discursive openness of novels like *La región más transparente* (1958) and *Cambio de piel* effectively figure forth suppressed, alternative dimensions of experience which belong to the category of 'the Other'. In *Aura, Cumpleaños* and *Una familia lejana* (1980), the Other manifests itself in the themes of reincarnation and the double; in *La muerte de Artemio Cruz* and *Terra nostra*, it is constituted by the possibilities which have been negated in the lives of an individual and the Mexican nation, respectively; in *Gringo viejo* (1985), it is latent in the potentialities of a historical mystery (that of the disappearance of a retired North American soldier during the Mexican Revolution) which conventional historiography has failed to articulate. In *Gringo viejo*, as in *La muerte de Artemio Cruz* and the futuristic pages of *Terra nostra* and *Cristóbal Nonato*, Fuentes is particularly interested in investigating the relationships of alterity, antagonism and complementarity between Mexico and the United States of America. The later novels debate issues of national identity and integrity on a grand scale: in relation to the values and traditions of post-Renaissance Europe (*Terra nostra*) and against the hypothetical backdrop of a North American occupation of Acapulco, Veracruz and other provinces of Mexico (*Cristóbal Nonato*). The broad perspective of these narratives complements the narrow focus, found in earlier works such as 'Chac Mool' and *La región más transparente*, on 'subterranean' indigenous elements which survive in contemporary Mexican culture, contributing something vital and disruptive to a national identity which has engaged Fuentes's attention throughout his career.

La muerte de Artemio Cruz is generally regarded as his first major novel and a landmark in Mexican and Latin American fiction. Written between May 1960 and December 1961 in Havana and Mexico City, it absorbs many of the energies released by the Cuban Revolution, feeding consciously on a newly awakened spirit of solidarity and commitment to the struggle for greater freedom and self-determination in Latin America. Like *Rayuela*, it is a conjunctural text, and one which made an immediate impression on fellow writers like García Márquez and the Mexican Gustavo Sainz. García Márquez incorporated a reference to its protagonist in the final sections of *Cien años de soledad*: Sainz admitted that 'this book changed me, as the fall from the horse changed Funes the Memorious, in a provocative and highly stimulating fashion'.[8] Translated into some fifteen languages, *La muerte de Artemio Cruz* continues to be read in many parts of the world a quarter of a century after it was first published.

Essentially, the novel explores the legacy of the Mexican Revolution of 1910–17, filtered through the fragmented consciousness of Artemio Cruz whom we visualise lying on his death-bed on 10 April 1959. Cruz is 70 years old and the owner of a huge personal fortune amassed without scruple or restraint over the past forty years. The major events of his life are recounted in retrospect, in a disjointed series of twelve fragments that are narrated in the third person; the remainder of the narrative comprises twenty-six fragments divided equally between a first person – YO – and a second person – TÚ – whose interaction provides the necessary dynamics of narrative progression. In part a showcase of technical experimentation, *La muerte de Artemio Cruz* more importantly explores themes of individual psychology and morality, national history and identity, and certain regional and continental concerns. In this essay I shall examine each of these aspects of the novel in turn, paying attention to technical features of the writing when they seem to have a direct bearing on points of interpretation.

As a starting point for discussion, we may consider *La muerte de Artemio Cruz* as a novel of the psyche focused primarily on the maze-like mind of the dying Cruz. Access to this world of jumbled thoughts, memories, perceptions, sensations, feelings and desires provides insights into the minds and motivation of secondary characters including his wife, Catalina, and their daughter, Teresa, but these are strictly subordinate to Cruz's ego, as they have been throughout his life. Cruz's conscious and subconscious minds may usefully be visualised as the site of innumerable conflicts, a theatre in which are played out complex preoccupations with self and identity, affirmation and the will to power, pride and courage, frustration and guilt. These clusters of themes are presented systematically within the broad parameters of an Existentialist enquiry which highlights notions of responsibility and commitment, alienation and authenticity, freedom and identity, chance and destiny.

Beginning *in media res*, the novel depicts Cruz's interior struggle to salvage something of value from a life characterised by political opportunism, intimate personal failure and the abuse of human relationships. After a childhood which is reconstructed by memory as an idyllic age of innocence and ambiguous promise, the teenage Cruz becomes enmeshed in 'el tejido de lo incierto'[9] which obliges him to define himself and choose between multiple courses of action. Armed with indestructible self-confidence and a Nietzschean will to power which drives him ever onwards – 'siempre había mirado hacia adelante desde la noche en que atravesó la montaña y escapó del viejo casco veracruzano' (p.189) – he proceeds to impose himself on his natural and social surroundings, sweeping obstacles aside and creating new rules 'como si nada hubiese sucedido antes, Adán sin padre, Moisés sin tablas' (pp.103–4). Just minutes before he is whisked away by ambulance to be operated on in hospital, he finds the spiritual strength to reaffirm his will to live and to feel pride once again in a sexual relationship which had been the source of an ecstatic 'encuentro con el mundo' almost half a century ago (p.67). Through a selective operation of memory, Cruz contrives to forget the horror of Regina's death, an event which provoked 'su primer llanto de hombre' (p.81) and coincided with his first experience of a sense of shame, during a battle in the military phase of the Mexican Revolution when he deserted from his regiment and abandoned a wounded companion whose life he could, and should, have saved. In the overall pattern of his life, this is a crucial turning point when he lost a sense of direction, symbolised by the 'hilo perdido': 'El hilo que le permitió recorrer, sin perderse, el laberinto de la guerra. Sin perderse: sin desertar. . . . El hilo quedó atrás' (p.78).

Cruz's desertion is the first in a series of reactions to specific test-situations where he fails to live up to standards of conduct which his son Lorenzo's example proves are a wholly attainable ideal. It is a lapse which has immediate and inescapable consequences, both for the subsequent direction of his life and for the reader's evaluation of him. Straightaway it narrows the range of options open to Cruz, on the basis that a choice between alternative forks on the path of life simultaneously creates and denies experiential possibilities: 'decidirás, escogerás uno de los caminos, sacrificarás los demás: te sacrificarás al escoger, dejarás de ser todos los otros hombres que pudiste haber sido' (p.209). And it projects a shadow onto his entire future which will forever be contaminated by the past.

In this latter respect, his experience resembles a fall from grace into a state of existential inauthenticity which is illustrated in various ways. Since 1947 Cruz has led a double life, grudgingly devoting time and attention to his family in their house in Las Lomas, and cohabiting with Lilia in a residence in Coyoacán which he regards as 'mi verdadera casa' (p.31). The retrospective episode of Lilia's sexual infidelity in Acapulco at the beginning of their relationship pointedly reveals its foundation in artificiality and pretence. Flanked by two scenes in which Cruz contemplates his reflection uneasily in a mirror, it awakens in him feelings of vulnerability, world-weariness, impotence, suspicion and rage:

> No podía tenerla más. Esta tarde, esa misma noche, buscaría a Xavier, se encontrarían en secreto, ya habían fijado la cita. Y los ojos de Lilia, perdidos en el paisaje de veleros y agua dormida, no decían nada. Pero él podría sacárselo, hacer una escena... Se sintió falso, incómodo y siguió comiendo la langosta...
>
> (p.159)

Cruz's embarrassment is plainly visible shortly after, when, as he prepares to shave, he turns to the mirror 'quer(iendo) descubrir al mismo de siempre', and sees an image of himself stripped of comforting illusions: 'Al abrirlos, ese viejo de ojos inyectados, de pómulos grises, labios marchitos, que ya no era el otro, el reflejo aprendido, le devolvió una mueca desde el espejo' (p.162). The motifs of the mask and the mirror are constant reminders of the fragmented and inauthentic basis of his life.

That lack of wholeness manifests itself in Cruz's inability to establish integrated relationships with other people. The relationships on which he embarks after his personal Fall characteristically pit one person's will and needs against those of another, excluding any harmonious resolution of contraries. His marriage to Catalina is an extreme example. Locked in a conflict of self-assertion and mutual mistrust, Artemio and Catalina are twinned in complex ways: they are identical in their pride, their disenchantment and sense of loss (Catalina senses that they have both been expelled from their respective 'paradises'); they are potential complements to each other, 'quizás dos mitades y un solo sentimiento' (p.222); yet, they are sadly unable to communicate when the occasion demands and remain unreconcilable in their antagonism.

At a further level of psychological analysis each of these characters embodies contradictory features. On the critical night of 3 June 1924, Catalina feels torn between an instinctual sexual desire for Cruz and a vengeful rejection of the man who was responsible for her brother's death: 'Me vences de noche. Te venzo de día', she reflects, later lamenting the division of her life 'como para satisfacer a dos razones' and imploring '¿Por qué no puedo escoger una sola, Dios mío?' (p.105). For his part, at this stage of their relationship Cruz is still convinced of his love for Catalina and would openly beg her: 'Acéptame así, con estas culpas, y mírame como a un hombre que necesita.... No me odies. Tenme misericordia, Catalina amada. Porque te quiero' (p.114). But, he lacks the courage to admit his weakness and culpability, and responds to Catalina's recriminations by taking a frightened, compliant Indian girl to his bed, thus reinforcing the barriers between them.

The sequence of events under consideration illustrates Cruz's tragic inability not only to compromise in his relationship with Catalina but also to integrate opposing sides of his personality. This applies particularly in respect of the feminine side of his nature which he resolutely denies, both figuratively and literally, in his relations with his daughter, Teresa. Fuentes probably had the mythological character of Artemis in mind when he chose his protagonist's Christian name. Artemis, a redoubtable huntress renowned for her vindictive and bloodthirsty nature, was a virgin who refused any contact with the opposite sex, in dramatic contrast to the conduct of her brother and alter ego, Apollo. In Fuentes's novel the name 'Artemio' is at once ironic, inasmuch as it reverses the gender of the mythological referent and a telling comment on Cruz's suppression of half of his sexual being. The surname 'Cruz' reinforces this interpretation: among its many connotations is that of a coin (the Spanish equivalent of English 'Heads or tails' is 'Cara o cruz') flipped to decide who wins and who loses a contest. Here, Cruz turns out to be simultaneously a winner in life's contest for material gains and a loser in the moral and spiritual stakes. A faceless man who has fulfilled only half of his potential, he might also be described as 'Cruz sin cara'.

Cruz reacts to his circumstances in a variety of ways. One reaction consists in redoubling his challenge to the established moral order, in a triumphant reassertion of pride: 'Les gané a muchos. Les gané a todos', he boasts on his death-bed (p.32). This diabolical egotism, coupled with cunning and perversity, provides a yardstick with which Cruz may be judged. Crucially, it establishes a perspective from which to evaluate some of the more positive traits of his character such as the courage that he displays on occasions throughout his life (for example, at a political rally when he was fired on by Don Pizarro's thugs and stood his ground, or on the flight from Sonora to Mexico City where a mechanical failure causes consternation amongst all of the passengers except him); the dignity which informs some of his personal relations; and his capacity for experiencing emotions of love, nostalgia and regret, as in a memorable moment, steeped in pathos, when he wishes he could recall every feature of his dead son, Lorenzo: the smell of his body, the colour of his skin. . . . It is a measure of Fuentes's grasp of the subtleties of Existentialist morality that he recoils from presenting any of these qualities in a pure, unadulterated state. It may be that Artemio's courage is no more than the mask of aggressive bravado associated with the Mexican *chingón*: his pride is double-edged ('Nos salvó el orgullo. Nos mató el orgullo', he mentally confesses to Catalina (p.204)); his nostalgia may be a cover for cowardice. Overall, Fuentes's presentation of Cruz captures the internal contradictions of a man who is 'capaz. . . de encarnar al mismo tiempo el bien y el mal' (p.33).

Cruz's nostalgia for a lost garden of Eden (cf. 'jardín', 'paradiso') is a second reaction to his Fall, and one which invariably leads to disappointment because, as Catalina learns from experience, there can be no return to the source of purity, no recovery of innocence (pp.113–14). Cruz's private realisation that this is so intensifies the pathos of his nostalgia. Yet, the suspicion is never dispelled that his nostalgic attitude may not be yet one more aspect of a general bad faith. That objection does not hold for the third of his reactions, which consists of a mature acceptance of guilt. For, ever since he abandoned the anonymous soldier in December 1913, Cruz has harboured feelings of guilt which he has so far managed to suppress by dint of will and self-deceit. Years of living 'como si no hubiera atrás, siempre atrás, lápidas de historia e historias, sacos de vergüenza, hechos cometidos por [Catalina], por él' (p.158) have effectively numbed 'la herida que nos causa traicionarnos' (p.267), and protected Cruz from the provocations of conscience. However, on 10 April 1959 the voice of that conscience – the TÚ voice – breaks through his defences and visits on him spectres of the past, from which there is no escape. As the twelve sets of narrative fragments unravel like a ball of twine, we witness the gradual return of the repressed, orchestrated by a mind which is straining to come to terms with its history. In the first YO fragment, a minimal and uncontextualised reference to 'Regina. Soldado' sets in motion a process of recovery which is sustained in the fourth fragment through a simple repetition, and expanded in the eighth and eleventh with the recitation of a full list of 'nombres muertos' of people who died in order that Cruz might survive: 'Regina. . . Tobías. . . Páez. . . Gonzalo. . . Zagal. . . Laura, Laura. . . Lorenzo' (p.271). The exhumation of these names gives Cruz the chance to relive events which took place on days 'en que tu destino. . . te encarnará con palabras y actos' (p.17) and enables him to face up to the truth about his relationships with other people.

Fuentes seems to envisage a positive outcome to Cruz's experience, 'hoy que la muerte iguala el origen y el destino y entre los dos clava, a pesar de todo, el filo de la libertad' (p.279). A prefatory quotation from Montaigne, 'La prémeditation de la mort est prémeditation de la liberté', had already anticipated the possibility of a secular form of redemption. Yet the message of salvation contained in *La muerte de Artemio Cruz* is a conditional one which allows contradictory interpretations: on the one hand, it asserts the possibility of finally attaining freedom, while on the other, it is shot through with a streak of irony redolent of Jorge Luis Borges's speculations about imminent revelation and mystical enlightenment at the moment of death, as illustrated in the story of Jaromir Hladík in 'El milagro secreto'.

In any case, the promises held out in Fuentes's novel must be weighed against much more sombre insights into the human condition, encapsulated in two other quotations which make up the Preface: these are an *estribillo* from a popular Mexican song which claims that 'No vale nada la vida. La vida no vale nada', and a quatrain from *El gran teatro del mundo* by Pedro Calderón de la Barca which reads 'Hombres que salís al suelo/ por una cuna de hielo/ y por un sepulcro entráis,/ ved como representáis. . .'. Elaborating on these ideas in the text of his novel, Fuentes conveys an often overwhelming impression of the utter worthlessness and fragility of life. The scene in which a fat policeman plays Russian roulette with Cruz illustrates a horrifying contempt for life which is supposed to typify the Mexican outlook, as examined by Octavio Paz in *El laberinto de la soledad* and dramatised by Malcolm Lowry in the *cantina* episode of *Under the Volcano*.

Elsewhere in *La muerte de Artemio Cruz*, the human body is the focal point of Fuentes's wholly conventional but nonetheless striking thoughts about suffering and death. The opening fragment spares Cruz few indignities as it records his physical collapse into a dehumanised state:

Los párpados me pesan: dos plomos, cobres en la lengua, martillos en el oído, una. . . una como plata oxidada en la respiración. Metálico todo esto. Mineral otra vez. Orino sin saberlo.

(p.9)

This graphic picture of physical disorder confirms TÚ's prophecy that 'serás un depósito de sudores nervios irritados y funciones fisiológicas inconscientes' (pp.14–15), at the same time as it emphasises Cruz's vulnerability to the ravages of time and sickness. Having previously taken the workings of his body for granted ('vivirás y dejarás que las funciones se las entiendan solas' (p.90)), Cruz now experiences their ephemerality and acknowledges the shocking vulnerability of what Fernando del Paso in a central chapter of *Palinuro de México* terms the body's 'sacred symmetry'.[10] In this regard, Cruz's perception of fragmented images of an eye, a nose, an unshaven chin and a sunken cheek which are reflected on the surface of his wife's handbag, and his piecemeal account of the sensations he feels in various other parts of his body, underline the vanity of his thoughts about the unity of 'El propio cuerpo. El cuerpo unido' (p.10).

A similar mood of disenchantment informs Fuentes's evalution of human life in relation to the astronomical duration of the universe. At a point when approximately two-thirds of the narrative have elapsed, the TÚ voice insists on the futility of Cruz's previous attempts to stall and buy time, assuring him that 'tu quietud no detendrá al tiempo que corre sin ti, aunque tú lo inventes y midas, al tiempo que niega tu inmovilidad y te somete a su propio peligro de extinción' (p.207). And, near the end, it evokes the chilling emptiness of interstellar space where 'los inmensos astros. . . giran en silencio sobre el fondo infinito del espacio' (p.312), anticipating the ultimate degradation of the universe on a day when 'no habrá ni luz, ni calor, ni vida' (p.313). Reminiscent of the final section of James Joyce's *Finnegans Wake* and of Spanish writing of the Baroque generally, these themes reveal a deep-seated pessimism which is at odds with the requirements of humanistic and Marxist philosophies alike.

Turning to Fuentes's treatment of Mexican themes, we note the same acuteness and breadth of vision and the same spirit of passionate debate as evidenced in his exploration of Existentialist concerns. Collective psychology, race, history and culture are the principal foci of an enquiry which is conducted at all three levels of the narrative: the YO voice acts as the vehicle of ancestral memory and collective desire; the TÚ voice ranges over two thousand years of Mexican history and transcends the bounds of national and regional geography; the narrative fragments in the third person, besides following the course of Cruz's life from the cradle to the grave, also survey the history of his family over four generations. These expansive patterns of the narrative are supplemented by allegorical and figurative procedures which serve to deflect the reader's attention away from the particular aspects of Cruz's experience to a broader frame of reference where his behaviour has a more general significance. For, as well as being the protagonist of an individual biography, Cruz represents a class – of bourgeois entrepreneurs – an age – that of burgeoning capitalist investment in mid-twentieth-century Mexico – and successive periods of the nation's history from the late *porfiriato*, through the years of the Revolution to the narrative present when President López Mateos is in charge of the country's affairs.

In the very first fragments of *La muerte de Artemio Cruz*, Fuentes reveals the extent of his character's financial holdings and gives a detailed description of the social values, aspirations and way of life of a bourgeois parvenu. Multiple business interests allied to the political status quo support a life-style which we are asked to believe was typical of the Mexican bourgeoisie after 1940. Cruz's conspicuous consumerism and sophisticated tastes in food, clothes, music, painting and so on, characterise a social type which compensates for its insecurities by aping foreign life-styles and values, in particular those of white urban society in North America. The TÚ voice observes:

> Desde que empezaste a ser lo que eres, desde que aprendiste a apreciar el tacto de las buenas telas, el gusto de los buenos licores, el olfato de las buenas lociones, todo eso que en los últimos años ha sido tu placer aislado y único, desde entonces clavaste la mirada allá arriba, en el norte, y desde entonces has vivido con la nostalgia del error geográfico que no te permitió ser en todo parte de ellos.
>
> (p.32)

The admiration which Cruz and those like him feel for the social and economic achievements of North America is shot through with jealousy and remorse: 'te duele saber que por más que lo intentes, no puedes ser como ellos, puedes sólo ser una calca, una aproximación' (p.33). Yet, Fuentes suggests, few Mexicans acknowledge the deep-seated motives and implications of their behaviour as they routinely order waffles with Pepsi Cola or Canada Dry from a waitress

107

'vestida de tehuana' at Sanborn's; in effect, they are collaborating in their own economic and cultural colonisation (p.22).

Fuentes's most pungent satire of the mental set of the Mexican bourgeoisie is contained in the ÉL fragment which describes 'la fiesta de San Silvestre' celebrated on New Year's Eve 1955 in Cruz's house at Coyoacán. This grotesque tableau, worthy of Hieronymus Bosch, portrays the collective greed, pettiness, vanity and *mauvaise foi* of those whom in another context the author deprecatingly calls 'los de arriba'.[11] Antedating the narrative present by only four years, it sharpens the historical perspective of Fuentes's novel.

The actual death of Artemio Cruz occurs at a critical moment in a turbulent period of Mexican history which Fuentes examines in his essay, 'Radiografía de una década: 1953–1963'. There, Fuentes surveys political events in contemporary Mexico and records 'las luchas obreras de 1958 y 1959, la represión brutal contra el sindicato ferrocarrilero de Demetrio Vallejo y el deterioro de las condiciones de vida y de trabajo de la gran mayoría de los mexicanos'.[12] On the day before he dies, Artemio Cruz flies into Mexico City and is driven to his office along streets impregnated with mustard gas, 'porque la policía acabará de disolver esa manifestación en la plaza del Caballito' (p.15). The bloody repression of striking railway workers, which will shortly provide the backdrop to *José Trigo* by Fernando del Paso (1966), is referred to in a conversation between Cruz and a North American, Mr. Corkery, who would like to use Cruz's newspaper to discredit 'los ferrocarrileros comunistas de México' (p.118). Cruz manages the interview with Corkery shrewdly and acts quickly to protect his own financial interests by sanitising reports about 'la represión de la policía contra estos alborotadores' (p.87). He is thus inextricably implicated in contemporary events.

Delving into the past, the novel traces the immediate roots of Cruz's political and financial influence to the new order which arose out of the Mexican Revolution. When Cruz visits the Bernal household in Puebla in 1919, don Gamaliel, the failing patriarch, reflects: 'Artemio Cruz. Así se llamaba, entonces, el nuevo mundo surgido de la guerra civil: así se llamaban quienes llegaban a sustituirlo' (p.50). Don Gamaliel's judgement turns out to be prophetic: Cruz wheedles his way into the home and, by marrying Catalina Bernal, becomes master of the family estate.

Don Gamaliel's lapidary assessment uncovers an allegorical dimension in Cruz's character and fortunes: he is the personification of the Revolution, an emblem of its origins, course and results. Several commentators have documented coincidences between the fictional life of Cruz and the process of the Revolution, positing a common progression from an initial stage of idealism, through corruption and betrayal to an institutionalised atrophy. They accordingly identify the young Cruz with Francisco Madero's principled opposition to Porfirio Díaz's re-election, and chart his faltering course through late December 1913 (the temporal setting of the third ÉL fragment) and October 1915 (the seventh ÉL fragment) up to May 1919 (the second ÉL fragment) when he arrives in Puebla. As the Mexican critic, María Stoopen, observes, '1913 es el año del fin de la revolución y del gobierno de Madero; es el año del golpe de Huerta y del ascenso del traidor; es el año de las lealtades y de las traiciones'. Significantly, Cruz's biography is similarly ambivalent at this time:

> Es Artemio Cruz, en estos momentos, como tantos otros participantes de la lucha armada, un representante del pueblo que no posee una conciencia clara de movimiento, pero que tiene la intención justa de 'llegar a México y correr de la presidencia al borracho de Huerta, el asesino de don Panchito Madero'.
> (in the words of the text, p.70)[13]

By 1915 the Revolution has entered a third phase of partisan military activity which effectively destroys any chance of its radical potential being realised. At this stage of the conflict, Cruz is fighting for General Álvaro Obregón in alliance with the troops of Venustiano Carranza, and is taken prisoner by the *villista* colonel, Zagal. In the circumstances, he appears to face certain death, along with his wounded Indian companion, Tobías, and Gonzalo Bernal, 'enviado del Primer Jefe Venustiano Carranza' (p.186), who shares their cell in the prison at Perales. But, a combination of treachery and good fortune allows Cruz to escape, leaving behind the corpses of his two cell-mates along with that of Zagal whom he kills in a duel made possible when *carranclán* troops launch a surprise attack on the town.

María Stoopen interprets Cruz's behaviour in this episode as a triple betrayal, of (1) the Indian peasant class, represented by the *yaqui* Tobías, (2) the popular cause championed by Villa, and (3) untainted revolutionary idealism personified by Gonzalo Bernal who, according to his father, 'Fue siempre tan puro' (p.36). Yet, when he learns that Tobías is to be shot, Cruz asks Zagal to spare his life (p.198); also, he does not kill Zagal, as he could have, by shooting him in the back during the confusion of the *carranclán* attack, but grants him the chance to fight a duel with loaded pistols across an imaginary line in the prison courtyard. It is therefore wrong to accuse Cruz of blanket treachery: plainly, his treatment of the three men involves different degrees of culpability. His treachery is greatest with Bernal who represents the moral and intellectual direction of the Revolution, a value nicely illustrated in the image of his corpse lying next to that of Zagal: 'El brazo muerto del coronel Zagal se extendió hacia la cabeza muerta de Gonzalo' (p.201). In abandoning Bernal to his fate, Cruz simultaneously sacrifices that part of himself which comprises 'ideas y ternuras' (p.197) and destroys the integrity of the Revolutionary movement.

So, when he visits Gonzalo's family in Puebla in 1919, Cruz is already the standard-bearer of betrayed ideals 'en el mundo destruido y confuso que dejaba la Revolución' (p.43). He is also the prototype of instinctive opportunism: 'Todo el camino de Puebla: cuestión de puro instinto' (p.43), ready to exploit the embattled position of don Gamaliel whom he finds locked in 'una lucha pasiva' with the recalcitrant local peasantry (p.48). As soon as they meet, don Gamaliel, who 'se imaginaba a sí mismo como el producto final de una civilización peculiarmente criolla: la de los déspotas ilustrados' (p.50), seals a 'pacto tácito' with the self-possessed Cruz who, he tells Catalina, can save the old order – 'Este hombre puede salvarnos' – by accommodating it within the new regime of land tenure, political influence and power being forged in the early days of post-Revolutionary Mexico. From this point on, the fortunes of the Bernal family and those of Artemio Cruz merge and become a mirror of the motley affairs of the nation.

Cruz's semiotic status as a type is signalled repeatedly throughout the narrative. In an early section, the TÚ-voice, wondering 'cuáles datos pasarán a tu biografía y cuáles serán callados', answers: 'No lo sabrás. Son datos vulgares y no serás el primero ni el único con semejante hoja de servicios' (p.17). Near the end of the novel, the same voice considers Cruz's legacy to the nation in terms which confirm his role as a personification of Mexico: 'legarás este país; legarás tu periódico, los codazos y la adulación, la conciencia adormecida por los discursos falsos de hombres mediocres; tengan su México: tengan tu herencia' (p.277).

Other allegorical dimensions of *La muerte de Artemio Cruz* centre on Cruz's family history and origins, which are the subject of the last two fragments narrated by the ÉL voice. At this late stage we discover that Cruz is the illegitimate child of a black servant-girl known as Isabel Cruz, and Atanasio Menchaca, the elder son of a *criollo* family settled since the early nineteenth century on a large estate in Cocuya in the province of Veracruz. Atanasio's father, Ireneo, had been an associate of General Santa Anna – the *supremo* of Mexican politics during the 1830s, 1840s and 1850s – and had lived 'una vida de azar y loterías como la del país mismo' (p.293). His wife, Ludivinia, is a symbolic counterpart, having been born in 1810, the year in which Mexico broke its colonial ties with Spain. In January 1903, which is the temporal setting of the penultimate ÉL fragment, Ludivinia still occupies the dilapidated remains of the family estate, whose doors she remembers opening 'al largo desfile de prelados españoles, comerciantes franceses, ingenieros escoceses, británicos vendedores de bonos, agiotistas y filibusteros que por aquí pasaron en su marcha hacia la ciudad de México y las oportunidades del país joven, anárquico' (p.291). Clearly, Cocuya is a microcosm of nineteenth-century Mexico, and the Menchacas typical representatives of the nation's tendency to accept *caudillo* figures and submit to colonising forces. It is no accident that these faults reappear in the character of Artemio Cruz a century later: in Fuentes's diagnosis, they constitute a *damnosa hereditas* which hangs like a dead weight around the country's neck.

In the case of Artemio, that heritage is handed down through his father Atanasio, a violent man who drove Isabel Cruz off his estate as soon as she gave birth, and would have killed the baby if Lunero had not made himself available as surrogate father. Interestingly, Atanasio had a brother, Pedro, who differed markedly from him in character and behaviour, striking up a contrast which the narrative mediates through the thought processes of their mother, Ludivinia:

> Ah– suspiró Ludivinia, encaramada en su lecho revuelto–, ése no es Atanasio, que era como la prolongación de su madre en la virilidad: éste es la misma madre, pero con barba y testículos– soñó la vieja–, no la madre como hubiese sido en la hombría, como fue Atanasio.

> (p.296)

In a brilliant analysis of this aspect of the novel, Steven Boldy has explained Pedro and Atanasio's role as the first pair in a series of brothers or doubles of opposing tendencies, who represent stark moral and political alternatives between which the nation must choose at crucial moments in its history. Following the sequence through to the fictional present, Pedro and Atanasio are succeeded by Gonzalo Bernal and Artemio Cruz who stand respectively for revolutionary commitment and cynical self-interest; their antagonism, which acquires its most dramatic expression in the prison sequence at Perales, is reproduced in the following generation in the relation between Lorenzo and Jaime Ceballos. As Boldy sees it, this cyclical scheme is intended to evoke 'the unfulfilled, censured promises of the Mexican heritage'.[14] Yet, one might argue just as convincingly that Fuentes paints a profoundly dispiriting picture of recurrent frustration and determinism in Mexican history since 1810: looked at from the vantage point of 1959, Artemio Cruz seems to have been fated to repeat the excesses and shortcomings of his grandfather, Ireneo, and his uncle Pedro. What is more, prospects for the future are glum, since the death of Lorenzo in the Spanish Civil War leaves the way open for the unscrupulous and scheming Jaime Ceballos to inherit Cruz's legacy, setting in motion a new cycle of injustice and sterility.

Cruz's status as Atanasio's illegitimate child yields a further set of meanings which have relevance here. First and foremost, his illegitimacy marks him as an 'hijo de la chingada' who is the very type of his nation, born in 1519 of the conjunction between imperial Spain – its power delegated to Hernán Cortés – and the Aztec empire of Anáhuac to whose seat Cortés gained access by using the political, linguistic and sexual services of an Indian woman known as La Malinche. According to Paz and Fuentes, modern Mexican man's obsession with legitimacy and betrayal follows directly from that founding event which is pictured as a violation of the national psyche and body politic.

In complicated ways, Cruz stands for all three terms in the equation Spain + Anáhuac = Mexico. He is portrayed as a *conquistador* setting foot on Mexico's Gulf Coast at Veracruz (p.35), like Cortés in a famous mural painted by Diego Rivera. A New World Atlas, he carries on his shoulders the whole of Mexican antiquity, including its landscapes, languages, customs and civilisations (p.275). And, he embodies the Mexican nation's two-pronged obsession with sexual betrayal and abuse, which is summed up in the repertoire of phrases featuring variants of the verb 'chingar'. The immense referential range of this 'palabra de honor' makes it the 'blasón de la raza. . ., resumen de la historia: santo y seña de México' (pp.143–4). Used by the malevolent *chingón*, the word is a weapon that can hurt and humiliate, but also one that can be turned against its user. This is exactly what happens in *La muerte de Artemio Cruz* where the TÚ voice turns on the protagonist and reminds him that 'Eres un hijo de la chingada/ del ultraje que lavaste ultrajando a otros hombres' (p.147). The ÉL fragments also conspire to shatter Cruz's pretensions to power and respectability, tracing his origins back to the day when he was born and, imaginatively, to the moment of his conception during one of 'los mil coitos feroces, descuidados, rápidos [de Atanasio Menchaca]' (p.299). The overall pattern of the narrative thus tends towards the revelation and re-enactment of a violation in which the origins of Cruz's personal identity and that of modern Mexico reside.

Comparisons of Cruz with the archetypal figures of Quetzalcóatl and Jesus Christ enhance his significance as an emblem of the nation. In *Tiempo mexicano* (1970) Fuentes represents the Conquest of Mexico as a process of interaction between one mythical and religious type identified with the Mesoamerican tradition, and another central to European culture. Fuentes recalls how in 1519 the Mexican Indians were awaiting the return of their chosen god, Quetzalcóatl, who had earlier fled the country in disgrace. Fortuitously, on the very day when he was expected to return, Hernán Cortés disembarked at Veracruz and instigated a chain of substitutions which caused native Mexicans subsequently to confuse Quetzalcóatl and Jesus Christ: 'México impuso a Cortés la máscara de Quetzalcóatl. Cortés la rechazó e impuso a México la máscara de Cristo. Desde entonces', Fuentes writes, 'es imposible saber a quien se adora en los altares barrocos de Puebla, de Tlaxcala y de Oaxaca'.[15]

This psycho-historical analysis of the Conquest provides an insight into processes of cultural syncretism in sixteenth-century Mexico and establishes a context for understanding the symbolic portrayal of Artemio Cruz as both a Christ-figure and an avatar of Quetzalcóatl. Parallels between Cruz and Christ are varied and oblique. In the opening pages of the novel Cruz suffers '[un] dolor del costado' which brings to mind Christ's suffering on the Cross (p.12). The surname 'Cruz' contributes a vital element to the comparison, connoting the weight of collective guilt which rests on the character's shoulders like the sins of the world on those of Jesus. Indeed, the sum of 'hechos cometidos por todos' is a burden that Cruz finds intolerable: 'Ésa era la palabra intolerable. Cometidos por todos' (p.158). In a complicated set of equivalences, Cruz is also likened to God the Father, at the moment when his daughter Teresa remarks, apropos of his relationship with Lorenzo, '¿No envió a la muerte a su propio hijo mimado?' (p.242). That the analogy is meant seriously and not ironically is confirmed by the author's declaration to Walter Mauro that he was moved to write *La muerte de Artemio Cruz* partly by 'una obsesión trinitaria de la que siempre he sufrido'.[16] In narrative terms, that obsession translates into the three levels of Cruz's consciousness which correspond to the Holy Trinity of God the Father (YO), God the Son (ÉL) and God the Holy Ghost (TÚ). The figure of Cruz combines aspects of all three in a heretical synthesis which challenges conventional notions of moral authority.

The role of Quetzalcóatl is assigned most conspicuously in the novel to Lorenzo Cruz who is identified with fertility and self-sacrifice and other positive values. As he leaves Mexico to go and fight for freedom on the side of the Republic in the Spanish Civil War, Lorenzo follows in the fabled footsteps of Quetzalcóatl who, in the author's words, 'Huyó, hacia el oriente, hacia el mar. Dijo que el sol lo llamaba'. The manner of Lorenzo's death is suitably heroic, making him a worthy successor of Quetzalcóatl. However, to emphasise Lorenzo's positive attributes and achievements is to overlook the ambivalence of Quetzalcóatl and of Mesoamerican deities in general. For the fact is that Quetzalcóatl symbolises vice as well as virtue, lust as well as chastity, shame as well as honour. Fuentes incorporates these negative traits into the character of Artemio Cruz who cuts a cowardly figure no less reminiscent of Quetzalcóatl than his son Lorenzo. Referring to a legendary event in the god's experience, Fuentes relates how Quetzalcóatl, faced with the reflection of his body in a mirror, 'Sintió gran miedo y gran vergüenza. . . Presa del terror de sí mismo – del terror de su apariencia – Quetzalcóatl, esa noche, bebió y fornicó. Al día siguiente, huyó. . .'. Cruz's experience overlaps with this account in some important details: he indulges in repeated acts of self-contemplation which cause him to feel disgusted with himself and anxious about his identity; also, he has a substantial record of adultery. In short, he resembles the mortal and fallible Quetzalcóatl whom Fuentes elsewhere compared interestingly to more familiar archetypes: 'Quetzalcóatl, protagonista simultáneo de la creación, la caída y el sacrificio: Yavé, Adán y Cristo de un mundo sin secuelas históricas, mítico'.[17]

This hybrid characterisation of Artemio Cruz conforms to the dominant patterns of the cultural history of Mexico. Yet it should not be forgotten that the worship of Quetzalcóatl was a regional phenomenon, extending beyond the territorial boundaries of modern Mexico. Similarly, the fusion of Christian and Amerindian traditions was not unique to the colony of New Spain, but typified the cultural *mestizaje* of the New World generally. With these points in mind, we may briefly consider the regional and continental resonances of Fuentes's novel.

A Caribbean perspective linking the Eastern seaboard of Mexico with the 'archipiélago tropical de ondulaciones graciosas y carnes quebradas [de las Antillas]' (p.278) is defined in the final sections of *La muerte de Artemio Cruz*, tying the history of that part of Mexico in with the slave trade emanating from 'las islas del Caribe' (p.292) and identifying the Gulf as an important point of intersection where the pre-Colombian civilisations of Meso-America met with a multiplicity of cultures arriving from Africa as well as Europe. The Menchaca estate in Veracruz exemplifies a synthesis of historical, racial and cultural factors which set it apart from the 'México seco [del] altiplano' (p.278). In that setting, the figure of Lunero is of special importance. Described by Helmy Giacoman as '[el] primer gran personaje mulato de la novela mexicana',[18] he may be regarded as a fictional cousin of Carpentier's Ti Noel and other black characters who populate the literary landscape of the Caribbean, particularly that of Cuba.

Cuba is in fact a prominent point of reference in *La muerte de Artemio Cruz*. At one moment in the narrative a tape-recording is played back of a conversation between Cruz and Mena in which Cruz comments on the changes that have taken place in Cuba since Batista's departure; the same conversation also mentions General Trujillo whose presidency of the Dominican Republic came to an end in 1960 (see p.140). At another point on the tape, a citizen of the United States who is visiting Cruz's office announces his Ambassador's intention 'to make a speech comparing this Cuban mess with the old-time Mexican Revolution' (p.206) – a project which reflects ironically both on Cruz, who had seen active service in the Mexican

Revolution, and on the Revolution itself, now largely institutionalised and ineffectual. In a very real sense, Fuentes, as he writes from Havana, invites his Mexican readers to look at the achievements of their own revolution through the prism of the new Cuba of 1959–61.

As stated earlier in this essay, events in Cuba sent reverberations all over the Americas, altering political perceptions and creating new perspectives on areas of common interest. In such circumstances it was inevitable that certain writers of the period should register a sense of community and take it upon themselves to represent continental opinion. Fuentes's dedication of *La muerte de Artemio Cruz* to C. Wright Mills, whom he salutes as the 'verdadera voz de Norteamérica, amigo y compañero en la lucha de Latinoamérica', indicates a clear and conscious intention to pitch the message of his novel beyond local boundaries, onto a wider plane of significance.

While the text of *La muerte de Artemio Cruz* makes overt references only to Cuba and the Dominican Republic outside Mexico, a supra-national perspective may readily be inferred from a range of historical data which are valid for the entire subcontinent. At a general level, these include the experiences of conquest, colonial and neo-colonial status and the consequences of political and economic dependence. More specifically, they embrace the phenomena of *caciquismo* or bossism, government repression of labour organisations, financial corruption and social inequality. As he denounces these and other ills in Mexican society under President López Mateos, Fuentes articulates the grievances of people throughout Latin America, prefiguring his systematic treatment of some of the same themes in *La nueva narrativa hispanoamericana*.

The climax of that essay is an analysis of linguistic alienation north and south of the Rio Grande, where the name of C. Wright Mills is invoked once again to exemplify continental experience. In Fuentes's opinion, the linguistic falsification of reality 'is an enormous fact in Latin America',[19] which he describes as a 'continente de textos sagrados' requiring immediate 'profanation' by writers of an iconoclastic disposition.[20] On the evidence produced in this essay, *La muerte de Artemio Cruz* is a seminal contribution to that enterprise. In it Fuentes mounts a vigorous and coherent assault on moral and political dogmas, with the aid of formal and linguistic procedures which shortly become common currency in the writing of the Boom. A quarter of a century later, when other writers have renounced their faith in formal experimentation, Fuentes retains an unswerving commitment to exploration and iconoclasm, forever producing new and unsettling novels. Histories of the Boom and after will remain incomplete as long as he continues to write them.

NOTES

1 See José Donoso, *Historia personal del 'boom'* (Anagrama, Barcelona, 1972), pp.56–7.
2 See Herman P. Doezema, 'An interview with Carlos Fuentes', *Modern Fiction Studies*, vol. 18 (1972–3), pp.491–503; 'Carlos Fuentes at UCLA: an interview', *Mester*, vol. 11 (1982), pp.3–15; and John King, 'Carlos Fuentes: an interview', in *Modern Latin American Fiction: A Survey* (Faber & Faber, London, 1987), pp.136–54.
3 Carlos Fuentes, *La nueva novela hispanoamericana*, 5th edn (Joaquín Mortiz, Mexico, 1976), p.49.
4 'Carlos Fuentes at UCLA', p.15.
5 John King, 'Carlos Fuentes: an interview', p.143.
6 Carlos Fuentes, *La nueva narrativa hispanoamericana*, pp.30–2.
7 For a hostile reaction, see Manuel Pedro González's comparison of *La muerte de Artemio Cruz* with James Joyce's *Ulysses* in his *Coloquio sobre la novela hispanoamericana* (Fondo de Cultura Económica, Mexico, 1967), pp.90–7.
8 Gustavo Sainz, 'Carlos Fuentes: a permanent bedazzlement', trans. Tom J. Lewis, *World Literature Today*, vol. 57, no. 4 (Autumn, 1983), p.569.
9 Carlos Fuentes, *La muerte de Artemio Cruz* (Fondo de Cultura Económica, Mexico, 1978), p.62. All subsequent page references are included in the text.
10 Fernando del Paso, *Palinuro de México* (Alfaguara, Madrid, 1977), p.578.
11 Carlos Fuentes, 'Radiografía de una década: 1953–1963', in *Tiempo mexicano*, 4th edn (Joaquín Mortiz, Mexico, 1972), pp.75–9.
12 Ibid., pp. 86–7.
13 María Stoopen, *La muerte de Artemio Cruz: una novela de denuncia y traición* (UNAM, Mexico, 1982), pp.113–15.
14 Steven Boldy, 'Fathers and sons in Fuentes' *La muerte de Artemio Cruz*', *Bulletin of Hispanic Studies*, vol. 61 (1984), p.39.
15 Carlos Fuentes, 'De Quetzalcóatl a Pepsicóatl', in *Tiempo mexicano*, p.22.
16 Walter Mauro and Elena Clementelli, 'Carlos Fuentes', in *Los escritores al poder* (Luis Caralt, Barcelona, 1975), p.185.
17 Carlos Fuentes, 'De Quetzalcóatl a Pepsicóatl', p.24.
18 Helmy Giacoman (ed.), *Homenaje a Carlos Fuentes* (Las Américas, New York, 1971), p.12.
19 Herman Doezema, 'An interview with Carlos Fuentes', p.499.
20 Carlos Fuentes, *La nueva novela hispanoamericana*, p.30.

6

JULIO CORTÁZAR: *RAYUELA*

STEVEN BOLDY

Cortázar's *Rayuela*, which in 1963 changed for ever the novel in Spanish, is the cosmopolitan novel of the 1960s and a nostalgic celebration (and bitter denunciation) of a country, Argentina, and a city, Buenos Aires. The novel is excitingly of the 1960s in its hail of cobblestones against the *gendarmerie* of moral, vital and verbal automatisms and conformity, but is markedly free of the slogan or password or flower-power or Che-power panaceas which also characterised the period. As a passionate and open dialogue with the most radical literary texts of its decade and of the century, *Rayuela* is an important and lasting work. Published when Cortázar was 49 years old, but had the wisdom to mistrust wisdom and experience, *Rayuela* quickly became the 'evangelio para las nuevas generaciones'.[1] Its sustained novelty and attraction for many people, even after many readings, lies in its paradoxical combination of multi-voicedness, ambiguity and rejection of ideology with a highly personal, crusading and utopian voice.

Cortázar was born in Brussels in 1914 to Argentinian parents and went to Argentina when he was four. Brought up in Banfield, near Buenos Aires, in a predominantly female household, he was an extremely precocious and avid reader. He attended university for a while before training as a teacher and lived for some years in distant provincial towns where he chose to build up a vast and catholic (very Argentinian) knowledge of world literature. He later moved to Buenos Aires where he qualified as a translator, an activity which he has cultivated extensively (both working for UNESCO much of his life and in the literary field, translating the complete works of Poe) and which he recommends as an excellent training for young writers. During this period, Cortázar wrote much, including a full-length study of John Keats, but, out of a spirit of rigorous self-criticism, published little.

Like many intellectuals from his generation and especially those connected with the magazine *Sur* such as Jorge Luis Borges who published his first major story, Cortázar was a Europeanist, perhaps even elitist writer with little interest in the Argentinian or even Spanish tradition. It is thus not perhaps surprising that he was fiercely hostile to the populist Peronist movement as the vulgar irruption of an excessively local reality. In his first novel, *El examen*, written in 1950 but published posthumously in 1986, he is painfully aware of this situation. His character Juan exclaims that all the folk in the street not like his intellectual friends 'me da asco', while 'los que son como nosotros me dan lástima'. Anticipating much of the problematics of *Rayuela*, he laments, 'Me jode no poder convivir, entendés.'[2] The threatening yet attractive presences which he calls 'los monstruos' in early short stories such as 'Las puertas del cielo', he later admits represent the Peronist 'cabecitas negras'.[3] While the character Juan leaves Buenos Aires never to return, like Cortázar in 1951, Horacio Oliveira, the hero of *Rayuela* returns to Buenos Aires in the second part of the novel where he and his friend and double Traveler are referred to as 'los monstruos' of the wife of the lunatic asylum director.[4] The change in attitude towards the establishment in this example is radical, and *Rayuela* is in many ways the chronicle of that reversal. In a purely literary fashion, however, the reversal had been foreshadowed by his early play *Los reyes* (1949), where a monster, the Minotaur, represents joy and liberation against the repression of the King and the stupidity of Theseus. Cortázar later admitted that he had been wrong in his judgement of the nature of Peronism.[5]

In the same year as he came to live in Paris, Cortázar published *Bestiario*, the first in a series of eight collections of short stories over some thirty years up to the publication of *Deshoras* in 1983, a year before his death. Many of the stories belong to the fantastic genre, but to a fantastic which is psychological or existential in origin and mimetic in its rhetoric, as opposed to the literary-philosophical fantastic of Borges.[6] Both writers share the fascination with what might lie beyond the limits of culture, but Cortázar has more faith in this beyond, this other of convention and reason (the animal, the primitive, the popular, the incongruous, violence), even though contact with it frequently destroys his characters. The impulse behind Cortázar's stories remains much the same throughout, though many of those contained in *Todos los fuegos el fuego* (1966) are formally more complex than others, and his later collections tend to be more self-referential,[7] but include some fine political stories such as 'Graffiti' in *Queremos tanto a Glenda* (1980) or 'Apocalipsis de Solentiname' in *Alguien que anda por ahí* (1977).

There is much disagreement as to which is the greater Cortázar, the novelist or the story-teller. The latter is certainly a consummate master at his art, the greatest in Spanish together with Borges. Cortázar has said that the short story is closer to poetry than to prose, that it is a neurotic product of obsessions and nightmares exorcised through writing, and as such has a large degree of autonomy once free from the author, like a bubble which emerges from a clay pipe. He claims to have written many of his stories in a trance-like state, as if he were simply painting magic ink over a pre-existing text. Communication in a story, then, is not through it, but from it, as the reader is affected by the same archetypal forces which created the story, and in almost the same way as the writer, who becomes a reader of himself:

> Si algunos se salvan del olvido es porque he sido capaz de recibir y transmitir sin demasiadas pérdidas esas latencias de una psiquis profunda, y el resto es una cierta veteranía para no falsear el misterio, conservarlo lo más cerca de su fuente, con su temblor original, su balbuceo arquetípico.[8]

Communication in a novel such as *Rayuela* is of a very different nature, a more urgent, self-conscious and critical engaging of all the discourses of modernity which the writer shares with his reader, or wishes him to share.

Genre, however, is just one of the barriers which Cortázar's work questions, and indeed many of his works are multi-genre, or defy generic classification. *Prosa del observatorio* (1972) is a typical example. The text, which has many elements of the prose poem, is interspersed with photographs of an observatory in India. The text itself includes two seemingly heterogeneous thematic lines, one far from 'poetic' in the conventional sense (the life cycle of eels and the stars) while winding into its 'own' language, which is at once poetical and ideological (Rimbaud and Marx), the scientific language which aims to classify the stages of the eels' evolution. Even more openly collage works (or as Cortázar liked to call them 'almanaques', after those read by countryfolk in the Argentina of his youth) are *La vuelta al mundo en ochenta días* (1967) and *Último round*

(1969), where many types of visual material, mainly from friends of Cortázar or artists admired by him, interact in a controlled but not always predictable manner with a series of essays, stories, poems, vignettes and so on. The dialogue between genres and even artistic media is paralleled by the extreme intertextuality which has always been a mark of Cortázar's work. The collage, as we shall see, is also an integral part of the functioning of novels such as *Rayuela* and *Libro de Manuel* (1973).

Cortázar's personal and political life changed radically in the first two decades of his residence in France. It was in Paris, like so many Latin Americans such as Asturias and to a certain extent Carpentier, that Cortázar discovered Latin America. The Cuban Revolution in 1959 was a fundamental landmark, as was his visit to that country in 1963, after which time Cortázar became ever more committed to the struggle for socialism and freedom from imperialist intervention in Latin America, for all that he simply summed up as 'justice'. His twin preoccupations of literature and politics followed parallel but basically separate paths through the 1960s and early 1970s, a fact which involved him in occasionally unpleasant exchanges with critics and other writers who demanded committed literature from him, some form of social realism perhaps. Cortázar's position was basically that the Revolution needed revolutionary writing to push back the frontiers of liberation on many fronts, the erotic, the ludic, the irrational, more than it needed official writers of the Revolution.[9] In 1971 there came a crisis in the relations of the most important writers of Latin America with the Cuban regime when the poet Heberto Padilla was imprisoned for anti-revolutionary writing. While Cortázar initially joined the protest of writers such as Mario Vargas Llosa and Carlos Fuentes, he firmly realigned himself with the Revolution after Fidel Castro reproached the protesters, while at the same time demanding a margin of freedom to widen the scope of revolutionary literature.[10] In his later years, at the expense of his failing health and his overwhelming desire to write literature, Cortázar was a staunch and effective defender of the Nicaraguan Revolution and an indefatigable denouncer of the horrors committed by the military regime in Argentina. Two posthumous collections of essays, published in 1984, document this dimension of his life: *Nicaragua tan violentamente dulce* and *Argentina: años de alambradas culturales*.

While living in Paris Cortázar published four novels. Only in the last one, *Libro de Manuel,* do politics and literary experiment, sexual and political liberation, finally come together in one text. While the result is a fascinating, brave and exciting work, Cortázar will (perhaps, who knows?) be remembered for *Los premios* (1960), and especially for *Rayuela* and his most arcane (and yet most amusing) novel *62. Modelo para armar* (1968). In *62,* the notion of the individual, independent character is broken open as impersonal or rather transpersonal constellations of forces, referred to as *figuras* and associated here with literary archetypes or classical myths, are seen to emerge from the fragments of his text to control the destiny of the characters. Whether the characters can rebel against the fatality of these forces and reverse their repressive determinism seems to depend on the attitude of the narrator, Juan, and that part of him and of other characters associated with narration which becomes a sort of semi-character in his own right and is referred to as 'mi paredro'. Their attitude towards events, which in the language of realism have already happened, actually determines and dictates those events and their consequences in the text. The sense of an alternative and more authentic reality underneath surface psychology and habit, which can only be discovered by chance or in privileged moments of decentred vision and which can either destroy or else totally transform personal and social life, is fundamental to Cortázar's work, and not alien to his great and productive affinity with Surrealism. This intuition of an alternative order which denounces what we accept as reality is the obsession of Oliveira and the deep motivating force behind *Rayuela.* Before socialism became an absolutely central part of Cortázar's vision, the demand that life, self and reality be different, together with the refusal to use any of the accepted means of changing these things, suspecting that they are part of the problem, lend to *Rayuela* a particularly painful, exhilarating and human intensity.

Rayuela is the story of a middle-aged Argentine intellectual, Horacio Oliveira, in many ways similar to Cortázar, though described by him as both morally and intellectually mediocre,[11] who lives a semi-artistic, bohemian life in Paris among friends who refer to themselves as the Club de la Serpiente. Dissatisfied with life and his own hyper-intellectual relation to it, he finds in la Maga an example of a more authentic, less hierarchical approach to existence. Not wishing, however, to be trapped in an emotional or biological corner as automatic as his own intellectual reactions, he mistreats la

Maga until she disappears after her son Rocamadour dies. After encounters with a series of semi-archetypal female figures[12] he seems gradually to shed his intellectualism and even his very condition as a civilised being before being deported to Buenos Aires. Back home from his odyssey, he finds that he has in a way not come back, that he has (intentionally) ceased to be Argentinian and must now discover a new way of coming to terms with his homeland. Society is represented by the couple Manuel and Talita Traveler, doubles of Oliveira and la Maga. As they live together and move from working in a circus to the lunatic asylum, the mythical, fantastic presence of la Maga, presumed long-dead, and the values she represented seem to emerge in their relationship. The resolution of the novel will depend on the characters' reaction to this new presence, as will Oliveira's possible reconciliation with his fellows. In an open-ended finale, where Oliveira is seen possibly to go mad or to commit suicide, the reconciliation, change and understanding is passed firmly into the camp of the reader.

Structurally, the novel has three parts. The thirty-six chapters of 'Del lado de allá' are set in Paris, and the twenty of 'Del lado de acá' in Buenos Aires; the Proustian echoes in the titles and the desire to reconcile the two 'côtés' and establish a new unity under the discontinuities of existence is not ironic but not totally dismissive. The third part consists of what the author calls the 'optional' 'capítulos prescindibles', often quotations from other authors and, sometimes, literary theory from Morelli, a fictional author who is in many ways the double of Cortázar as Traveler is of Oliveira. These chapters are intercalated at more or less regular intervals into the main text, with the exception of blocks such as the twenty-two 'capítulos prescindibles' between Chapters 28 and 29. A 'Tablero de instrucciones' is provided to indicate to the reader the order in which the chapters are to be read, and the reader physically re-enacts the jumping of the hopscotch player and the spiritual search of the protagonist in his flicking through the volume to find the next section. There is, then, in the very structure of the novel an opposition between two places and between two sorts of writing. Similar oppositions are present in all the other novels, e.g. in the main text of *Los premios* and the monologues of Persio or in the intercalated paper cuttings of political events in Latin America in *Libro de Manuel*. Other authorial doubles are Persio, 'mi paredro' in *62* and 'el que te dije' in *Libro de Manuel*.

The relation between Buenos Aires and Paris is relatively complex. The tone of the two sections is totally different and it is almost impossible to recognise the lazy, amusing, provincial Oliveira we see there as the cynical and anguished intellectual from Paris. From the notes and drafts of *Rayuela* recently published as *Cuaderno de bitácora* (1983), we know that some of the Buenos Aires scenes were written before the rest of the text. The poetic and tragic tone of the Paris episodes is replaced by the grotesque and ludic in Buenos Aires. What may initially be perceived as a flaw in the homogeneity of the work, however, is best viewed within the author's avowed intention to make the reader himself make the links between characters, episodes and areas of experience.

There is of course a linear reading of the text in which Oliveira sets out on a quest for the paradisal state or awareness he variously calls 'el centro', 'el kibbutz del deseo', 'armonía', and so on; he returns after finding it (or not, according to one's reading), bringing the mythical boon back to his homeland. If one reads the trip in conjunction with Cortázar's autobiographical comments on his move to Paris, the return to Buenos Aires signifies the return of Oliveira to a humanity which the author admitted to having discovered late in life in the 1950s. His discovery of fellow man not only necessarily involves a discovery of self, but also of the Latin American reality to which he had been so wilfully blind in Argentina. He relates the process in an interview with González Bermejo:

> Años con experiencias humanas que yo no había hecho en la Argentina donde viví siempre muy solitario, metido en una especie de carrera docente, por un lado, y lecturas en bibliotecas, por otro. París fue un poco mi camino de Damasco, la gran sacudida existencial.

> Ese proceso que, en un plano más privado se había iniciado aquí en París conmigo en la época de 'El Perseguidor' y de 'Rayuela', esa especie de descubrimiento del prójimo y, por extensión descubrimiento de una humanidad humillada, ofendida, alienada.[13]

Related to this autobiographical reading is the cultural and social role that Paris has traditionally played for the middle-class Latin American intellectual. The novelist and critic David Viñas in his powerful *De Sarmiento a Cortázar* (1971) examines the dual role of the retreat to the *hacienda* and the trip to Paris as the escape of the

124

oligarchy from an historical reality and an increasingly urban reality which they preferred to avoid or sublimate. Cortázar's life and text in this reading is the trip from the earth of the Hopscotch of the title, the inert and disgusting body of America to the Heaven represented by its tenth and final square, the spirit of Paris. While this reading, as we have seen, works for *El examen* and stories such as 'Casa tomada', in *Rayuela* Cortázar is critically aware of the cultural pattern, even though this awareness is characteristically placed in inverted commas when voiced by the parody Spanish intellectual Perico: 'Aquí has venido siguiendo el molde de todos tus connacionales que se largaban a París para hacer su educación sentimental. Por lo menos en España eso se aprende en el burdel y en los toros, coño' (p.69). Though Oliveira agrees with this outburst, his experience is in fact radically different. Oliveira's Beatrice in Paris, la Maga, who carries the whole weight of the quest in the novel, refuses to fulfil the role of pure spirituality. It is la Maga's example which breaks Oliveira's confident faith in his own hyper-intellectualism. Uncerebral to the extreme ('No era en la cabeza donde tenía el centro' (p.40)), she insists on recounting to all minimally willing to hear her unspiritual rape in a Montevideo slum, and her presence is inseparable from her sick child Rocamadour and the constant references to the smell of urine and faeces. Indeed faeces and bodily filth become the very sign of the supposedly spiritual Paris. Oliveira's cultural hero Morelli is hit by a car when he slips on a pile of shit; the middle-aged homosexual Valentin daubs his neighbour's door and himself with cat muck; his pianist wife Berthe Trépat (the 'syncrétisme fatidique' of whose music is a grotesque parody of the intertextuality of Cortázar's text) has her mouth compared with the anus of Rocamadour. This descent into the faecal which started as something of a shock to Oliveira, culminates almost programmatically, as he emulates Heraclitus who is said to have immersed himself in dung to cure his dropsy: 'Entonces tal vez fuera eso, estar en la mierda hasta el cogote' (p.247). His particular dung is the final woman he faces in Paris, the *clocharde* Emmanuèle, whose stench he shares together with a couple of litres of red wine and whose preparations to suck his penis are interrupted by the hostile arrival of the gendarmerie. The spiritual vision, the key hierarchies of the Western civilisation that Oliveira finds increasingly hard to accept are finally reversed by the whole Paris experience, traditionally designed to bolster it:

La gente agarraba el calidoscopio por el mal lado, entonces había que darlo vuelta con ayuda de Emmanuèle y de Pola y de París y de la Maga y de Rocamadour, tirarse al suelo como Emmanuèle y desde ahí empezar a mirar desde la montaña de bosta, mirar el mundo a través del ojo del culo.

(p.253)

Paris is thus the zone where Oliveira comes up against everything that he, like Juan in *El examen*, had rejected in Argentina and repressed in his own experience. Having gone beyond the repression in Argentina and beyond civilisation, become an animal, 'una especie de mono entre los hombres' (p.358), Oliveira then in the second part returns to face the world and people he left. His presence and the knowledge that he only half-consciously embodies are perceived as a threat to the certainties and values of his friends. Oliveira plays the role of the haunting, invading force felt in many of the short stories as figures from one geographical zone infiltrate another. He becomes like the beggar from Budapest, who gradually takes over the consciousness of the society girl Alina Reyes from Buenos Aires in 'Lejana', or like the Paris whores, writers and murderers who become part of the staid Buenos Aires life of the protagonist of 'El otro cielo'.

What then is Buenos Aires? Argentina is the summary of the automatism, conformism and unthinking, dogmatic faith in one's own language against which Oliveira is rebelling. But Argentina is also Oliveira's homeland and thus what he would most like to belong to, the origins to which he would like, transformed, to return. The epigraphs of the first and second parts express this paradoxical or dual nature of Argentina, which applies to the whole of culture and reality in *Rayuela*: 'Rien ne vous tue un homme comme d'être obligé de représenter un pays' and 'Il faut voyager loin en aimant sa maison.' Much of the tension and pleasure of the reading process of the novel springs from such contradictions. The text is at once deconstructive and mystical. What, for example, he rejects about language and reason is that it gives individuals a false sense of stability and centrality: 'La razón segrega a través del lenguaje una arquitectura satisfactoria . . . y nos planta en el centro' (p.194); the activity of the text is constantly referred to as a 'decentrar' or 'desencasillar'; and yet Oliveira's ultimate goal is described as a 'centre': 'el centro del mandala' (p.374).

Apart, then, from being his homeland and humanity, 'Argentina' is culture used as a means of evading reality, doubt, nothingness: 'defenderse mediante la rápida y ansiosa acumulación de una "cultura", truco por excelencia de la clase media argentina para hurtar el cuerpo a la realidad nacional y a cualquier otra, y creerse a salvo del vacío que la rodeaba' (p.31); and irrational affirmation used to give authority to a personal, ideological or otherwise dubious statement: 'el tan hispanoítaloargentino "¡Se lo digo yo!", acompañado de un puñetazo rotundo que debía servir de ratificación iracunda' (p.33). The naturalisation of similar constructs in high culture proceeds from an identically arbitrary weight of 'las autoridades y las influencias'. The ego and unity of personality is seen as coming from a similarly spurious and unquestioned linguistic hardening of the arteries: 'una supuesta unidad de la persona que no pasaba de una unidad lingüística y de un prematuro esclerosamiento del carácter' (p.99). The quest of Oliveira and the text is to undo the rigidity of the arbitrary elevated to authority, the national elevated to the natural by the weight of ego, hierarchy, fear, intolerance and at the same time stay within these structures, which are the only ones humanity has: to fight against language with language, intelligence with intelligence: 'El alacrán clavándose el aguijón, harto de ser un alacrán pero necesitado de alacranidad para acabar con el alacrán' (pp.189–90).

This project can only be a process, not a message, 'no hay mensaje, hay mensajeros y eso es el mensaje' (p.453): a series of contradictions, dialectical confrontation, dialogue. Indeed, the dilemma of Oliveira and the practice of Cortázar corresponds exactly to Bakhtin's definition of the essential nature of the novel (what many critics have described in *Rayuela* as 'anti-novel'). For Bakhtin the novel is a dialogue between the languages within and without a society, a taking up of the languages of others ('heteroglossia'), which both breaks down the univocality of authoritarian discourses (which can never form a true novel) and reflects and helps mould a new, richer and more fluid consciousness, often in the name of the pre-class consciousness he claims existed before ideology and sublimation split life up into separate compartments (the dualism about which Oliveira so often complains). What Bakhtin writes about Rabelais could equally well apply to *Rayuela*:

Turning away from language (by means of language, of course), discrediting any direct or unmediated intentionality and expressive excess (any 'weighty seriousness') that might adhere in ideological discourse, presuming that all language is conventional and false, maliciously inadequate to reality – all this achieves in Rabelais almost the maximum purity possible in prose.[14]

In a manner very relevant to our discussion of Argentina, Bakhtin links the emergence of the novel to the critical consciousness of national languages. Such consciousness is necessarily polyglot and associated with homelessness, which helps to explain why Oliveira's exile is inseparable from the writing of the novel, and indeed why the novel has been perceived as so important:

The novel is the expression of a Galilean perception of language, one that denies the absolutism of a single and unitary language – that is, that refuses to acknowledge its own language as the sole verbal and semantic centre of the ideological world, a certain linguistic homelessness of literary consciousness, which no longer possesses a sacrosanct and unitary linguistic medium for containing ideological thought. . . What is involved here is very important, in fact a radical revolution in the destinies of human discourse: the fundamental liberation of cultural-semantic and emotional intentions from the hegemony of a single and unitary language, and consequently the simultaneous loss of feeling for language as myth, that is, as an absolute form of thought.[15]

A nation's coming of age, then, its consciousness of itself as a plural community related to other consciousnesses is inseparable from the emergence of the novel, the locus of the dialogue between different national and social groups and their literary genres. *Rayuela* is an essentially dialogic novel, polyglot to a degree, multi-voiced and highly intertextual. It is probably significant, then, that as Latin American nations emerge into modernity, their most important novels are intensely dialogical and intertextual and at the same time highly local and national. *Rayuela* combines quotations from a good number of European languages with the freest and most extensive use of Buenos Aires Spanish ever attempted. A similar process is at work in novels like *La región más transparente* (1958) or *Cristóbal Nonato* (1987) by the Mexican Carlos Fuentes, or *Tres tristes tigres* (1970) by the Cuban Cabrera Infante or in a slightly different way Onetti's *Tierra de nadie* (1941). The Andean countries have their own perhaps more urgent internal heteroglossia and polyglossia to incorporate into the novel, as in José María Arguedas, a more arduous birth than that of the European novel from the Hellenistic and Latin worlds.

The critical heteroglossia and decentring which Bakhtin has as the essence of the novel is present throughout the text of *Rayuela*, but especially in the 'capítulos prescindibles', the optional chapters which in a full reading are intercalated in those of the two main sections. A good many of these chapters are quotations from foreign writers in some way related to the main text (or pointedly unrelated). Cortázar here is foregrounding the process which Bakhtin distinguished at the root of the European novel, i.e. the voice of another incorporated into one's 'own' discourse through translation: 'European novel prose is born and shaped in the process of a free (that is, reformulating) translation of others' works.'[16] The 'capítulos prescindibles' stand in the same relation to the main text of the novel as does Paris to the reality of Buenos Aires: they question, pluralise, decentre, reveal what is hidden. It can be argued that many of the quotations in the novel do not pluralise, but rather dictate the way the text should be read, that they are even didactic in nature,[17] fix its genealogy, give its ideology the prestige of tradition. But as Borges shows in 'Pierre Menard, autor del Quijote', any quotation is already a creation of new meaning. Moreover, the very number of voices involved at times in the quotations throws a highly critical light on the notion of the univocal, authoritative text. Many of the quotations are quotations from the reading of Morelli, a figure related to Cortázar but not to be confused with him, and furthermore reported and commented on by Oliveira and other characters of the novel. When the quotation, as in Chapter 136, is accompanied by an exclamation on quotation, 'la manía de las citas en Morelli', and goes on to quote a translation of a text of Bataille which is itself self-referential and talks of including in itself various incompatible pieces of writing from yet another set of voices, 'el diario de un muerto y las notas de un prelado amigo mío', the 'yo' of the '¡se lo digo yo!' is far from monolithic. Intertextuality, the collage, can be seen as an opening onto the collective. As Yurkievich says of the poems of the Chilean Nicanor Parra but in the context of *Rayuela*: 'El autor descentra o desegocentra el poema hacia el decir colectivo; renuncia a la singularidad estilística, al apropiamiento personal del lenguaje.'[18] As Morelli, who believes that any salvation must be collective, and for this reason publishes in the most collective, intertextual genre, i.e. the novel (p.491), puts it: 'La novela cómica ... le da algo así como una arcilla significativa, un comienzo de modelado, con huellas de algo que quizá sea colectivo humano y no individual' (p.454). Carlos Fuentes in a similar spirit talks of the 'lugar común' as being not only a cliché but a common place, a place of sharing and communion.[19]

The theorising of Morelli, on his own literary work, work which we do not actually read, especially concerning his relationship with the reader, the critical 'lector cómplice' which his writing wishes to encourage, is certainly relevant to the intentions of Cortázar, but it would be naive to take it as a description of *Rayuela*. The function of the 'capítulos prescindibles' is a large and complex theme. Suffice it here to say that they sometimes metaphorically expand our understanding, make us more critically aware of our reading, often by discursively theorising about reading. At other times, they constitute an amusing or shocking change of tone from the preceding chapter, juxtaposing different genres or registers in a way which deprives each of its natural status and invites the reader to consider its conventionality and his own reaction to it. After the virtuoso, pathos-filled description of the death of Rocamadour, for example, a piece is reproduced from *The Observer* in which helpful advice is given on the risks of encounters between trouser zips and foreskins. Similar generic incongruities, ironical foregrounding and critical *mise en abîmes* are not exclusive to the 'capítulos prescindibles', but are present throughout the text.

Such little tricks, effective and amusing as they may be, should not distract the reader from the more basic contradictions, ironies or paradoxes of the writing which are central to the perplexing and rich effect of the text. I will briefly enumerate a few, most of which are obvious enough. One is the simultaneous celebration of culture, in the whole text of the novel, and of ignorance in the figure of la Maga and the general process of 'deseducación' to which Oliveira subjects himself. Another is the coexistence of high seriousness and game, of the sacred and irony. Love, for example, is as central to Cortázar as it was to Breton. At one point, la Maga is referred to in the phrase from the second Canto of the Chilean poet Huidobro's *Altazor*, 'dadora de infinito' (p.484), and elsewhere we read a variation on the expression: 'Amor, ceremonia ontologizante, dadora de ser' (p.120). And yet Oliveira goes to great lengths to ruin in la Maga any impression that there was a transcendental side to their love: 'evitar como la peste toda sacralización de los juegos' (p.44). Similarly, the initial title of the novel, *Mandala*, with its religious connotations is replaced by the desacralised 'hopscotch'. The intention is similar, yet the expression less pedantic, as Cortázar explained to Yurkievich in an interview: 'Yo creo que el juego es la forma desacralizada de todo lo que para la humanidad inicial son ceremonias sagradas.'[20] There are many other similar desacralised/ metaphysical ceremony/games in the novel, such as the crossing of the plank from Traveler towards Oliveira by Talita, and the descent to the morgue/ Hades where the beer is kept in one of the freezers. The sacred does not cancel out the irony, nor vice-versa. Perhaps the most pervasive of the contradictions we have examined is that between the bleak pessimism of Oliveira's judgement of humanity (that it quite simply took a wrong turning into rationalism many centuries ago), and the constant presence, evocation or glimpsing in love, dream and poetry of Eden, utopia, a state of release and happiness. Cortázar himself sums up this tension well in an important 1967 article, 'Acerca de la situación del intelectual latinoamericano' published in Cuba and reproduced in *Último round* (no reference to socialism is made in the novel, where political action is provocatively seen as a form of escapism from deeper existential dilemmas). He suffers

> un problema metafísico, un desgarramiento continuo entre el monstruoso error de ser lo que somos como individuos y como pueblos en este siglo, y la entrevisión de un futuro en el que la sociedad humana culminaría por fin en ese arquetipo del que el socialismo da una visión práctica y la poesía una visión espiritual.[21]

One final example of the rich complexity of tone and intention in the novel can be given. Lida Aronne-Amestoy rightly describes Cortázar's work as 'ni más ni menos que una revolución ética'.[22] The clearly parodic first two epigraphs of the novel ('la presente colección de máximas' (p.9); 'Y ojalá lo que estoy escribiendo le sirbalguno para que mire bien su comportamiento' (p.11)) together with the irony, irreverent and demystifying humour and generalised ambiguity of the text would seem to negate any such intention. The ethical lesson is perhaps precisely in critical and self-critical activity of the reader demanded to overcome such tensions.

These ambiguities, however, do little to detract from the urgency established in the first line of the novel and underlying our reading throughout: '¿Encontraría a la Maga?'. The whole first part of the novel is suffused with the poetical presence of the mysteriously simple la Maga and coloured by her loss: 'Hablo de entonces. . ., no de este balance elegíaco en que ya sabemos que el juego está jugado' (p.487). To the end of the novel the question is kept open, and the very ambiguity as to how, according to what generic instructions, one should read her presence/absence lends an even greater numinosity to the question. Oliveira and la Maga do not arrange to meet, but wander round their favourite haunts in Paris and perhaps meet by chance. A chance meeting, for Cortázar, as for the Surrealists, would be far more authentic a meeting than one organised by conventional, social rules; it would be the sign of an alternative order of greater reality. All the novels involve an important image of chaos and chance (lottery, kaleidoscope, insects flying round a lamp, and so forth) and the emergence of significant patterns, *figuras*, from it. In some short stories, such as the terrifying 'Manuscrito hallado en un bolsillo', the need to make the trajectories of the lovers coincide by chance in the labyrinth of the underground if they are to deserve their relationship becomes a fatal tyranny. Coincidence and analogy are a sign of poetical truth in a world where society, logic and language simply serve to hide reality.

La Maga is authenticity on two legs in the face of the intellectual bad faith of Oliveira. As such she is a highly mythified character, with a long literary tradition. Cortázar makes it clear that he knows Oliveira is mythifying her, spiritualising her and, as we have seen, a series of episodes is used to lend an irreducible physicality to her nebulosity, but this process reacts ambiguously with the mythification and enriches it rather than satirically cancelling it. La Maga does not understand, is ignorant, disordered and spontaneous, yet endowed with powers of intuition and a direct, unmediated contact with reality, which Oliveira can only see through a series of literary or philosophical grids. These characteristics of Cortázar's Uruguayan Nadja destroy Oliveira's confidence in his own relation with the world, and suggest a better one to him that he is incapable of knowing or embracing. She was 'perfecta en su manera de denunciar la falsa perfección de los demás' (p.365). In a sense her role is one used in eighteenth-century satire by Montesquieu or Swift, and described by Bakhtin: 'The device of "not understanding" . . . takes on great organizing potential when an exposure of vulgar conventionality is involved.'[23] In suggesting a world beyond that which is normally accepted as reality, Maga plays a role similar to dreams, where 'nos asomamos a lo que éramos antes' (p.523), and from which one is expelled on waking as if from Eden (p.577), with the certainty that reality is an 'increíble equivocación' (p.515). Such 'paravisiones', 'corrimientos a un costado' (p.84), which the surprises of the novel try to reproduce in the reader, have the effect of making Oliveira painfully aware of the limitations of his intellect, indeed realise that intellect, thought and language prevent him from a better relationship with the world. His painful lucidity awards him an intense sense of the absurd, but also such a mistrust of any 'solution', which he fears will simply be part of the trap, that his position becomes one of sterility and paralysis. Wishing to join humanity after the example of la Maga, he is excluded from it by the very heightened sense of inauthenticity which had given him the desire to belong in the first place. Sadly, la Maga seems to him the largest trap, and his mistreatment of her and their love is his first unpleasant task in his liberation from convention, biological reflexes, and inauthentic humanity: what he sums up as 'la piedad'. Having no way to know what is truly human and what is conventional, he opts more and more for a path of blanket destruction.

One interlude offers him the opportunity of joining humanity almost by grace only to throw him more starkly back into solitude. He finds himself absurdly moved to sympathy by the pathetic nymphomaniac and psychotic Berthe Trépat and the prospect of literally coming in out of the cold streets to have a drink with her and her homosexual husband. 'Sólo viviendo absurdamente se podría romper este absurdo infinito' (p.123), he muses. 'Les hommes sont si nécessairement fous que ce serait fou par un autre tour de la folie de n'être pas fou', comments Pascal.[24] But the episode ends in a misunderstanding, Oliveira's party backfires and the deluded pianist-composer believes he is making an indecent proposition, slaps his face and screams to the delighted neighbours to save her from his advances.

Almost as if as a result of this failure, when Oliveira returns to la Maga's room, he finds that her infant son Rocamadour has died without her realising. The death of the child in Cortázar's work is a sign of the ultimate absurdity, rather like in Camus's *La Peste*, but without the rousing solution of communal action. Illness in children, who are often seen to represent a sort of knowledge which is lost to adults, is the sign of the inauthenticity of the life of the main characters. In *Los premios*, Jorge becomes ill when the passengers fail to reach the stern of the boat where they are travelling, which is out of bounds and symbolises censured areas of their experience, but recovers when they do so. In *62*, the censoring or repressing of various traits in Hélène leads to the death of the 'muchacho muerto' under anaesthesia, and something similar happens in 'La señorita Cora'. In most cases medicine is seen as the cause or accomplice of the death or illness rather than its solution. Only in the explicitly socialist *Libro de Manuel*, where the child is a central character, does he escape illness, though concern is expressed that he might be poisoned by Lonstein's mushroom. Oliveira certainly toys with the idea that his own situation is in a way responsible for the death: 'nos ha matado porque somos culpables de su muerte. Culpables, es decir fautores de un estado de cosas. . .' (p.185). It is here that Oliveira most radically and shockingly breaks with normal human patterns of behaviour, first sitting for over an hour talking philosophy by the corpse, then refusing to show any pity towards the mother, la Maga, to 'calzar en el guante, hacer lo que debe hacerse en estos casos' (p.176). The step outside society is more or less definitive and Oliveira is squeezed out of the Club de la Serpiente. His final and paradoxical cleansing himself of civilisation through immersion in filth, in his wonderfully obscene night with Emmanuèle, is now almost inevitable, and effective in allowing Oliveira to reach some sort of zero point.

Around this time la Maga disappears: departed, drowned, elsewhere. Her supposed death and subsequent role are complex and handled with skill and ambiguity by Cortázar. The question is basically whether her death and possible return to Buenos Aires has a deep mythical and poetic-archetypal dimension or whether such issues are simply in the mind of an increasingly deranged Oliveira. Cortázar in his *Cuaderno* significantly jots down 'No tener miedo a lo fantástico'.[25] Ana María Barrenechea in a very interesting and perceptive discussion concludes that he abandons this option in the text of the novel, moving rather onto a symbolic plane.[26] Cortázar characteristically offers possible reading cues not in an authorial voice, but through the mouths of characters. I believe, however, that the effect of the final pages lies in a coexistence of genres in the novel, and we should perhaps recall Todorov's definition of the fantastic as a hesitation in the reader between a reading according to the 'merveilleux' or the 'étrange', i.e. the fantastic lies in an ambiguity of reading. Cortázar would in fact seem to be using in the novel techniques developed in his short stories. The characters themselves, especially towards the end of the novel, have similar difficulties in reading the situation.

La Maga at one point hopes that Oliveira will kill her so that she can be reborn, transformed: 'la Maga esperaba verdaderamente que Horacio la matara, y que esa muerte debía ser de fénix' (p.45). Oliveira himself is at least momentarily attracted by this ritual murder which would be a release of cosmic forces:

Oliveira sintió como si la Maga esperara de él la muerte, algo en ella que no era su yo despierto, una oscura forma reclamando una aniquilación. . . Sólo esa vez, excentrado como un matador mítico para quien matar es devolver el toro al mar y el mar al cielo, vejó a la Maga en una larga noche de la que hablaron poco luego.

(p.44)

Other literary archetypes are evoked in various places of the text involving an enhancing of love through destroying the beloved object. There is then a reading whereby la Maga's death is a ritual murder by Oliveira, which releases impersonal forces beyond the control of individuals, perhaps of the sort that in Chapter 62 are described as 'fuerzas habitantes, extranjeras, que avanzan en procura de su derecho de ciudad; una búsqueda superior a nosotros mismos como individuos y que nos usa para sus fines, una oscura necesidad de evadir el estado de homo sapiens' (p.417). Another way that Oliveira uses to rid himself of la Maga is significant according to a different sort of code. He alleges that she is unfaithful to him with Gregorovius as an excuse to leave her. Jealousy is usually a sign of bad faith in Cortázar: a dishonest reading of a situation which blocks or censures a significant process in the individual or group. Traveler is in a similar position at the end of the novel, as is Andrés at the end of Libro de Manuel where the ambiguity lies in the question whether he joins the revolution for genuine reasons, or because he is jealous of the leader Marcos's relation with his girlfriend Ludmilla.

Nothing is further from the tone of the first few chapters of the 'Del lado de acá' than such mythical considerations. The characters, however, are structurally doubles in a way reminiscent of the mirror structure of the short stories where presences from one area or period are projected onto another; one set of characters haunts or dictates the actions of another. Oliveira (like other Cortázar protagonists) in Paris has an orderly intellectual bourgeois lover (Pola) and a chaotic, intuitive working-class lover (la Maga), and is half-heartedly jealous of Gregorovius. In Buenos Aires there are also two couples. Oliveira lives with Gekrepten ('aunque hacía pésimamente el amor y la pasta asciutta' (p.268), an irresistible phrase), who shares with la Maga the fact that she is rather simple. Traveler is very much what Oliveira would have been had he not gone to Paris, and is explicitly referred to as his *doppelgänger*. His wife Talita, though basically faithful, is torn between what the two men represent, while Traveler is torn between jealousy and an understanding of the (half-conscious) aims of Oliveira.

Traveler is described as 'el hombre del territorio', superficially anarchical but generally reconciled with life. Oliveira has become 'un perro entre los hombres', has gone beyond society but perhaps has something to offer, something that he learned from la Maga. He acts as the same sort of irritant to the Travelers as had la Maga to him, becoming 'una especie de mensajero' (p.318), or 'inquisidor cariñoso' (p.451). Traveler on the other hand is seen by Oliveira as 'el abanderado, el heraldo de la rendición, de la vuelta a casa y al orden' (p.397), as a champion of all that Oliveira had rebelled against, though his life-style is painted in an attractive, humorous manner, very much that of the *cronopio*: he works in a circus, half-plucked geese slither across the kitchen floor, there are idealised *mateadas* and games of *truco* in the patio with the neighbours, and so on. Talita, though she shares this aura, nevertheless has negative points against her: she is a 'farmacéutica', and associated like the anaesthetist Hélène in *62* with medicine and thus repression. She is also described as a 'lectora de enciclopedias' (p.257), though she reads with the others the delirious systems of Ceferino Piriz which send up the sort of hardened and fixed mental order symbolised by the dictionary, and which is further subverted by the word games played across the street which symbolically separates the world of the Travelers from that of Oliveira.

Underneath the jollity, a tense and expectant atmosphere develops in Buenos Aires. Traveler feels the challenge to change and account for his life; he and Oliveira are seen as vampires with a common circulatory system; Talita feels almost that she is being inhabited by Oliveira. It is Oliveira who first suggests that their relationship goes beyond the merely individual plane: 'Ma da por pensar que nuestra relación es casi química, un hecho fuera de nosotros mismos' (p.328). Things come to a head when he mistakes Talita for la Maga, and especially when he goes with her down to the morgue of the lunatic asylum where they all work and kisses her thinking her la Maga, or kisses la Maga through her. In all the novels there is a symbolic descent to Hades, like that for example of Orpheus to recover Eurydice, to recover a lost vital force. La Maga of course has been associated throughout with all that has been lost by modern civilisation, all that which Oliveira, without exactly embodying it, has reproached the Travelers with lacking or ignoring. The text thus suggests various contradictory things: that la Maga has returned in spirit through Talita as a sort of medium or zombie; that Oliveira is going mad; that a sort of collective psychic and existential revolution has overcome the group. These readings belong in a sense to the different genres that *Rayuela* combines, and the resolution of the novel is very much a question of reading, not only on the part of the reader himself, but also on that of the characters. What Cortázar is perhaps asking is that we should read the novel and the world simultaneously according to several genres.

Oliveira very much wants to be reconciled with his reality, friends and country, but equally fears reconciliation as renunciation of all he has so painfully achieved. For there to be any true reconciliation of the opposite worlds, the world and that which questions it, its other, there must be a certain acceptance by the Travelers of the point of view of Oliveira, of the non-exclusive nature of their own values. After all it is Traveler who says that the world of Ceferino Piriz can only seem strange to 'los tipos que creen en sus instituciones con prescindencia de las ajenas' (p.469). What they must accept is the real presence, spirit and force of la Maga and what she represents, i.e. that which undermines the security and authoritativeness of their own discourse, 'denounces' it as partial.

In the final episode of the main part of the novel, Oliveira barricades himself into his room in the asylum after kissing Talita, afraid that Traveler is out to kill him. If he believes this, it is in part because he does not dare to believe that the woman he kissed was la Maga. The onus, however, is mainly on Traveler to come to accept a non-realistic reading of what happened between his wife and Oliveira. To declare Oliveira 'mad' is the easiest and most traditional way of not accepting what is different, and this he does at one point: 'Eso se llama locura' (p.401). A fantastic story, read according to the generic codes of realism must attribute madness to some party. When, however, Traveler and Talita see the automatic labels thrown about by the other staff of the asylum (e.g. 'histeria matinensis yugulata' (p.403), and the crude attempts to lure Oliveira down), they eventually come out on his side, at the risk of their jobs and to the delight of Oliveira. Madness, moreover, within the novel has taken on a series of rich connotations. As the opposite of 'sanity', it forms another of the dualisms which Oliveira, after Breton and the Surrealists, had longed to transcend, such as 'sueño' and 'vigilia', dualisms which at this point are represented by the two men and the two readings of the novel. Madness also has another very important meaning. Before meeting the *clocharde*, Oliveira muses on the possibility of 'unirse al mundo, a la Gran Locura, a la Inmensa Burrada, abrirse a la cristalización del deseo, al encuentro' (p.239). It is the world itself, in all its absurdity, which is the 'Gran Locura', and to join the world is to go mad and in a way to cease to be mad. When walking the wet streets of Paris with Berthe Trépat, Oliveira had wondered whether the only way to destroy the absurd was to live absurdly. Here, faced with the world of Traveler, what he calls the 'territorio', he comes to an identical conclusion: 'la única manera de escapar del territorio era metiéndose en él hasta las cachas' (p.402).

The solidarity of the Travelers produces in Oliveira an intense feeling of friendship and a joyful acceptance of their humanity. The solution that he had not been able to accept from la Maga without being exasperated by his automatic reaction to physical or emotional stimuli, 'la obediencia al deseo' (p.51), he is now able to accept without coercion, having won for himself the right to return and having, albeit momentarily, fused his world with that of the Travelers: 'cuánta hermosura en esos ojos que se habían llenado de lágrimas y en esa voz que le había aconsejado: "Metele la falleba, no les tengo mucha confianza", cuánto amor en ese brazo que apretaba la cintura de una mujer' (p.402). Oliveira's long path has transformed his country and world from a prison into a home, social and emotional bonds from coercion into freedom.

Maybe, though, the harmony will not last, maybe Oliveira throws himself out of the asylum window. The whole experience of the text suggests that there can never be a perfect reconciliation, an ecstatic union between habit, alienation and closure and the forces which deny, question and open such structures. The text of *Rayuela*, however, offers us a working example, in the sort of reading the text elicits from us, of a more fluid and porous apprehension of reality, a more dynamic relation with what Cortázar often calls 'lo otro', with what we deny, because it questions the exclusiveness of our attitudes and lives. The paradisal unity which the novel constantly evokes may not be round the corner, but Cortázar is one of the modern writers most likely to make us glimpse and desire it, and thus see in a different light our unthinking acceptance of the given as natural and inevitable.

NOTES

1 Lida Aronne-Amestoy, *Cortázar: la novela mandala* (Fernando García Cambeiro, Buenos Aires, 1972), p.98.

2 *El examen* (Sudamericana/Sudamericana-Planeta, Buenos Aires, 1986), p.90.

3 In an interview with Evelyn Picon Garfield, *Cortázar por Cortázar* (Universidad Veracruzana, Xalapa, 1981), p.97.

4 *Rayuela* (Sudamericana, Buenos Aires, 1969), p.600. All future page references to *Rayuela* will be from this edition and be incorporated parenthetically into the text.

5 In Ernesto González Bermejo, *Conversaciones con Cortázar* (Edhasa, Barcelona, 1978), p.119.

6 See Saúl Yurkievich's interesting comparison of the two writers, 'Borges/Cortázar: mundos y modos de la ficción fantástica', in his *Julio Cortázar: al calor de tu sombra* (Legasa, Buenos Aires, 1987), pp.71–82.

7 See Jacques Poulet, 'Poétique du conte de Julio Cortázar', especially the section 'Le conte comme métatexte', in J. Poulet (ed.), *Julio Cortázar*, Co–Textes, no. 11 (CERS, Montpellier, 1986), pp.124–80.

8 'Del cuento breve y sus alrededores', *Último round* (Siglo XXI, Mexico, 1969), upper deck, p.42.

9 See, for example, Cortázar's important statements in O. Collazos, M. Vargas Llosa and J. Cortázar, *Literatura en la revolución y revolución en la literatura* (Siglo XXI, Mexico, 1971).

10 See Cortázar's 'Policrítica a la hora de los chacales', reproduced in 'Documentos: el caso Padilla', *Libre*, vol. I (Sept.–Nov. 1971), pp.126–30.

11 See Picon Garfield, *Cortázar por Cortázar*, p.22.

12 This aspect of the novel is intelligently analysed from a radically Jungian and pychoanalytical point of view by Ana Hernández del Castillo in *Keats, Poe, and the Shaping of Cortázar's Mythopoesis*, Purdue University Monographs in Romance Languages, vol. 8 (John Benjamins, Amsterdam, 1981).

13 In González Bermejo, *Conversaciones con Cortázar*, pp.12, 120.

14 Mikhail Bakhtin, 'Discourse in the novel', in his *The Dialogic Imagination*, ed. M. Holquist (University of Texas Press, Austin, 1986), p.309.
15 Ibid., pp.366–7.
16 Ibid., p.378.
17 See Cynthia Stone, 'El lector implícito de *Rayuela* y los blancos de la narración', in Fernando Burgos (ed.), *Los ochenta mundos de Cortázar: ensayos* (Edi-6, Madrid, 1987), pp. 177–84.
18 S. Yurkievich, 'El collage literario; genealogía de *Rayuela*', in *Julio Cortázar: al calor de tu sombra*, p.129.
19 Carlos Fuentes, *La nueva novela hispanoamericana* (Joaquín Mortiz, Mexico, 1972), p.9.
20 In 'Contar y cantar: Julio Cortázar y Saúl Yurkievich entrevistados por Pierre Lartigue', in Yurkievich, *Julio Cortázar: al calor de tu sombra*, p.95.
21 *Último round*, bottom deck, p.213.
22 Aronne-Amestoy, *Cortázar: la novela mandala*, p.12.
23 'Forms of time and chronotope in the novel', in *The Dialogic Imagination*, p.164.
24 In *Pensées*, ed. L. Lafuma (Seuil, Paris, 1978), no. 412, p. 173.
25 In Julio Cortázar and Ana María Barrenechea, *Cuaderno de bitácora de 'Rayuela'* (Sudamericana, Buenos Aires, 1983), p.226.
26 See Barrenechea, 'Estudio preliminar', in *Cuaderno de bitácora*, pp.40–1, 53–4.

7

GABRIEL GARCÍA MÁRQUEZ: *CIEN AÑOS DE SOLEDAD*

JAMES HIGGINS

Born in 1928, Gabriel García Márquez spent the formative years of his childhood in Aracataca, a small town in the tropical Caribbean region on Colombia's north coast. In the early years of the century the North American United Fruit Company had moved into the area to exploit its banana-producing potential and in the 1910s Aracataca became something of a boom town. By the time of the author's birth the boom had passed, but it was still a bustling, prosperous little community. However, following United Fruit's withdrawal from Colombia in 1941, the economy of the region collapsed and a few years later, when the writer and his mother returned to arrange for the sale of his grandparents' house, they were to find that the once-thriving Aracataca had become a dilapidated ghost town.

Because of the unusual circumstances of his upbringing García Márquez was to experience solitude from an early age. His mother Luisa, the daughter of one of the region's long-established families, had married a humble telegraphist, Gabriel Eligio García, against her parents' wishes, but to placate them she returned home for the birth of her first child and left the boy behind to be brought up by them. In his grandparents' large, rambling house, shared by three aunts he grew up as a solitary little boy among elderly adults. Later experiences were to reinforce the deep-rooted sense of solitude that runs through all his writing.

Nonetheless, his childhood was a happy one in which he enjoyed a particularly close relationship with his grandfather, and he was raised in a story-telling environment in that the elders were constantly reliving the past and recounting anecdotes about the history of the family and the town. His grandfather, Colonel Nicolás Márquez, had fought on the Liberal side against the ruling Conservatives in the Thousand Days' War (1899–1902), the last of a

141

succession of civil wars that had rent Colombia, and would often reminisce about those stirring times. For their part, his grandmother and aunts were credulous, superstitious women who believed in the supernatural and recounted all sorts of magical happenings as if they were everyday events, and the author has often claimed that it was from his grandmother that he learned his narrative manner. That childhood world was to come to an end, however, with the death of his grandfather in 1936, and García Márquez has frequently stated that no other period in his life has matched his first eight years for richness of experience.

García Márquez spent most of the next ten years as a boarder at a school in Zipaquirá, near Bogotá, and in 1947 he entered the National University in the capital to study law. Coming as he did from the Caribbean region, he never felt at home in the alien environment of the Andean highlands, whose cold climate and formal, traditionalist atmosphere proved uncongenial to him. He found solace in books, among which he singles out Kafka's *Metamorphosis* as exercising a profound influence on him, and himself began writing short stories. In 1948 he abandoned his studies and returned to the north coast, where he worked as a journalist, first in Cartagena, and then, from 1950, in Barranquilla. The latter city was to have a decisive influence on his literary development, for there he took up with a group of bohemian literati, who introduced him to the work of modern Anglo-Saxon writers, especially Joyce, Virginia Woolf and William Faulkner. Later he was to render homage to this so-called Barranquilla Group by portraying them in the latter pages of *Cien años de soledad*.

It was in Barranquilla that he wrote most of his early short stories and his first novel, *La hojarasca*, writing at night and in his spare time. The novel was eventually published in 1955, but he encountered difficulty in establishing himself as a novelist and was, in fact, achieving greater success as a reporter. In 1954 he had joined the staff of *El Espectador* in Bogotá and soon became one of Colombia's best-known journalists, boosting the paper's circulation with articles such as 'Relato de un náufrago' a serialised account of the ordeal of a shipwrecked sailor.

Like his fellow Colombians García Márquez was deeply affected by the years of political violence unleashed by the assassination in 1948 of the Liberal presidential candidate, Jorge Eliécer Gaitán, violence which claimed 200,000–300,000 lives in the period 1949–62 and led to the dictatorship of General Gustavo Rojas Pinilla (1953–7). An indication of his own political leanings is that in 1955 he was briefly a member of the Communist Party. As a child he had come under the influence of his grandfather's radical liberalism, a lasting impression was made on him by accounts of the massacre of striking United Fruit Company workers in Ciénaga in the year of his birth,[1] and at school in Zipaquirá he had been introduced to Marxist thought by leftist teachers. His flirtation with the Communist Party was transitory and he · has always rejected hard-line Marxist dogmatism, but he has consistently championed left-wing causes and has always maintained that the future of the world lies with socialism.

In 1955 García Márquez was sent to Europe by *El Espectador* as a foreign correspondent, only to discover shortly after his arrival in Paris that the paper had been closed down by the government, and for several months he endured the struggles and hardships of the impecunious artist. In 1957 he moved to Caracas, working there as a journalist for almost two years, and in 1959, following the Cuban Revolution, he joined the Cuban news agency Prensa Latina, first in Bogotá and then in Cuba and New York. In 1961 he resigned in protest against the manoeuvres of the Communist Party hard-liners and with his wife – he had married in 1958 – moved to Mexico City, where he continued his journalistic career, worked for a public relations firm and wrote film scripts. In the meantime he had persevered with his writing and achieved modest success with the novella *El coronel no tiene quien le escriba* (1961), the novel *La mala hora* (1962) and a collection of short stories, *Los funerales de la Mamá Grande* (1962), and in 1967 he was to win an international reputation almost overnight with the publication of his masterpiece, *Cien años de soledad*.[2]

While considerable works in their own right, García Márquez's early writings are also stages in the maturation of *Cien años*. *La hojarasca* and several of the short stories introduce us to Macondo, the fictional representation of the world in which the author grew up. The former shows the effects of the short-lived 'banana boom' and the subsequent depression on that small rural community, while 'Los funerales de la Mamá Grande' portrays the traditional dominance of the land-owning oligarchy through the mythical story of the legendary matriarch who ruled over the region from time immemorial. *El coronel no tiene quien le escriba* and *La mala hora* recreate the climate of political violence which prevailed in the Colombian countryside in the 1950s, the former linking it to a long tradition of such violence and the latter depicting its corrosive effect on the community. Many of the characters of these early narratives are also forerunners of the Buendías of *Cien años de soledad* in that they are lonely, isolated individuals leading a solitary existence. With regard to style, 'Los funerales de la Mamá Grande' marks a major evolution. In all of his fiction García Márquez endeavours to achieve a poetic transposition of reality, but in most of his early work he does so in a style that by and large is still essentially realistic. However, in this story he was to hit on the narrative manner best suited to give literary expression to the world he had known as a child. Here the narrator introduces himself as someone who sits down at his front door to tell a tale as a kind of spokesman for the community. The story, in effect, has the character of popular oral narrative, privileging the legendary and depicting the world in larger-than-life terms, but at the same time its 'magical realism' is counterbalanced by an ironic, irreverent tone which subverts the very legend it is propagating. In *Cien años* García Márquez was to perfect that narrative manner and to create an all-encompassing fictional world which incorporates the principal themes treated separately in his earlier work.

Following his success with *Cien años*, García Márquez went on to consolidate his reputation with a number of other books, notably *La increíble y triste historia de la cándida Eréndida y de su abuela desalmada* (1972), *El otoño del patriarca* (1975), *Crónica de una muerte anunciada* (1981) and *El amor en los tiempos del cólera* (1985). His status as one of the world's great novelists was recognised by the award of the Nobel Prize for Literature in 1982.

Cien años narrates the history of the town of Macondo and of its founding family, the Buendías. Following his killing of a neighbour who insulted his honour, José Arcadio Buendía, his wife Úrsula and a group of friends abandon their native town and set out in search of a new home, settling eventually in an isolated region in the swamplands. For some time Macondo lives in a state of primeval innocence, its only contact with the outside world coming through the occasional visits of a tribe of gypsies, led by Melquíades, who introduce the inhabitants to wondrous inventions such as false teeth, ice and the magnet and arouse in José Arcadio the thirst for scientific experiment and the ambition to see the town enjoy the benefits of technological progress. In the course of time progress does come to Macondo as it gradually emerges from its isolation, but although it brings relative prosperity, it does not turn the town into the Utopia envisaged by its founder. A magistrate is sent by the central government to assume authority over the district and, as it is drawn into the sphere of national politics, the town becomes embroiled in a series of bloody civil wars. The establishment of a railway link paves the way for the commercial exploitation of the region's natural resources by the North American Banana Company and overnight Macondo is transformed into a boom town; disgruntled by their low wages and poor working conditions, the workers declare a strike and are shot down by government troops; subsequently, torrential rain destroys the plantations, the Banana Company withdraws and Macondo declines into a ghost town. The history of the Buendías began with an 'original sin' in that José Arcadio and Úrsula were first cousins and succeeding generations likewise betray a propensity to incest, and throughout the novel the family is haunted by the fear of punishment in the form of the birth of a monstrous child with a pig's tail. That fear is eventually realised when the love affair between the last remaining Buendías, Aureliano Babilonia and his aunt Amaranta Úrsula, produces the dreaded monstrosity. Shortly afterwards, when Aureliano finally succeeds in making sense of the puzzling manuscript written by Melquíades decades earlier and which over the generations various members of the family have vainly attempted to decipher, he discovers that it is a prophetic account of the history of Macondo and that the Buendías and their world will come to an end when he reads the last sentence.

Cien años is a novel which maintains a tension or dialectic between different perspectives. It is, first of all, a comic novel, an entertainment, which adopts an irreverent attitude towards literature – 'the best plaything ever invented for making fun of people' (p.462) – as something not to be taken seriously.[3] Yet at the same time it is a deeply serious and highly ambitious book which sets out to rewrite the history of Latin America and to offer a view of the human condition. Again, it proclaims its fictionality when, on the closing page, Aureliano Babilonia discovers that, in effect, the Buendías are no more than creatures of Melquíades's imagination with no existence outside the pages of his manuscript, an ending which serves, among other things, to warn the reader that the novel is 'a fictive construct, a creation, and not a mirror that meticulously reflects reality'.[4] Lurking behind the book is the ontological uncertainty of our times, as is revealed by an earlier episode when the same Aureliano, trying to persuade others of the truth of his version of Macondo's history, runs up against the scepticism of the local priest, who, ironically, is conspicuously lacking in the certainties which he is supposed to embody:

> El párroco lo midió con una mirada de lástima.
> −Ay, hijo − suspiró −. A mí me bastaría con estar seguro de que tú y yo existimos en este momento.

(p.484)

Unable to share traditional realist fiction's confident assumption of man's ability to understand and describe the world, García Márquez effectively waives any claim to be 'telling it the way it is'. And yet, despite his awareness of the limitations of literature, he nonetheless endeavours to do what novelists have always sought to do: to depict the world around him. Paradoxically, he attempts to translate reality into words while casting doubt on the feasibility of such an undertaking.

García Márquez has stated that his primary aim in writing *Cien años* was to recreate the lost world of his childhood.[5] He does so through the vehicle of a so-called magical realism which eschews the documentary approach of realist fiction and instead gives expression to the world-view of a rural people living in remote isolation from the modern developed world. It should be stressed that the magical realism of *Cien años* does not imply that Latin American reality is somehow inherently magical, though the novel does highlight the prodigious dimensions of the natural environment and the excesses of political life. Nor does the much-bandied term 'fantasy' have much meaning in relation to *Cien años*, since every event described, no matter how fantastic it might appear, has a perfectly logical explanation. What the novel does is to present events, not as they actually occurred, but as they were perceived and interpreted by the local people. Thus, for example, the narrative points to the real explanation of Remedios's disappearance by recording that outsiders were of the opinion that she had run off with a man and that the story put about by her family was an invention designed to cover up the scandal, but it is the family's version − that she ascended into heaven − which the text privileges and recounts in full and plausible detail, since it was the one which was widely accepted in the

146

community (pp.313–14). Likewise, the systematic use of hyperbole – José Arcadio's prodigious virility, Colonel Aureliano's thirty-two armed uprisings, the seventy-two schoolgirls queuing up to empty seventy-two chamber-pots, to cite but a few examples – corresponds to the way in which the popular collective memory blows events up to larger-than-life proportions. The narrative, too, has an Old Testament ring to it – there is an original sin, an exodus, the discovery of an (un)promised land, a plague, a deluge, an apocalypse – which is a reflection both of the cultural environment and of the myth-making tendency of popular history. In effect, *Cien años* transmits the history of Macondo as it was recorded and elaborated over the generations by popular oral tradition, and by so doing, it permits a rural society to give expression to itself in terms of its own cultural experience.

Yet *Cien años* is a written text, and a story that gives the impression of being an oral narrative turns out on the final pages to be recorded in Melquíades's manuscript.[6] Another layer of tension informing the novel, therefore, is that between the oral and the written. By incorporating popular oral history into literature to convey a Third World experience, García Márquez accords it the status and prestige associated with the written word. He also highlights the relativity of all world-views, for events which appear fantastic to the sophisticated reader – Remedios's ascent into heaven, trips on flying carpets, the parish priest's feats of levitation – are accepted as everyday realities in the cultural environment of Macondo and by contrast the modern technology which the sophisticated reader takes for granted – ice cubes, false teeth, the locomotive – is greeted with awe as something wonderful and magical. *Cien años* thus not only challenges conventional assumptions as to what constitutes reality, but subverts the novelistic genre's conventional Eurocentrism and, indeed, the whole rationalist cultural tradition of the West. At the same time, though, the narrator writes in an ironic, tongue-in-cheek manner which distances him from the oral history which he is transmitting. Thus, for example, in the episode discussed earlier, the story of Remedios's ascent into heaven is recounted straight-faced but is undermined by insinuation of the real, more prosaic explanation of the facts. In effect, if *Cien años* sets out to subvert Eurocentric attitudes, it also simultaneously subverts Latin Americans' perceptions of their own history.

As has already been implied, García Márquez is writing against the Western novelistic tradition and *Cien años* demands a reading which, eschewing the kind of narrow Eurocentrism that disguises itself as universalism, approaches the novel in terms of its own specificity. However, at the same time, the novel draws heavily on literary sources and if Borges would seem to be the main influence, it should be remembered that behind the latter lies the whole corpus of Western culture.[7] It is significant that in the provincial environment of Macondo a privileged space should be allotted to Melquíades's room, representing the timeless world of literature, and significant, too, that, having had his horizons broadened by the Catalan bibliophile, the younger writer Gabriel should leave Macondo for Paris. For while challenging the Western novelistic tradition, García Márquez is also writing within it and in *Cien años* he has set out, not only to portray a Latin American reality, but to express the universal through the local.

In giving a literary depiction of the world of his childhood, García Márquez has also created in the fictional community of Macondo a microcosm of a larger world. The story of Macondo, in fact, reflects the general pattern of Latin America's history. It is founded by settlers fleeing a homeland haunted by the spectre of violence and is born of a utopian dream, being built on the spot where José Arcadio has a vision of a luminous city of houses walled with mirrors (p.97). By the final page, however, the city of mirrors has become a city of mirages. Macondo thus represents the dream of a brave new world which America seemed to promise and which was cruelly proved illusory by the subsequent course of history. *Cien años*, in effect, is a demystifying rewriting of the history of the subcontinent. The ruling establishment's tradition of manipulating history is exposed in the latter part of the novel when the authorities hush up the massacre of the striking banana workers and the round-up and disappearance of all potential subversives, claiming that Macondo is a peaceful and contented community where social harmony reigns (p.383). Later, young Aureliano, brought up by his uncle to regard Macondo as the victim of the Banana Company's imperialist exploitation, discovers that the school history books portray the company as a benefactor which brought prosperity and progress (pp.422–3). *Cien años* sets out to debunk the official myths by offering an alternative history. In part, this is a popular view of a local community subjected to domination by outside forces. At the same time, however, it is the view of a privileged class, since the dominant perspective is that of the Buendías, the local provincial elite, and their version of history is undermined in its turn by the narrator's ironic distancing of himself from it.

While in strictly chronological terms the events of the novel roughly span the century from the years after Independence to around 1930, the early phase of Macondo's history evokes Latin America's colonial period, when communities lived isolated from one another and the viceroyalties themselves had little contact with the distant metropolis. Latin America's isolation from intellectual developments in Europe is hilariously brought out when José Arcadio's researches lead him to the discovery that the earth is round (p.75) and colonial underdevelopment is reflected in his acute awareness of Macondo's backwardness in relation to the outside world:

'En el mundo están ocurriendo cosas increíbles', le decía a Úrsula. 'Ahí mismo, al otro lado del río, hay toda clase de aparatos mágicos, mientras nosotros seguimos viviendo como los burros.'
(p.79)

The novel thus ironically debunks Spain's claim to have bequeathed to America the benefits of European civilisation. Indeed, the Conquest itself is parodied, in a passage reminiscent of the chronicles (pp.82–3),[8] by the expedition in which the men of Macondo re-enact the ordeals of the Spanish explorers and conquistadores in order to make contact with the civilisation which Spain allegedly spead to its colonies.

Furthermore, the Spanish colonial heritage is identified as one of the principal factors in Latin America's continuing underdevelopment. Significantly, the Macondo men's expedition fails to make contact with civilisation and succeeds only in finding the hulk of an old Spanish galleon, stranded on dry land and overgrown with vegetation (p.83), symbol of a heritage that is anachronistic, out of context and ill-equipped to tackle the awesome American environment. Above all, that heritage takes the form of a mentality, personified in the novel by Fernanda del Carpio. An incomer from the capital, she embodies the Castilian traditionalism of the *cachacos*, the inhabitants of the cities of the Colombian *altiplano*, and, beyond that, a whole set of values and attitudes which Latin America has inherited from Spain. Nursing aristocratic pretensions that are

149

reflected in her name – an echo of that of Bernardo del Carpio, a legendary Spanish hero of medieval times – she lives the illusion of a grandeur that no longer exists and clings to antiquated customs in a world that no longer has any use for them; and as Macondo falls into the hands of the Banana Company and is invaded by lower-class upstarts, she comforts herself with the belief that she is spiritually superior to the vulgar tradesmen who have taken over the world, an attitude which echoes the response of Spanish American intellectuals of the Arielist generation to North American expansionism.[9] The heirlooms which she receives from her father as Christmas presents are ironically described by her husband as a family cemetery and, as though to confirm the truth of his words, the last present turns out to be a box containing the father's corpse (pp.289–90). What they symbolise, in fact, is an outmoded, traditionalist mentality which prevents Latin America from coming to terms with the modern world.

The advent of the republican era is marked by the arrival of Don Apolinar Moscote to assume authority over the town as representative of the central government. Reversing the conventional wisdom which has traditionally attributed the political instability of the nineteenth century to the 'barbaric' countryside, whose backwardness and lawlessness supposedly hindered the 'civilised' cities' efforts to lead the subcontinent towards order and progress,[10] the novel identifies government intervention in local affairs as the origin of Macondo's troubles. Till then it had always been a well-ordered community and, far from bringing law and order, the new magistrate immediately stirs up unrest by decreeing that all houses are to be painted blue (pp.133–4), the colour of the ruling Conservative party, an act symptomatic of the autocratic and insensitive impositions of central government. Moreover, if Don Apolinar introduces Macondo to parliamentary democracy, he also introduces it to the cynical manipulation of democratic institutions, the first elections being rigged to ensure the victory of the government party (p.173). And as Macondo is incorporated into the national political system, it becomes caught up in the civil violence engendered by that tainted system.

For much of the novel Macondo is afflicted by the civil wars between Liberals and Conservatives that were a feature of the nineteenth century in Colombia and other Latin American countries. The futility of that bloodshed is conveyed by the progressive disillusionment of Colonel Aureliano Buendía, the champion of the Liberal cause. A principal cause of his disenchantment is the ideological fanaticism typified by the agitator Dr Alirio Noguera, who conceives a plan for liquidating Conservatism by a coordinated nationwide campaign of assassination (p.175). While such fanaticism leads extremists on both sides to forget their common humanity, Aureliano establishes a friendship with General Moncada across the ideological divide and at one point the two men consider the possibility of breaking with their respective parties and joining forces to establish a humanitarian regime which would combine the best features of the warring doctrines (p.223). Yet he later has Moncada executed, for he himself falls prey to the same fanaticism and is ready to sacrifice even his friends to achieve his political objectives, and before his death his old friend warns him that his obsessive hatred of his political enemies has dehumanised him (p.235). Fortunately, Aureliano is sensitive enough to realise what is happening to him and his subsequent determination to bring the war to an end is born in part of the wish to save himself as a human being.

The irony is that, despite their ideological differences, both parties are dominated by the same privileged elite and in practice the distinction between them ultimately becomes blurred, just as the houses in Macondo take on an indeterminate colour as a result of being constantly repainted red or blue according to which group is in control (p.201). In power the Liberals commit the same abuses as the Conservatives. As Governor, Arcadio Buendía behaves like a petty dictator, and the deal which he strikes with the second José Arcadio, whereby he legalises the latter's right to lands which he has usurped in exchange for the right to levy taxes (pp.190–1), exemplifies and reinforces the traditional pattern of oligarchic domination and, significantly, is later ratified by the Conservatives. Committed to a programme of radical reform, Colonel Aureliano finds himself not only fighting the Conservatives but at odds with his own party. The Liberal landowners react to the threat to their property by entering into secret alliances with the Conservatives, financial backing is withdrawn, and eventually the party strategists drop all radical policies from their programme in order to broaden their support (p.244). At this point Aureliano comes to realise that they have been fighting not for change but for power, for access to office and the spoils that go with it, and, disillusioned, he brings the war to an end and withdraws from political life. In the end a compromise is reached whereby the two parties share power, a solution which restores peace but which leaves the socio-economic status quo intact. Liberals and Conservatives are thus exposed as ultimately representing the same class interests.

As peace and stability return to Macondo, the region enters a period of neo-colonial domination. Early in the novel José Arcadio articulates the dream of a world transformed by scientific and technological progress:

> Trató de seducirla con . . . la promesa de un mundo prodigioso donde bastaba con echar unos líquidos mágicos en la tierra para que las plantas dieran frutos a voluntad del hombre, y donde se vendían a precio de baratillo toda clase de aparatos para el dolor.
> (p.86)

What he is voicing, in effect, is a constant of Latin American thought since Independence, the aspiration to 'modernise' on the model of the advanced industrial nations in order to achieve a similar level of development. In the event, Macondo does come to enjoy a period of economic growth. However, 'modernisation' does not come about as the result of internal development but is imported from the outside, and hence José Arcadio's original dream of a city of mirrors takes on an ironic significance in that Macondo's role becomes that of reflecting the developed world. And though Macondo does undoubtedly prosper and progress, it continues to trail behind the rest of the world and, furthermore, it finds itself the victim of foreign economic and cultural imperialism.

In fact, the story of the later Macondo illustrates Latin America's neo-colonial status as an economic dependency of international capital, particularly North American. No sooner has Macondo embarked on a phase of autonomous economic development than it falls under the domination of North American capital and, incorporated into the world economy as a source of primary products, becomes subject to cycles of boom and recession determined by the fluctuations of the international market. Aureliano Segundo accumulates a fantastic fortune quite fortuitously, thanks to the astonishing fertility of his livestock (p.267), and the whole community enjoys an equally fortuitous prosperity generated by the banana boom. Macondo's experience of prosperity is thus due not to any real economic development but to the amazing richness of the region's natural resources and to international demand for those resources. Hence it is defenceless against sudden slumps in the market. Symbol of such slumps is the great deluge which ruins Aureliano Segundo by killing his stock and which halts banana production and leads to the departure of the company, turning Macondo into a ghost town. The extent to which the Latin American economy is manipulated by foreign capital is indicated by the suggestion that the crisis was deliberately engineered by the company, whose directors were so powerful that they were able to control the weather (p.422). In the wake of his ruin Aureliano Segundo is reduced to running a lottery to make ends meet and is nicknamed Don Divina Providencia. He comes, in fact, to personify Latin America, whose economic role in the world is passively to wait for the stroke of good fortune which will bring it another period of prosperity.

Furthermore, such progress and prosperity as are brought to Macondo by foreign capital are achieved at a price. The Banana Company exploits its work-force quite cynically, as is indicated by the list of complaints presented by the workers (p.372), and Macondo effectively becomes a colony, a company town run by company men backed up by armed thugs dressed as policemen. And such is the power exercised by the company that when the workers take strike action the authorities send in troops to break the strike by force, massacring the strikers and liquidating the union leaders. The dominant influence exerted by foreign capital in Latin America is thus seen to extend beyond the economic to the political sphere.

The patrician Buendías represent that oligarchy which has traditionally ruled Latin America. Macondo's founding family, they develop into a land-owning class, the process by which the latifundia system was established being encapsulated in the episode in which the second José Arcadio makes use of his enormous physical strength to appropriate the best lands in the district (p.190), and subsequently they evolve into an entrepreneurial bourgeoisie by branching into business. The solitude that is their dominant family trait is directly related to their egoism: living exclusively for themselves, they are incapable of loving, of sharing, of giving themselves to others. Perhaps the most extreme examples are the introverted Aureliano, who lives in a private world of his own which no one is allowed to enter, and Amaranta, who ruins the lives of four men by arousing their passion without being able to bring herself to satisfy it, but their egocentric attitude is shared by the whole family, for everyone in the Buendía household is too wrapped up in his own affairs to think of anyone else: 'nadie se daba cuenta de nada mientras no se gritara en el corredor, porque los afanes de la panadería, los sobresaltos de la guerra, el cuidado de los niños, no dejaban tiempo para pensar en la felicidad ajena' (p.432).

Relating to that egoism is the family's propensity to incest. The Buendía dynasty originates with an incestuous marriage and successive generations become involved in more or less incestuous relationships. Their phobia about the monstrous child with a pig's tail ironically highlights their blindness to their failings, for the apparently normal Buendías are, in fact, deformed by their monstrous egoism, as Úrsula glimpses on more than one occasion (pp.98, 245). García Márquez himself has pointed out that, as the negation of solidarity, solitude has political implications.[11] The solitude of the Buendías, in effect, is a reflection of the egoistic, individualistic values by which they live. And their propensity to incest mirrors the selfish, inward-looking attitude of a privileged oligarchy jealously defending its class interests against other sectors of society.

Yet, contrary to the view of many critics, there is in the novel a notable progression which seems to offer a way out of the vicious circle in which Macondo/Latin America is caught. For as the Buendías fall on hard times in the wake of Macondo's economic decline, adversity teaches them how to love. The once frivolous Aureliano Segundo and Petra Cotes not only discover a sense of mutual solidarity but take pleasure in making sacrifices to help others in need. The same pattern is repeated with Aureliano Babilonia and Amaranta Úrsula and the latter is convinced that the child born of their love will represent a fresh start for the Buendías (p.486). In the event, he turns out to be the long-feared monster with the pig's tail whose birth marks the end of the line. For the emergence of love in the novel to displace the traditional egoism of the Buendías reflects the emergence of socialist values as a political force in Latin America, a force which will sweep away the Buendías and the order they represent.

The ending of the novel reflects, at least on the socio-political level, the optimism generated throughout Latin America in the 1960s by the triumph of the Cuban Revolution. The sense of the ending is clarified by an early episode where Melquíades comes across a prophecy of Nostradamus which he interprets as predicting a future Macondo which will be the luminous city of José Arcadio's dream but where there will be no trace of the Buendías (p.130). In effect, what Aureliano Babilonia reads in Melquíades's manuscript is the imminent demise of his own class. The Buendías' attempts to make sense of the manuscripts can be interpreted as a metaphor of Latin Americans' attempts to understand their history and it is no accident that it should be Aureliano who finally succeeds where all others in the family have failed.[12] Not only is he one of a new breed of Buendías who have learned to love, but he has been educated by his uncle José Arcadio Segundo, a union activist, who has taught him history from a working-class viewpoint. Aureliano, in other words, has broken out of the narrow perspective of his own privileged class and developed a social awareness. That awareness enables him to arrive at an understanding of Macondo's history and to see that it must culminate in a new socialist ethos which will do away with the old oligarchic and neo-colonial order.

First and foremost, then, *Cien años* is a novel which has to be read in its own Latin American context. But it is also a novel about the human condition and the story of the Buendías is susceptible to being read as a Latin American version of the history of Western man. Despite its humour, the novel presents an essentially pessimistic view of man's condition. The novel's central theme, highlighted by the title, is human isolation. If, as we have seen, the solitude of the Buendías is directly linked to their egoism, it is so only in part, for it is too pervasive to be explained away so easily and appears, in fact, as an existential condition. Disfigured 'forever and from the beginning of the world by the pox of solitude' (p.469) which prevents all communication with others, the Buendías share a common condition which, paradoxically, isolates them from one another: 'the unfathomable solitude which separated and united them at the same time' (p.448). Rather than a family, the Buendías are a group of solitary individuals living together as strangers in the same house. As such, they personify the predicament of the human race.

The story of the Buendías also reveals the limited nature of the individual's control of his own destiny. Experience teaches Pilar Ternera that 'the history of the family was a mechanism of irreversible repetitions' (p.470), while Úrsula observes that 'time wasn't passing . . . but going round in circles' (p.409). These insights

155

are sparked off by the perception that the same character traits are passed on from generation to generation (p.258) and that each new generation engages in activities which echo those of its predecessors. Thus, Aureliano Triste's sketch of the railroad is 'a direct descendant of the diagrams with which José Arcadio Buendía illustrated his scheme for solar warfare' (p.297), and when José Arcadio Segundo, following the precedent of other members of the family, shuts himself away to study Melquíades's manuscript, his face reflects 'the irreparable fate of his great-grandfather' (p.387). Implied here is not merely that the human personality is largely shaped by heredity and environment, but that individual life is subject to generic laws in that, since all men live out a limited range of experiences, every human existence corresponds to an archetypal pattern.

The world which the Buendías inhabit is one which fails to come up to the level of man's expectations and their history is a catalogue of 'lost dreams' (p.438) and 'numerous frustrated enterprises' (p.452). Again and again the characters find fulfilment denied them: the only crown that Fernanda gets to wear – that of a Carnival Queen – makes a mockery of her regal pretensions; Pilar Ternera wastes her life away waiting for the lover who never comes; the virginity which Amaranta preserves to her death is an emblem of her sterile life. José Arcadio re-enacts man's perennial striving to surmount the limitations of his condition, first when he attempts to break out of Macondo's narrow confines and reach the utopian land of the great inventions, and later when he endeavours to realise the alchemists' dream of converting base metals into gold, but in the former case he finds himself hemmed in by the sea and in the latter he succeeds only in reducing gold to a molten mess that reminds his son of dog shit (p.102). Not only are the Buendías' hopes and aspirations thwarted by life, but misfortunes arbitrarily befall them, as when Colonel Aureliano sees first his wife die and later his sons or when Rebeca and Meme tragically lose the men who brought them happiness, and the unexplained murder of the second José Arcadio stands as a metaphor for the inexplicable mystery of evil and suffering. For many of the characters, indeed, life becomes synonymous with suffering and a recurring motif is withdrawal from the world in a symbolic retreat to the refuge of the womb. In *Cien años* peace of mind is achieved only when the Buendías opt out of active emotional involvement in life.

The character with the acutest sense of life's futility is the disillusioned Colonel Aureliano. After undertaking thirty-two armed uprisings he comes to the conclusion that he has squandered twenty years of his life to no purpose and withdraws to his workshop, where he devotes himself to making the same little golden ornaments over and over again. This routine represents a recognition of the vanity of all human enterprises: it is completely senseless, but for the Colonel it is no more absurd than his previous activities and it is a means of filling in the time while he waits for death. A few moments before he dies a circus parades down the street and in it he sees a tableau of his own life, a showy, ridiculous spectacle that has given way to an emptiness as bleak as the deserted street (p.342).

If the story of Macondo reflects the general pattern of Latin America's history, it also reflects the evolution of Western civilisation and the progressive alienation of Western man. The mythical account of its history depicts Macondo's early years as a Golden Age and the town itself as an earthly paradise where men lived in happy innocence, in harmony with their world. The Fall comes with its incorporation into the modern age and, as Macondo keeps changing around her, Úrsula feels reality becoming too complicated for her to cope with: '"Los años de ahora ya no vienen como los de antes", solía decir, sintiendo que la realidad cotidiana se le escapaba de las manos' (p.321). In a local version of a universal myth which attributes man's alienation to his development of reason as a tool for dominating the world, the expulsion from paradise is depicted as a punishment for the sin of acquiring forbidden knowledge. The mysterious gypsy Melquíades appears as a personification of the intellectual curiosity which impels man to pursue knowledge and progress. It is Melquíades's tribe which brings the first scientific advances to Macondo, but the tribe is punished with extinction 'for exceeding the limits of human knowledge' (p.113). However, Melquíades himself survives and, like the serpent in the Christian myth of the Fall, plays the role of the tempter, inviting men to partake of the fruit of knowledge, and at one point Úrsula identifies the odour of his experiments with the Devil (p.77). Under his influence José Arcadio is seduced by the fascination of science and feverishly devotes himself to all kinds of experiments, but his passionate pursuit of knowledge distances him more and more from reality and brings him to a state of madness which leaves him completely alienated. Disorientated in a world turned chaotic, he vents his rage by destroying the laboratory and the apparatus which have brought him to this sad condition and, like Prometheus chained to his mountainside, lives out the rest of his days bound to a tree (the tree of knowledge?).

Moreover, when the progress so desired by José Arcadio reaches Macondo, it brings with it a general alienation as the town suffers a plague of insomnia which causes loss of memory. Lapsing into a kind of idiocy in which they cease to know the function of things and the identity of people and are no longer aware even of their own being, the inhabitants of Macondo are cast adrift in a world bereft of order and coherence. To counter the effects of the plague they identify things with labels and in the main street they erect a banner proclaiming the existence of God. This represents a desperate attempt to preserve the old values which gave life a meaning, to cling to a coherent vision of an ordered world, but elusive, shifting reality slips away from them as they forget the written word (p. 123). Reality, in other words, refuses to adapt itself to the old moulds, no longer conforms to the old concepts of order and its meaning becomes increasingly inaccessible. And although the town apparently returns to normality after Melquíades restores its memory, things are never quite the same again and, indeed, the memory-restoring potion would seem to be a metaphor of the process whereby men become conditioned to change after the first traumatic impact of progress.

Various members of the Buendía family have the image of Melquíades imprinted in their mind as a hereditary memory (p.77), and several of them devote themselves to the task of deciphering his manuscript. That image would seem to represent the human urge for knowledge and the study of the manuscript is a metaphor of man's attempts to discover the secret of existence. For most of the novel the manuscript, like life, remains an incomprehensible enigma and it is ironically implied that the search for truth is a useless activity when Melquíades's room is converted into a store-room for chamber-pots. When Aureliano Babilonia finally succeeds in decoding the manuscript in a denouement reminiscent of Unamuno's *Niebla* and Borges's 'Las ruinas circulares', the truth he comes face to face with is a disheartening one. For what he discovers is that the Buendías are no more than fictions created by Melquíades's imagination, that life is a dream, an illusion, that ultimately existence has no meaning. It is significant that that truth should be arrived at by the last of the

Buendías, for it is, in effect, the world-view of the last representative of a worn-out, declining society whose perception of life becomes more and more disillusioned as its world collapses around it. The novel's ending, therefore, can be seen as an expression of the existential anguish of twentieth-century Western man.

Given the narrator's ironic distancing of himself from the version of Macondo's history which he is transmitting, it would seem that to some extent he is dissociating himself from the world-view conveyed by the novel and identifying bourgeois individualism as one of the root causes of Western man's existential anguish. Nonetheless, the novel also communicates a sense of the ultimately tragic nature of life, one that goes beyond the subjective perceptions of the characters and resists explanation as the consequence of human failings, and the dénouement would appear to express a view of the world held by the author himself. Such a pessimistic world-view does not seem to me to be incompatible with faith in social progress, as Shaw suggests.[13] Other writers such as Peruvian poet César Vallejo have managed to balance both attitudes, and the ambivalence of the dénouement and of Aureliano Babilonia as a character epitomises the way in which the novel maintains a tension between differing perspectives, playing off against each other a passionate social commitment and a belief that in the long run nothing has any meaning. Furthermore, it has to be stressed that García Márquez's pessimism with regard to life is tempered by a number of factors. The first of these is his conviction that the advent of socialism will create a healthier and more harmonious world. Then again, the image of humanity projected in the novel is far from being entirely negative, for, despite their many failings, the Buendías come across as sympathetic characters and possess optimism-inspiring virtues: José Arcadio's heroic striving to triumph over circumstances; the tireless tenacity with which Úrsula struggles to keep the family going; Colonel Aureliano's stubborn refusal to be beaten, exemplified by his dying on his feet after urinating on the tree of life (p.342). Last but not least, *Cien años*'s exuberant humour conveys a sense that if life is tragic, it is also a great joke.

NOTES

1 This incident is incorporated into *Cien años de soledad*. See L.I. Mena, 'La huelga de la compañía bananera como expresión de lo "real maravilloso"

americano en *Cien años de soledad*, *Bulletin Hispanique*, vol. 74 (1972), pp.379–405.

2 See G. García Márquez, *Cien años de soledad*, ed. Jacques Joset (Cátedra, Madrid, 1984). All references are to this edition. Henceforth the abbreviation *Cien años* will be used. Certain quotations incorporated into the body of this text have been rendered into English.

3 See C. Griffin, 'The humour of *One Hundred Years of Solitude*' in B. McGuirk and R. Cardwell (eds.), *Gabriel García Márquez: New Readings* (Cambridge University Press, Cambridge, 1987), pp.81–94.

4 D.P. Gallagher, *Modern Latin American Literature* (Oxford University Press, Oxford, 1973), p.88.

5 P.A. Mendoza, *The Fragrance of Guava*, trans. A. Wright (Verso, London, 1983), p.72.

6 It does not follow, of course, that the novel replicates Melquíades's manuscript. In his above-mentioned edition of the text J. Joset argues that the narrator is an unknown person who rescued Melquíades's manuscript from oblivion by transcribing the translation, using the key discovered by Aureliano Babilonia (p.44). He further points out that *Cien años* includes elements which could not possibly have been contained in Melquíades's manuscript (p.491, n.42).

7 On the influence of Borges see R. González Echevarría, 'With Borges in Macondo', *Diacritics*, vol. 2, no. 1 (1972), pp. 57–60.

8 On García Márquez's use of the chronicles as a source, see I.M Zavala, '*Cien años de soledad*, crónica de Indias', *Ínsula*, no. 286 (1970), pp.3, 11.

9 The most influential expression of that response was the Uruguayan José E. Rodó's essay *Ariel* (1900). See J. Franco, *The Modern Culture of Latin America: Society and the Artist* (Pall Mall Press, London, 1967), pp.49–53.

10 This view, essentially that of the Europeanised urban elites, was given its clearest formulation in Argentina by Domingo F. Sarmiento in *Facundo* (1845), but was widely held throughout Latin America.

11 See E. González Bermejo, 'Gabriel García Márquez: ahora doscientos años de soledad', *Casa de las Américas*, vol. 10, no. 63 (1970), p.164.

12 See G. Martin, 'On "magical" and social realism in García Márquez' in McGuirk and Cardwell (eds.), *Gabriel García Márquez: New Readings*, pp.95–116.

13 D.L. Shaw, 'Concerning the interpretation of *Cien años de soldedad*', *Ibero-Amerikanisches Archiv*, vol. 3, no. 4 (1977), p.321.

8

MARIO VARGAS LLOSA:
LA CASA VERDE

PETER STANDISH

One newspaper reporter described it as one of the best dressed demonstrations this century: it was early 1987 and one of Lima's main squares had filled with protesters against President Alan García's proposed nationalisation of the Peruvian banking system. They were to be addressed by Mario Vargas Llosa. Yet this man, the new darling of the Right, was the same whose first novel had been ceremoniously burned in that same city, no doubt by some of the same people, as subversive and immoral; it was the same man who, on receiving a major literary prize for *La casa verde* twenty years earlier, had turned the occasion into propaganda for the Left. The biography of Mario Vargas Llosa is material fit for a novel; as we shall see, it has in fact been a source of much of his own work.

Until the early 1960s, few people had heard of Vargas Llosa, although he had already published a collection of short stories, *Los jefes* (1959). Then, at about the same time as more established writers like Fuentes and Cortázar produced major works in *La muerte de Artemio Cruz* and *Rayuela* respectively, Vargas Llosa, only in his late 20s, burst on to the literary scene with *La ciudad y los perros* (1962). The product of a broken home, he had been brought up by his grandparents in Bolivia, where his grandfather was consul for Peru. Later, Vargas Llosa would rejoin his parents when they became reconciled, and would spend formative periods in Piura (in northern coastal Peru, and a major setting for *La casa verde*) and in Lima; here, he was sent to the Leoncio Prado military school, which his father thought would make a man of him, and which was to be the scenario of *La ciudad y los perros*. This novel caused controversy because it hit out at certain parts of the establishment, because it was sordid and used crude language; but the literary world was impressed by the variety and mastery of technique: there was little that was comparable in previous Spanish American writers, and certainly nothing in Peru. *La ciudad y los perros* won him the Biblioteca Breve prize, and the Premio de la Crítica, as would *La casa verde* (1966). But this second novel was also to earn him the most prestigious prize in Latin America, the Rómulo Gallegos, and give rise to the notorious speech of acceptance in Caracas, to which I referred above.[1] *La casa verde* is a moving, complex book inspired by a deeply felt concern for social justice on the one hand, and a determination to achieve literary quality on the other. These early novels, together with the novella *Los cachorros* (1967) and *Conversación en La Catedral* (a two-volume work of 1969) are generally held to make up the first, and many would say best, period in Vargas Llosa's writing. All are intense, serious and unsugared works which are not easy to read but offer great rewards to those who persevere. Apart from *La casa verde*, they deal with sleazy life in Lima and arise from the author's personal experiences, as an adolescent or as a young newspaper reporter; *La casa verde*, though it shares many features of style with the others, has an altogether grander sweep.

The next novel, *Pantaleón y las visitadoras*, came out in 1973. It was short, it was a much easier read, but above all (and this was the most radical difference) it was funny. The author, who had previously recorded his view that humour had no place for him in literature, now wrote an elaborate joke, ridiculing the military precision with which prostitutes are despatched to jungle-bound troops. This was followed by another comic novel, directly drawn from the experience of Vargas Llosa's first marriage: *La tía Julia y el escribidor* (1977) stand for the aunt Vargas Llosa married at the age of 18, and the budding writer that he then was. Not surprisingly, that Mario married the former wife of an uncle caused a certain amount of family scandal; in the novel, as in real life, the failure of that marriage opens the way to another – with the author's first cousin! The book is an extremely funny and playful parody, with a biographical thread narrated alongside, but ever more entangled with, a farcical soap being written for radio. One can understand why the estranged Julia was offended.[2] Commercially, this has been one of Vargas Llosa's most successful novels, particularly in the English-speaking world, while in Colombia they actually turned it into a soap opera for television. Even more than *Pantaleón*, *La tía Julia* breaks with the image of the intense and campaigning writer of the early books.

Humour is very much in evidence in the three plays which appeared in quick succession in the early 1980s; in fact, Vargas Llosa's first play had been written when he was still a teenager, but until *La señorita de Tacna* (1981) there had been no more theatre. It is a play which seems to be about family relationships and memories, but is really about writing: the metaliterary interest is materialised in the form of a writer who occupies a part of the stage (in his 1980s world) while he observes, intrudes upon, and writes about the characters who occupy the rest of the stage (in the 1950s). Something similar characterises the second and most humorous play, *Kathie y el hipopótamo* (1983): a professional writer acts as ghostwriter for the recollections or fantasies of a Peruvian banker's wife. In the last play, *La Chunga* (1986), the emphasis is more squarely on the (fruitless) quest for truth, almost always a theme in Vargas Llosa; and here it is significant that he has resurrected characters and a setting from *La casa verde* (in which, as we shall see, the story of the founder of the Casa Verde itself is shrouded in hearsay and myth).

The novels of this same period are less ponderous and complex than those of the early one, though less playful than those of the 1970s. *La guerra del fin del mundo* (1981) is an epic work arising from the author's repeated trips into the Amazonian jungle, his collaboration in a 1973 screen-play about a nineteenth-century rebellion by a religious group against government forces in Brazil, and above all his reading an important documentary novel describing that event, the Brazilian Euclides da Cunha's *Os Sertões* (1902). Vargas Llosa rewrites and synthesises; the scope of this novel makes one think of the great writers of the last century; its technique is relatively unobtrusive. *La guerra. . .* has been a great commercial success in the Spanish-speaking countries. It was followed, in 1984, by *Historia de Mayta*. This date of publication might almost have been significant: against an apocalyptic political backdrop, a famous novelist tries to piece together the story of a 1950s Trotskyist activist.

Increasingly, the novels seem to insist that no ideology can be relied upon. Perhaps this is one reason why these later novels are not always satisfactory in their endings. Yet if the same comment cannot be levelled at the early ones, it is not because they offered facile solutions to the many problems they sketched: rather, they tended to be rounded off strongly by pages inviting a review of what had gone before, often accompanied by the aesthetic pleasure associated with perceiving an overall design.

There remain two recent novels. *¿Quién mató a Palomino Molero?* (1986) is one of Vargas Llosa's shortest and most readable books, marred (like *La Chunga*) by a certain amount of bad taste: two policemen investigate a gruesome murder, only to be frustrated. As in *La Chunga*, the message is that the truth is never simple, but that there is a human need to search for it, and a pleasure to be had in reading about that search. *El hablador* appeared in late 1987, similarly short but altogether more substantial. Here, two narratives unfold and converge: one, clearly autobiographical, recounts Vargas Llosa's student friendship with a young ethnologist enthralled by a little-known Amazonian tribe, and how these things turn into a recurrent obsession of the author's in subsequent years; the other presents chaotic anecdotes and myths as told by the tribal story-teller, or 'hablador'. Formally this novel has something in common with *La tía Julia*, while thematically it takes us back through *La guerra* . . . to *La casa verde*, raising such issues as the ethics of acculturation, the position of minority groups, the values of a materialist society, the status of belief. As on several occasions previously, Vargas Llosa sometimes gives in to the temptation to spell out what the reader can readily deduce for himself, but *El hablador* remains a significant novel.

Throughout all this time Vargas Llosa has been active as a critic (notably of books on García Márquez and Flaubert[3]) and as an essayist and journalist. The two volumes of articles which make up *Contra viento y marea* (1986) provide invaluable evidence of the political and artistic evolution over a quarter of a century of this most public of writers. Ever since the early success of *La ciudad y los perros* he has been in the limelight, with his lectures, his political polemics, his awards, his shoulder-rubbing with the influential, and his television appearances (including being presenter of a very popular Peruvian arts programme). He was even offered the Presidency of Peru.

For some fifteen years, Vargas Llosa lived away from his country – in Paris, London, Barcelona – travelled the world, enjoyed visiting posts in the USA. More recently he has settled into a pattern of dividing the year between London and Lima. The latter is a troubled city and doubly dangerous for an outspoken public figure; in London he can enjoy a degree of anonymity and more freedom to indulge his passion for telling stories.

That passion has never been in doubt: one of the reasons for Vargas Llosa's admiration for Flaubert is the latter's whole-hearted commitment to the vocation of writing. Flaubert and Sartre (at least in the early years) were major influences, together with the medieval novels of chivalry; Vargas Llosa was to evolve and frequently speak of a theory of the novel stemming from these influences. The novel, he said, was a superior genre, given its ability to incorporate and make use of other genres, to accommodate different perspectives, to represent reality in all its dimensions. Furthermore, good novels came from societies in turmoil, not from complacent ones, like those of modern Europe and the USA, where the novel was lost in arid formal experiments. The novelist had to seek to represent reality in all its complexity, whether rational, fantastic, abstract or concrete, and thus produce a 'total' novel:

> . . . abarcar la realidad a todos sus niveles. . . decirlo todo. . . Yo creo que las mejores novelas son las que se han acercado a esta posición, es decir, las que expresan las cosas desde todos los puntos de vista. . . Considero que las novelas que dan sólo una dimensión de la realidad tienden a mutilar la realidad; las grandes novelas no mutilan la realidad sino que la ensanchan; no sólo son novedosas sino que dan un testimonio nuevo, son totalizadoras.

And elsewhere:

> La realidad reúne. . . lo real objetivo y lo real imaginario en una indivisible totalidad en la que conviven, sin discriminación de fronteras, hombres de carne y hueso y seres de la fantasía y del sueño, personajes históricos y criaturas del mito, la razón y la sinrazón, lo posible y lo imposible.[4]

While the Caracas speech, his political sympathies in those years, and the social injustices evident in the novels he then wrote might have led to propagandist literature, Vargas Llosa always aspired first to literary quality. In this he was a little like his great friend of the time, Gabriel García Márquez, who declared (with a lightness that the early Vargas Llosa could never have managed) that, 'Tengo ideas políticas muy firmes, pero mis ideas literarias cambian con mi digestión.'[5] That friendship, however, was to turn sour, somewhat surprisingly in view of the courteous charm which Vargas Llosa has managed to preserve, for all his success. Then there has been the polemic with Günter Grass. The cynics might say, no doubt with some envy, that from the moment when he donned his first Savile Row suit he lost credibility as a crusader and reformer, and that his novels, once elitist in form, become elitist in content as the years go by. There may well be some truth in this; it would be human to be affected by material wealth and it is hardly unusual for age to mellow one's political views. A number of intellectuals who once enthusiastically espoused the Cuban Revolution later found it scarcely more palatable than the oppressive right-wing regimes. It is important to note that Vargas Llosa broke with Cuba over the oppression of a writer, the poet Heberto Padilla; even his fiercest critics must acknowledge his dogged consistency in defending the right of speech (and writing).

In the late 1960s, riding high on the success of his first two novels, Vargas Llosa travelled the world giving a lecture which he would later publish as *Historia secreta de una novela* (1971). It explains the genesis of *La casa verde* and makes an interesting and helpful adjunct to the novel, which can be bewildering to the reader who embarks upon it; perhaps the author wrote *Historia*. . . partly because he was aware of the impenetrability of the novel. Comparing writing to a kind of reverse striptease, in which the novelist clothes and disguises the truth as he proceeds, he explains that one of the experiences which underlies *La casa verde* is the year he spent in Piura (1945), his first in Peru. Two experiences stand out from this highly formative year in the life of the 9-year-old author-to-be:

> La primera era la silueta de una casa erigida en las afueras de Piura, en la otra orilla del río, en pleno desierto. . . La casa ejercía una atracción fascinante sobre mis compañeros y sobre mí. . . Todo era extraño en ella: el hecho de estar apartada de la ciudad, su inesperado color. . . Había algo maligno y enigmàtico, un relente diabólico alrededor de esta vivienda a la que habíamos bautizado 'la casa verde'. Nos habían prohibido acercarnos a ella.[6]

Most curiously, the house would only come alive at night, when the boys would hide and spy on the stream of visitors to it, recognising many of them and extracting bribes from them in exchange for silence, though they did not quite know what it was that had to be kept secret! During daytime, in the town, they would recognise the women who came from the house and taunted them with being 'habitantas', again without knowing why the taunts worked. The boys were sometimes punished for their curiosity by an old priest in their school, Padre García.

The other important recollection from 1945 was the suburb called 'La Mangachería', a poor area of shacks, also in the desert. This was full of life; its people were proud and independent, the arch rivals of those who lived in the lower-middle-class 'Gallinacera'. The *mangaches* were politically aware, were hostile to outsiders and had a reputation for violence.

After some time in Lima, the adolescent Vargas Llosa was to return to Piura and his former friends, and would find out for himself what the green house really was, from the inside – 'la realidad se hallaba por debajo de los ritos y tráficos con que la fantasía había poblado el verde palacio de las dunas'.[7] It was a primitive structure, its women were vulgar, but it *was* different; and among its personnel there was a stern harridan and a small band including a blind harpist.

The foregoing explains the origin of one of the main scenarios for the action of *La casa verde*: Piura, where all activity radiates from the brothel. But there is a second main scenario, and another (metaphorical) Casa Verde, the jungle. In 1957, having finished his first degree in San Marcos University, Lima, Vargas Llosa was working as a research assistant when he was invited to join a party of anthropologists on a trip into the interior; it was this that made him aware of the *aguarunas* and other primitive and exploited tribes of Indians. He saw the Mission at Santa María de Nieva, whose work, for all the dedication and self-sacrifice of the nuns, had led to alienation of young Indians from their culture, so that new pupils were being conscripted by force, taught menial skills, and entrusted to the representatives of 'civilisation', who would then ship them off to coastal towns to end up as servants or whores. Vargas Llosa learned, too, of Reátegui, a powerful man mixed up in rubber trafficking, and of the village chieftain Jum, who resisted exploitation and suffered appalling torture. He heard of another man involved in the rubber dealing, a fugitive Japanese called Tushía (sic), whose exploits were the subject of legend and rumour, and who had many 'wives', a small army of renegades, and his own realm.

All this serves to show how far the novel is inspired by what Vargas Llosa saw or was told in Piura and in the jungle. But a number of years were to elapse before *La casa verde* saw the light of day; Vargas Llosa would return to the jungle, and the initial details

– the author's own experiences and the stories he heard or imagined – would be modified by time, by subsequent experiences and by the very process of writing a novel, by the author's 'demonios personales', the striptease in reverse.[8]

We have seen how there are two settings for *La casa verde*: the coast and the jungle, with action related to the respective focal points of Piura and Nieva, to the brothel and the mission. In and out of these settings come some ninety characters. The novel spans something like three decades and there are five main storylines. But, as if this were not enough, even these broad outlines are somewhat difficult to discern until one has read the book, for information is not presented chronologically but is deliberately fragmented, undermining any sense of cause and effect, and almost without benefit of any authorial orientation. The story-lines can be 'recovered' with hindsight, and are these:

1　The nuns of the mission at Sta. María de Nieva are taking in young girls from the aguaruna and other Indian tribes in order to teach them Catholic and civilised behaviour. With the aid of the soldiers from the garrison, they take the girls by force, educate them and pass them over to families from the coast, to be domestic servants. However, the truth is that many end up as prostitutes. The key example is Bonifacia, who eventually becomes a 'habitanta', the 'Selvática' of the Casa Verde in Piura.

2　Fushía, a man of Japanese/Brazilian origin, has been a 'negociador de caucho' and a smuggler, and has spent time in prison. Now a sick and failed man, he travels the Marañón river with his old friend Aquilino, to whom he confesses his feelings and recounts his life. The boat is taking him to die in the jungle, of leprosy.

3　The Casa Verde is a brothel opened to satisfy a whim of the mysterious Don Anselmo. A stranger who once rode into town unannounced, he is the subject of speculation and rumour in Piura, an arid coastal town. Don Anselmo loses the Casa Verde in a fire at the hands of the righteous Padre García. A second Casa Verde is built by La Chunga, the daughter of the blind and dumb Antonia by Anselmo; the latter plays the harp in this second house.

4　Deep in the Amazonian jungle, the Borja garrison faces a rebellion by the Indians against their exploitation by the middle

men dealing in rubber, the 'patrones', Julio Reátegui being one of
them. But the attempt to form a cooperative and deal direct with
the people in Lima fails, and Jum, the leader of the Indians, is
brutally punished. Part of his punishment is the personal
vengeance of Corporal Roberto Delgado, himself previously
humiliated in an encounter with the Indians.

5 Four uncouth youths from the proud and patriotic Mangachería,
a suburb of Piura, gather in the Casa Verde to drink, gamble and
find sex. They are violent, insulting, and offensive in their
behaviour to others, but make great display of their group
solidarity with their 'himno' and their nickname: 'los inconquistables'. The group comprises José, El Mono, Lituma and Josefino.
(Lituma appears as 'el sargento' in the jungle setting, although it
is left to the reader to deduce that this is so. He married
Bonifacia, but due to a feud with the influential Seminario family,
he is sent to jail, during which time Josefino seduces her. Once
installed in the brothel, she maintains these characters with her
earnings.)

The following diagrams attempt to represent the main groupings
of characters and their interactions, first for the jungle setting and
then for Piura. The main focal point for events in the jungle is the
mission; the nuns are more important as a group than as individuals,
and the same goes for their pupils, with the exception of Bonifacia.
Not only is she representative of the kind of destiny I have referred
to previously, but with her marriage to Lituma, her translation to
Piura, and her transformation into Selvática she provides a
structural link between the two settings, and emphasises the
symbolic dimension of the novel. She becomes the anachronistic
'jungle woman' in that other anachronism, the Casa Verde which
springs from the desert. Otherwise, only Jum stands out among the
Indians; his main interaction is with Delgado and Reátegui, though
he trades with the 'caucheros' as a group and comes under the
influence of people from Lima, here represented as the 'autoridades'.
Within the garrison, three men have prominent roles, and it is the
sergeant who proves most important in the long run. (Introduced in
the very first words of the novel, but never identified by name, this is
Lituma, another key character in linking the two settings.)[9] Adrián
Nieves is a guide who works with Delgado and with the 'caucheros';
a significant character in the latter grouping is Lalita, who has

relationships with four men and children by three of them.

The second diagram represents Piura. Here, the focal point is obviously the brothel. Juana Baura, a washerwoman of Gallinacera, adopts Antonia (Toñita), who has been found abandoned as a baby in the desert, blind and tongueless after being attacked by vultures; loved passionately and deeply by Anselmo (see pp.320, 344 and 366), Toñita has a daughter, who as La Chunga comes to rule the green house.[10] The relationship between Anselmo and Padre García is tense and variable: although the latter sets fire to the first Casa Verde, by the end of the book he has become Anselmo's confessor and relents in his condemnation of him. A close friend of Padre García amongst the group of influential Piurans (I have dubbed them the 'piuranos de pro') is Dr. Zevallos. Lituma, after his confrontation with the Seminario family and his banishment to jail, returns to the place and to the friends he knew before: thus, although he has operated in the jungle and has married Bonifacia-Selvática, so that like her he is a link between the two settings, he does not carry similar cultural weight.

(1)

AMAZONAS

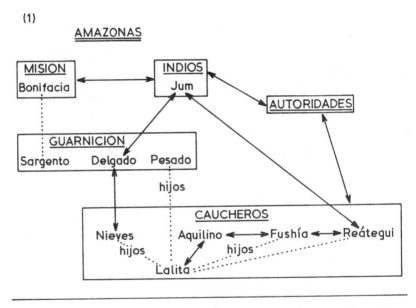

······· Love/Sex — · —▶ Parentage — — ▶ Adoptive Parentage
◀——▶ Main Contacts (group and personal)

(2)

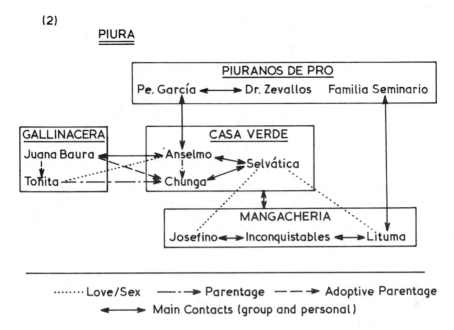

We now turn to more detailed comments on narrative form. The five 'story-lines' which I described earlier are related to the presentation of events in episodic fashion; we can illustrate this by taking a close look at the beginning of the novel, up to the beginning of its second chapter. These pages consist of an introductory section, followed by five other sections which comprise the first chapter.

The introductory section (Vargas Llosa was later to refer to such sections as 'umbrales') has nuns and men from the garrison arriving by boat to meet some Indians from whom they abduct new pupils for the mission. The prose is like the jungle itself, dense and unrelenting, with not a single paragraph break in all the section's twelve pages. Furthermore, without warning it conflates the conversation of various characters, inner thoughts, reported speech and the observations of the narrator, switching from one to another in mid-sentence. For example:

Y el Sargento furtivamente señala a las madres, don Adrián, estos trabajitos le reventaban el alma. La Madre Angélica tenía mucha sed y a lo mejor un poco de fiebre, el espíritu seguía animoso pero el cuerpo ya estaba lleno de achaques, Madre Patrocinio y ella no, no, que no dijera eso, Madre Angélica, ahora que subieran los guardias tomaría una limonada y se sentiría mejor, ya vería.

(p.12)

We might reconstruct a 'normalised' version as follows, but it should be pointed out that this is only one possible reconstruction: the fact that such passages are open to different readings is one way of justifying their use:

> El Sargento señaló furtivamente a las madres. 'Estos trabajitos me revientan el alma', le dijo a Nieves. 'Tengo mucha sed, y a lo mejor un poco de fiebre', dijo la Madre Angélica a la Madre Patrocinio, 'El espíritu sigue animoso pero el cuerpo ya está lleno de achaques.' 'No, no, Madre Angélica', le contestó, 'Ahora que han subido los guardias tomará una limonada y se sentirá mejor, ya verá.'

Clearly, another effect of this sort of writing is to come closer to representing the simultaneity of events: as a character talks, he brushes away an insect, another eyes him suspiciously, a nun recites a prayer, an Indian is held flailing to the ground; but language is linear and can never do more than approach this simultaneity in its account of events.

The second section (the first of the first chapter) is set in the Mission of Sta. María. The nuns discover that some of the recruits have escaped to return to the jungle; the irony underlying the Mother Superior's concern for their well-being says much about the mission's lack of understanding: 'Esas pobres criaturas por ahí, de su cuenta. . . – suspiró la Superiora–. Felizmente que no llueve' (p.27). One of the remaining pupils, Bonifacia, reveals that the others escaped not because of her negligence but with her help. We have no way of knowing whether the escapees of this section are the detainees of the previous one; nor can we be sure that the chronology of events is reflected by their sequence in print; however, the author's juxtaposition of detention and escape is clearly deliberate. It is also symptomatic of a technique he frequently employs, of using juxtaposition to highlight dramatic effect or to present conflicting perceptions of the 'truth'.

The style of this second section presents no difficulty in itself: it is omniscient third-person narrative with clearly oriented pieces of dialogue. Any difficulty for the reader stems from his partial grasp of the contextual details. Two observations might be added, relating to the wider structure of the novel. It is Bonifacia's freeing of the pupils that seals her destiny, determines her departure, and that destiny is covertly suggested in a passing description of her physical appearance, in particular her bare feet: once she is in the Casa Verde Vargas Llosa will fix in a similar way on her uneasy adaptation to high heels.

The third section deals with Fushía, and another escape, though a less noble one. Fushía recalls his early career, his escape from prison, his betrayals. There is no obvious temporal or causal connection between these events and those previously related; in fact, the Fushía story will always stand rather apart from the others, because (barring the fact of his 'present' conversation with Aquilino) virtually everything in his story is recalled. The style here is again third-person omniscient and similar to that of the previous section. Here, however, there is much use of free indirect speech, in a Flaubertian manner. Also, we have the first instance in this novel of the technique of the 'vasos comunicantes':

> —Pero eso ya me lo contaste al salir de la isla, Fushía— dijo Aquilino—. Yo quiero que me digas cómo fue que te escapaste.
> —Con esta ganzúa— dijo Chango—. La hizo Iricuo con el alambre del catre. La probamos y abre la puerta sin hacer ruido. ¿Quieres ver, japonesito?
> Chango era el más viejo, estaba allí por cosas de drogas, y trataba a Fushía con cariño. Iricuo, en cambio, siempre se burlaba de él. Un bicho raro que había estafado a mucha gente con el cuento de la herencia, viejo. El fue el que hizo el plan.
> —¿Y resultó tal cual, Fushía?— dijo Aquilino.
> —Tal cual— dijo Iricuo.
>
> (p.29)

The explanation of this passage is as follows: only Aquilino and Fushía are present in the boat, but characters from Fushía's past enter the conversation. Aquilino asks Fushía to explain how he escaped and the answer comes back from a fellow prisoner, Chango, who (one surmises) is/was answering a similar question put to him, in jail, by Fushía. The ensuing descriptive passage ('Chango era. . .') comprises the reported speech of Fushía to Aquilino, back in the boat; the 'proof' of this is the tagged 'viejo', itself a fragment of direct speech, at the end of a sentence. Vargas Llosa uses this device of the 'vasos comunicantes' a great deal in his novels, bridging gaps in space and time, and forging contacts between his characters which can be believed only on a narrative level.[11]

The next section is straightforward third-person description by an omniscient narrator, without dialogue. It paints the Piura of a time before the Casa Verde existed. 'La noche piurana está llena de historias' (p.32) hints at the importance hearsay and legend will later acquire in the novel. Most of the significant characters and groups of the Piuran setting are referred to, and the birth of the Casa Verde is anticipated at the end of the section.

The fourth section centres on the Borja garrison. Corporal Roberto Delgado seeks permission to undertake a trip to Bagua in the company of Nieves; this will be a decisive journey, because it will eventually be seen to have sparked off the Jum rebellion. The style of this section is like that of the opening 'umbral', albeit somewhat less confusing because of the limited number of participants in a simple situation.

Finally, the fifth section takes us back to Piura and to those musketeers of the Mangachería, the 'inconquistables'.[12] Arriving at Josefino's house, they announce Lituma's return from jail. Josefino reveals his unease, having betrayed Lituma with Selvática. Lituma is returning to stay: '–Está difícil que Lituma se vaya. .– dijo José–. No es como cuando regresó de la montaña, que todo allí le apestaba. En Lima se le despertó el amor por la tierra' (p.40). The final words of the section (and chapter) take the young men off to the Casa Verde.

We have seen something of the style and content of the opening pages of the novel, six fragments which are bound to bewilder the starting reader and can only be related to each other with benefit of hindsight. It even appears on occasion that any potential link the reader might perceive between them is deliberately undermined; the two references to the Casa Verde at the end of the last two sections are an example: the one speaks of a future entity which in the other, by inference, is well established, but no allowance is made for the divide. However, while the reader cannot know it, in these first forty-odd pages he has been introduced to the two major settings of the novel, to its five main story lines ((1) to (5) above, respectively in the five sections of Chapter 1), to the range of styles to be deployed throughout, and to most of the principal themes.

There is, in fact, also a parallel to be found in the novel's five parts. These parts, in turn, can be shown to have an integral symmetry. The following table demonstrates this:

LA CASA VERDE

Part 1	Part 2
Umbral	Umbral
Ch. 1 (five sections)	Ch. 1 (five sections)
Ch. 2 (five sections)	Ch. 2 (five sections)
Ch. 3 (five sections)	Ch. 3 (five sections)
Ch. 4 (five sections)	
Part 3	Part 4
Umbral	Umbral
Ch. 1 (four sections)	Ch. 1 (four sections)
Ch. 2 (four sections)	Ch. 2 (four sections)
Ch. 3 (four sections)	Ch. 3 (four sections)
Ch. 4 (four sections)	
Epilogue	
Umbral	
Ch. 1	
Ch. 2	
Ch. 3	
Ch. 4	

It will be seen that a formal link of four chapters each exists between Parts 1 and 3, and of three chapters each between Parts 2 and 4. In addition, the number of sections links Parts 1 and 2 (five sections in each case), and Parts 3 and 4 (four sections). Finally, the Epilogue (to which I shall return later)[13] has five components – the umbral plus four numbered chapters.

If one analyses the march of each story-line separately, even then one finds that information is fragmentary and not always chronologically presented. The result of all this is that the reader is plunged into an apparent chaos of unexplained and unrelated events, whose design can only be perceived in the long term. The reader, in short, is made to work. That, in itself, is not extraordinary: modern novelists have tended to require their readers to work, sometimes referring to a wish to make the reader contribute to the shaping of the fiction. If one looks at other novelists of the Boom, one finds plenty of examples (compare the experience of reading *Pedro Páramo* or *El obsceno pájaro de la noche*). Vargas Llosa saw life as being unstructured: experiences come upon us in disorder, not in neatly packaged concatenations of cause and effect. Furthermore, reality is complex, comprehending the tangible and the abstract, the definable and the elusive. We cannot know the truth because vital elements may be hidden from us, because individual perceptions of events vary, because we have recourse to reports by others, because 'historia' changes with the telling. Hence the fragmentation of events, the variety of narrative modes and perspectives, and the uncertain status of truth.

Nowhere is this last more apparent than in the story of Anselmo and the Casa Verde. The Piurans, we are told in the early pages, are suspicious of strangers; one day, like a character in a western movie, Anselmo rides into town. From the outset his actions and his origins are the subject of speculation. Even the existence of the first Casa Verde is put in some doubt: as the second Casa Verde is rising from the ashes, Anselmo is asked:

> 'Qué tal la Chunguita, arpista, se nos hace rica, ¿vio la casa que está construyendo?' Él sonreía gustoso pero, en cambio, cuando los viejos rijosos salían al encuentro, 'Anselmo, nos la está resucitando', el arpista se hacía el perplejo, el misterioso, el desentendido, no sé nada, tengo que irme, de qué me hablan cuál Casa Verde.'
>
> (p.290)

One of the most important passages in the novel is the conversation in the Epilogue, following Anselmo's death. Selvática claims Anselmo as a 'paisano' and Vargas Llosa makes use of the 'vasos comunicantes' again, to toy with this version of the truth:

> –. . .¿Acaso no era mi paisano?
> –¿Tu paisano?– dice el Dr. Zevallos, interrumpiendo un bostezo.
> –Claro, muchacha– dice don Anselmo–. Como tú, pero no de Santa María de Nieva, ni sé dónde queda ese pueblo.
> –¿De veras, don Anselmo?– dice la Selvática–. ¿Usted también nació allí? ¿No es cierto que la selva es linda. . .? ¿No es cierto que allá la gente es más buena?
> –La gente es igual en todas partes, muchacha– dice el arpista–. Pero sí es cierto que la selva es linda. . . por eso pinté de verde el arpa.
> –Es curioso– el Dr. Zevallos se rasca el cuello, mientras bosteza–. Pero posible, después de todo. ¿De veras tenía el arpa pintada de verde, muchachos?
> –Don Anselmo era mangache– dice el Mono–. Nació aquí, en el barrio, y nunca salió de aquí. Mil veces le oí decir soy el más viejo de los mangaches.

–Claro que la tenía– afirma la Selvática. . .

–¿Anselmo selvático?– dice el Dr. Zevallos–. Posible, después de todo, por qué no, qué curioso.

(p.427)

But moments later, Selvática is herself casting doubt on the subject.

The green house of the 1950s, that invited the imaginings of the young Vargas Llosa and friends in Piura, continues to do so for all concerned once translated to the novel:

Toda la historia de la Casa Verde y de Anselmo y esa serie de episodios que conforman el nivel mítico de la novela – están vistos a una cierta distancia y siempre a través de un intermediario, de una conciencia colectiva, que filtra, diluye, 'poetiza' los hechos, distorsionándolos sin duda, mitificándolos, irrealizándolos. ¿Quiénes forman esta conciencia colectiva? Los piuranos en general, los mangaches en particular. Son ellos los que cuentan la historia de la llegada de Anselmo a Piura, la fundación de la Casa Verde, el incendio que encabeza el Padre García.[14]

Don Anselmo's behaviour is mysterious, the content of his confession (p.345) is not revealed, his origins are obscure, his Casa Verde (the first) exists only in the recollections of the Piurans and the reader is never allowed 'direct' access to it. The consequence is myth, and myth in literature tends to carry symbolic weight. It is important to note that in *La casa verde* myth results primarily from the structure of the novel itself rather than from grafting on myths from biblical or classical sources. One exception is this: the second Casa Verde springs up, phoenix-like, from the ashes of the first. Each has stood, anachronistically green, in the desert; but they are a double-edged representation of nature and fertility, for in them the cruder instincts of man are released, and that in a seedy environment. Thus, the Casa Verde, like Fushía's island, becomes the symbol of paradise but also of decadence or hell. In fact, more than once it is suggested that Anselmo is not the hero or saviour who has helped the joyless Piurans by providing the means for them to satisfy their repressed desires, but the Devil who institutionalises reprehensible behaviour. That, at least, is the view of Padre García, even though it mellows with time: '¿Todavía cree que Anselmo era el diablo?' asks Dr. Zevallos. '¿De veras olía a azufre o era para asustar a los beatos?' (p.417). But, as the opening of the novel tells us (p.33), even in the pre-Anselmo era, couples would slip out of the bars into the desert to make love; perhaps there they planted the seeds of the Casa Verde.

Sex and love are recurrent elements in *La casa verde*, and the general picture is not edifying. Women are used by men (what better an example than Selvática, who gives herself to men in order to give her earnings to more men?), but other women aid this process (the nuns, unintentionally, and Chunga deliberately). Only two characters stand out against this negative background. Lalita is portrayed as long-suffering, practical and a survivor, a person who combines desire and the maternal instinct; but the price of survival is the loss of her beauty.[15] The other distinctive woman character is Toñita, in her relationship with Anselmo; his passion and love for her are made the more poignant by her disabilities, while the passage describing that love provides a rare access to the personality of the otherwise secretive Anselmo. However, the quality of this relationship is also put in doubt: in the Epilogue Dr. Zevallos suggests to Padre García that Toñita might willingly have gone to join Anselmo in the Casa Verde and have his child:

> –. . .Sólo digo que quién sabe lo que ella pensaba. La Antonia no sabía lo que era bueno ni malo, y después de todo, gracias a Anselmo fue una mujer completa. . .
> –¡Cállese, hombre!. . . ¡Una mujer completa! ¿Las monjas son incompletas? ¿Los curas somos incompletos porque no hacemos porquerías?
>
> (p.418)

Ironically, these very agents of religion are shown to be instrumental in making love a 'porquería', a matter of abuse: witness the violation of the virgin Bonifacia. But love is only part of it; the fact is that not much human behaviour is laudable in *La casa verde*. People betray each other (Lalita betrays Fushía, who betrays several others; Josefino betrays Lituma) while trust is thin on the ground. The solidarity of the 'inconquistables' is largely a matter of show.

A related issue is the loss of innocence; the violation of the jungle heralds the destruction of lives: Bonifacia (her name suggests innocence as perceived by the nuns) will become Selvática once uprooted from her environment and exploited. She stands for the Indians so exploited and drawn into the web of corruption. Formally, the process is reflected in the fact that each chapter starts in the selva and ends in the Casa Verde. Although he was not prey to the romantic illusion of the happy savage, Vargas Llosa does seem to be turning civilisation and barbarism on its head: European (i.e. coastal Peruvian) culture is civilising only in the minds of its proponents, and it is striking that Anselmo, with his brothel, is said by the narrator (p.276) to have brought civilisation to Piura.[16]

The Epilogue is one of the novel's great strengths. Unlike many epilogues which relate events subsequent to the main action, this one takes us back to the start. In the umbral, set, as they have all been, in the jungle, Reátegui brings an Indian girl to the mission; this may or may not be the girl who will be called Bonifacia, but the reader will undoubtedly make the association with Bonifacia's fate, and recall the first pages of the novel. In the following chapter, Fushía is left to die near Iquitos; the vegetation obscures the sight and smell of his body, suggesting that his journey, too, has come full circle and that Nature is reasserting herself. Fushía's story has dominated and interlaced with all those set in the jungle; during his river journey with Aquilino he has recounted his life in a series of interpolated dialogues involving various characters and times. Chapter 3 takes Lalita back to Iquitos, too, and there she re-encounters her son Aquilino.

The links between these two chapters are matched by those to be found between Chapters 2 and 4, thus revealing a certain symmetry which echoes that of the first four parts of the novel. In Chapter 2 Selvática summons the doctor and the priest to the dying Anselmo; in 4, Dr. Zevallos and Padre García leave his death-bed and there ensues a conversation between them which reveals new information about things past, such as the death of Antonia while giving birth to Chunga.

So the two lives which have dominated the two scenarios are drawn to a close. The dualism has in fact characterised the whole novel, often amounting to a set of oppositions: two settings, two brothels under the name Casa Verde, two meanings for that name (the literal and the metaphorical), two institutions (the brothel and the mission), Bonifacia/Selvática, Sargento/Lituma, two Aquilinos, the macho 'inconquistables' versus the 'inconquistables' maintained by a woman, and so forth.

But the Epilogue leaves much to be sorted out. Killing off Fushía and Anselmo does nothing to halt speculation about them. By leaving certain details unclear and indeed opening up new possibilities, Vargas Llosa invites his reader to reconsider. The truth does not come easily because the truth is not simple; in using different styles, representing objective and subjective views of reality and in the fragmentation of events such that time and causal order are undermined, Vargas Llosa has sought to produce a 'total' novel. No easy solution is offered for the social injustices that are undeniably denounced in *La casa verde* and one cannot speak of propaganda in the context of a novel which takes such delight in ambiguity. For artistic reasons, the author attempts to distance himself from the fiction and make it appear autonomous; apparently, at least, the reader is not directed or biased by authorial comment, but left to assess the data, such as they are, for himself.[17] The lives of the protagonists of *La casa verde* lead nowhere special: they are dictated by circumstances (often economic), and offered to the reader in a series of fragments which seem to emphasise their presentness, obscuring past cause and future consequence. The characters learn to survive in a perplexing world of injustice, complicity and betrayal; as in the jungle, the fittest survive in this world, and it is difficult to discern an order in it. Vargas Llosa makes his reader face a literary experience which is analogous to this: the title of the novel, as we have seen, has a physical referent (the brothel) and a metaphorical one (the selva), but it also points to that literary experience.

NOTES

1 The Caracas speech ('La literatura es fuego') is available in many sources, but most readily in *Contra viento y marea* (Seix Barral, Barcelona, 1986), pp.176–81.
2 See Julia Urquidi Illanes, *Lo que Varguitas no dijo* (La Paz, 1983). *La tía Julia* is openly dedicated to her.
3 *García Márquez: historia de un deicidio* (Seix Barral, Barcelona, 1971); *La orgía perpetua: Flaubert y 'Madame Bovary'* (Seix Barral, Barcelona, 1975).
4 Quoted, respectively, from 'Sobre *La ciudad y los perros*, de Mario Vargas Llosa' (round-table discussion including the author), *Casa de las Américas*, vol 5, no. 30, (1965), p.79, and from *La orgía perpetua*, p.177. Vargas Llosa was not reluctant to explain his own theory of the novel. See his *La novela* (Fundación de Cultura Universitaria, Montevideo, n.d.), his 'Carta de batalla por *Tirant lo blanc*', prologue to edition of same (Alianza, Madrid, 1969), and his interview with Luis Harss in the latter's *Los nuestros* (Sudamericana, Buenos Aires, 1966). See also Carlos Fuentes, 'El afán totalizante de Vargas Llosa', in Helmy F. Giacoman

and José Miguel Oviedo (eds.), *Homenaje a Mario Vargas Llosa* (Las Américas, New York, 1971), pp.161–72; R. Brody, 'Mario Vargas Llosa and the totalization impulse', *Texas Studies in Language and Literature*, vol. 19, no. 4 (1977), pp.514–21, and in C. Rossman and A.W. Friedman (eds.), *Mario Vargas Llosa: a Collection of Critical Essays* (University of Texas Press, Austin, 1978), pp.120–7; Alexander Coleman, 'The transfiguration of the chivalric novel' in *World Literature Today*, vol. 52, no. 1 (1978), pp.20–4; David Sobrevilla, 'Realidad, teoría y creación en Vargas Llosa', *Acta Herediana*, vol 5, no. 1 (1972), pp.29–39; Peter Standish, 'Acotación a la teoría novelística de Mario Vargas Llosa', *Revista de Crítica Latinoamericana*, vol. 10, no. 20 (1985), pp.305–11; Frank Dauster, 'Aristotle and Vargas Llosa: literature, history and the interpretation of reality', *Hispania*, vol. 53 (1970), pp.273–7.

    The best of many interviews with the author is included in R. Cano Gaviria, *El buitre y el ave fénix: conversaciones con Mario Vargas Llosa* (Anagrama, Barcelona, 1972). The major critical study of Vargas Llosa, updated in successive editions and including full biographical details, is José Miguel Oviedo, *Mario Vargas Llosa: la invención de una realidad* (Seix Barral, Barcelona, 1970). See also D. Gerdes, *Mario Vargas Llosa* (Twayne, Boston, 1985). The Twayne series is of very variable quality, but this is one of the better volumes.

    Unless otherwise specified, all other works by Vargas Llosa are published by Seix Barral.

5 Harss, *Los nuestros*, p.390. On the question of political commitment in literature, see Oscar Collazos, Julio Cortázar and Mario Vargas Llosa, *Literatura en la revolución y revolución en la literatura* (Siglo XXI, Mexico City, 1970).

6 *Historia secreta de una novela* (Tusquets, Barcelona, 1971), pp.11–12.

7 ibid. p.20.

8 For a definition of the 'demonios personales' see, for example, his book on García Márquez, p.87.

9 A number of characters from *La casa verde* reappear in later books; for example, Lituma in *¿Quién mató a Palomino Molero?*, Padre Venancio in *La señorita de Tacna*, and almost the whole cast of *La Chunga*.

10 All references to *La casa verde* are to the first edition (Seix Barral, Barcelona, 1966).

11 It, too, has its origins in Flaubert. For more on the 'vasos comunicantes' see my *Mario Vargas Llosa: La ciudad y los perros* (Grant & Cutler, London, 1982) pp.21 and 39.

12 The reference is deliberate: in *Historia secreta de una novela*, p.17, Vargas Llosa describes how, as a child reader of Dumas, he always imagined the three musketeers as *mangaches*.

13 The reduction from five story-lines to four is accounted for by the ending of the one dealing with Jum.

14 Vargas Llosa's own words, quoted by W.A. Luchting in *Pasos a desnivel* (Caracas, Monte Ávila, 1971), p.354.

15 With her multiple relationships, perhaps Lalita is intended as a kind of barometer, like Teresa in *La ciudad y los perros*.

16 See *Historia secreta*, pp.30–1. It is not surprising that many people have thought Vargas Llosa a pessimist, a charge he has always denied. In *Mario Vargas Llosa y la literatura en el Perú de hoy* (Colmegna, Sta. Fe, 1969) Rosa Boldori speaks of 'determinismo ambiental'. Oviedo in *Mario Vargas Llosa: la invención.* . . prefers 'fatalismo'. Boldori comes back at him in her *Vargas Llosa: un narrador y sus demonios* (Fernando García Cambeiro, Buenos Aires, 1974).

17 Paradoxically, the plethora of techniques tends to draw attention to the presence of the author in another way. Vargas Llosa admitted (in a private conversation) that this was 'una novela muy trabajada'.

9

JOSÉ DONOSO: *EL OBSCENO PÁJARO DE LA NOCHE*

PHILIP SWANSON

By the end of the 1960s the new novel was a well-established concept and the notion of the Boom a familiar one. The importance of precursors like Borges, Asturias (in *El Señor Presidente*) and Rulfo (in *Pedro Páramo*) was widely appreciated; the 'great' authors of the Boom had crystallised around the quartet of Cortázar, García Márquez, Fuentes and Vargas Llosa; and the literary canon of the Boom was already being settled, thanks to the existence of 'classics' such as *Rayuela* and *Cien años de soledad*. Indeed, in many ways, the Boom had reached a peak. Though several outstanding examples of fairly typical *nueva narrativa* were still to come, changes were clearly afoot. A new generation was emerging, for a start. Emblematic of this was the appearance in 1969 of Manuel Puig's *Boquitas pintadas* – a very 'new' kind of 'new novel' which intelligently exploited the formulae of popular culture. But equally the unity (such as there was) of the previous generation was under strain. The arrest in 1971 of the Cuban poet Heberto Padilla, whose work was alleged to be 'counter-revolutionary', had divisive consequences. As José Donoso himself explains in his 'personal history' of the Boom:

> Creo que si en algo tuvo unidad casi completa el *boom* – aceptando la variedad de matices – fue en la fe primera en la causa de la revolución cubana; creo que la desilusión producida por el caso Padilla la desbarató, y desbarató la unidad del *boom*.[1]

Moreover, this was roughly the time of the split within Seix Barral, a Barcelona publishing house which, together with its Biblioteca Breve prize, did much to promote the new novel and create the impression of a 'boom'. Donoso again:

> Justamente a finales de la década del sesenta se produjo la escisión

Barral Editores-Seix Barral, que dio al traste con el órgano más influyente en la internacionalización de la novela latinoamericana en la década recién pasada, e indisolublemente relacionada con el *boom*. La fecha de esta escisión coincide más o menos con . . . la dispersión y desilusión a raíz del caso Padilla.[2]

Interestingly, it is widely accepted that the novel which would have been awarded the Premio Biblioteca Breve, were it not suspended due to this rift, was Donoso's *El obsceno pájaro de la noche* (1970). In a sense, then, this novel marks the end of an era and the climax to the Boom. Long, tortuous and polysemic, it takes the complexity of the new novel to an extreme. It represents a crowning but pivotal moment, marking the culmination of one stage and opening up the possibility of an initiation of another. In the words of Promis Ojeda:

> Con esta novela se cierra y se cumple un ciclo, más allá del cual no existe otra posibilidad expresiva. Como en el caso de *Cien años de soledad*, la novela de Donoso es el broche que cierra una etapa, después de la cual sólo cabe cambiar de rumbo.[3]

Yet despite the success of *El obsceno pájaro* and its importance within the literary-historical trajectory of the *nueva novela*, Donoso was well into his mid-40s when it was published. This, Donoso's first major literary triumph, compares with the publication of Vargas Llosa's highly influential hit novel, *La ciudad y los perros*, when the Peruvian author was only 26 years of age. This belated 'arrival' was in part due to a later start: Donoso did not publish his first novel, *Coronación*, until the end of 1957, by which time he was 33 years old. Perhaps the reason for this slow beginning was the limitations of Donoso's character and background. The combination of his restless, somewhat neurotic nature, together with the social and cultural isolation of Santiago de Chile, meant that, for many years, his life lacked direction while his literary career lacked momentum.

He was born in Santiago on 5 October 1924 in a house on the Avenida Holanda in the suburb of Providencia. This house (and especially its garden) was later to become the inspiration for a central symbol in his 1981 novel of exile, *El jardín de al lado*, where the Santiago home appears as an image of a lost paradise. Indeed the family house is a common motif throughout Donoso's work, though usually the nostalgia for childhood innocence is tempered by the portrayal of an inevitable process of decay and corruption.

Hence, though he fondly remembers the dressing-up games he used to play as a child (like the children in *Este domingo* (1966)), he equally recalls his insane, dying grandmother (reminiscent of misiá Elisa in *Coronación*) whose 'madness brought the ironies of family life and the horrors of ageing and dying so cruelly into focus'.[4] In fact, the childhood games of disguise take on a more sinister tone when set against Donoso's comment that while mixing with 'underworld' prostitutes he also 'began going out with "nice" girls in the approved middle-class fashion': this sort of behaviour is not all that different to that of Álvaro in *Este domingo*, who makes love to his respectable wife Chepa while mentally substituting her with the earthy servant Violeta,[5] thus foreshadowing the nightmarish mistress-servant substitutions of *El obsceno pájaro*. Furthermore, Donoso's childhood seems to contain the roots of his own social, psychological and spiritual malaises. He tells us that his school-days at the English institution 'The Grange' merely alienated him from group or collective activities and coincided with his loss of the trappings of religion and adoption of atheism.

Early adulthood did not help the young Donoso settle. Having been moved to various schools where he would cut classes and consort instead with down-and-outs, he eventually dropped out of school in 1943, did odd jobs and then went off to the southern tip of Chile, where he worked as a shepherd on the pampa (a period reflected in his story 'Dinamarquero'). From there he hitch-hiked up the Patagonia to Buenos Aires to work on the docks and live in a doss-house. Illness then took him back to Santiago, where he finished his *bachillerato* and went to university to study English. In 1949 he was given a scholarship to study at Princeton. Having earlier been warned against literature by his father, Princeton taught Donoso to love art guiltlessly, and it was here that he wrote his first short stories.

This was the start of Donoso's career as a writer. He returned to Chile in 1952. Despite feeling 'imprisoned', he won a place in a much talked-of anthology of Chilean short fiction with his story 'China' in 1954 and his first book of short stories, *Veraneo y otros cuentos*, was published a year later, with a further collection *El Charlestón* following in 1960. In between appeared the first novel *Coronación* (1957). On the surface it is a fundamentally traditional novel whose realistic style is almost reminiscent of Spain's Pérez Galdós. So, though praised in Chile for its realism, it was unlikely to set the wider novelty-hungry literary world alight. Having said that, the novel does contain the seeds of an experimental technique and a finely-drawn grotesque, absurd climax in the coronation scene of the title. This, according to Donoso, was facilitated by the experience of reading Alejo Carpentier's *Los pasos perdidos*.[6] The problem, then, was simply a lack of any broader exposure to the new tendencies in Latin American fiction.[7] But this situation improved somewhat as Donoso travelled to Buenos Aires in 1958 (staying for two years) and attended an important Writers' Congress at the University of Concepción, Chile in 1962. The former trip allowed him to meet writers like Borges, Sabato and Roa Bastos, while the latter event gave him the chance to start up his friendship with Carlos Fuentes. Indeed Fuentes played a crucial role in Donoso's career: as Fuentes's guest in 1965 he wrote *El lugar sin límites* and a substantial part of *Este domingo* (both published in 1966). The latter novel was basically a more sophisticated and more experimental development of the themes of *Coronación*, while the former (populated by grotesque, inverted creatures) is usually regarded as providng the major link between the early Donoso and the Donoso of *El obsceno pájaro de la noche*.

After a spell in Iowa (1965–7), Donoso moved to Spain with his wife in order to finish writing the long-gestating *El obsceno pájaro*. Here he suffered ulcer pains and psychological problems which prevented him from writing. Then, during a lecturing break in Colorado away from his wife and adopted child, he had to undergo emergency surgery on his ulcer. His inability to tolerate morphine pain-killers induced a period of paranoia and hallucinations, the after-effects of which lingered on a couple of years when back in Spain. It was during this time that he rewrote *El obsceno pájaro* in a tormented style which attempted to recreate his own experience of madness. In 1970, the novel was published and, as a consolation prize for not receiving the suspended Premio Biblioteca Breve, Donoso was rewarded with a massive publicity campaign. Fame and fortune were now secured as Donoso joined the hallowed ranks of the major 'new novelists' of the Boom.

Interestingly enough, having struggled to incorporate himself into the mainstream of the Boom, Donoso seems to turn his back on it to some degree after 1970. His very useful essay *Historia personal del 'boom'* (1972) at once idealises the atmosphere of the Boom and suggests it is all over. His journalistic pieces, meanwhile, increasingly argue for a different direction in the *nueva narrativa* and a move away from excessively complex forms. Indeed his next work of fiction, *Tres novelitas burguesas* (1973) disappointed some critics with its undemanding fantasies in the tradition of River Plate writers. Similar reservations were raised concerning the soft-porn novel *A misteriosa desaparición de la marquesita de Loria* (1980) and the semi-autobiographical psychological realist novel *El jardín de al lado* (1981). Indeed, the only book to gain real, widespread acclaim in the post-1970 period was Donoso's 1978 work, *Casa de campo*, a political allegory on the rise of Allende and the Pinochet coup marked by an intriguing artificial narrative style where the narrator constantly intervenes to lay bare the devices by which he claims to be constructing the novel. Nonetheless, though the aforementioned texts all differ sharply from *El obsceno pájaro* on a formal level, it has been argued that they open up new possibilities for Latin American fiction: if *El obsceno pájaro* is a kind of final flourish or showcase of the typical features of the Boom, these later works recognise that what was once innovative is now familiar and attempt to challenge traditional realism in a new way, by shrewdly subverting from *within* the apparently realist pattern upon which the texts themselves seem to be based.[8]

The novels of the 1970s and 1980s mentioned so far were all written in Spain. But in 1981 Donoso and his family went back to live in Chile (something he had previously sworn never to do). One reason given for this was merely 'that I was beginning to feel old'.[9] This may partly explain the moderation in attitude and style in the later work after the sparkle and excitement of the period of the Boom – though some may feel that Donoso has simply gone off the boil, especially since his return to Chile. There he has published a book of poetry (mostly written in Spain) called *Poemas de un novelista* (1981) and a play, *Sueños de mala muerte* (1985), which came about as a collaborative project with the theatre company ICTUS three years earlier. The play's title is also that of one of the four novellas comprising the 1982 publication *Cuatro para Delfina* (dedicated to Delfina Guzmán of ICTUS). More recently, Donoso has published his most overtly political novel, *La desesperanza* (1986); though a powerful exposé of the hopelessness of life in Pinochet's Chile, it perhaps lacks the literary panache of some of his previous works. By his own admission, 'no tiene nada que ver con las otras novelas mías'.[10]

This last comment reminds us that we have come a long way since

El obsceno pájaro de la noche, that climactic novel of the Boom. As far as Donoso's own evolution is concerned, the novel constitutes a dual climax in that it represents the high point of the sense of scepticism and malaise traceable through the earlier works and the high point of the closely connected development of technical complexity. The extensive narrative is delivered in a fragmented, distorted fashion from the standpoint of its schizophrenic protagonist, Humberto Peñaloza. Given this fact, any outline of the plot has to be at best tentative or selective. Roughly, then, the 'story' is as follows. Humberto gets a job as secretary to don Jerónimo de Azcoitía, an aristocrat who has come back to Chile having been living in Europe. Don Jerónimo now gets involved in politics and marries the beautiful young Inés. Unfortunately, their marriage is badly shaken by the birth of a horribly deformed son, Boy. Jerónimo decides to isolate the child from the real world by shutting him away in La Rinconada, an estate administered by Humberto who – obeying his master's instructions – populates the property with freaks, grotesque statues and so on, so that the 'monstrous' should appear 'normal'. Some years later Humberto falls ill, eventually abandoning La Rinconada and taking refuge in the Casa de Ejercicios Espirituales, an old convent, owned by the Azcoitía family, which functions as a ramshackle home for orphans and elderly women. Here Humberto works under the name of Mudito, a mentally retarded odd-job man. Later, Inés retires to the Casa as well: she moves there to meditate following the failure of her marriage and her vain attempts to secure the beatification of an eighteenth-century ancestor, but is subsequently transferred to a lunatic asylum when she goes mad as a reaction to Mudito's attempted rape. With don Jerónimo also seemingly dead, the Casa goes into sharp decline and its inhabitants are shunted off to a more modern home. Mudito, however, is left behind. Apparently convinced that he is the offspring of a virgin birth and now sewn up inside an accumulation of sacks, he terminates his novel by imagining that he is cast by an old hag onto a fire where he is burnt to cinders.

This plot, however, is little more than a guide-line. The overwhelming impression to be gained from a reading of *El obsceno pájaro* is one of chaos and confusion. To borrow Russian Formalist terminology, the already complicated *fabula* (the chronological sequence of events) is not the same as the *syuzhet* (the order and manner in which they are actually presented in the narrative).[11]

Chronology is inverted, fragmented and contradicted, while narrative viewpoint, level and style chop and change at whim. Some random examples will illustrate this briefly. The first account of Humberto's youth is denied in Chapter 21, when we are given a variety of possibilities concerning Mudito's orphan childhood. When Humberto meets don Jerónimo (if he does), the latter is said to be famous even though his political campaign does not start until later. Multiple versions of the time and circumstances of the conception of Boy are offered (Boy is later confused with Iris Mateluna's (non-existent) child). The description of Humberto's delirium (which seems to take place both before and after his arrival at the Casa) confuses his flight from La Rinconada with his later flight from the Casa when he meets Boy again – though equally it is stated that Boy did not turn up at this meeting; indeed some references suggest he is not yet born (while others firmly indicate he is). We are also told that don Jerónimo is dead at this stage, even though he is still alive when Inés later returns from Rome. As for the narrator's presentation of himself: sometimes he is the deaf-and-dumb Mudito, sometimes Humberto Peñaloza, the writer and secretary to don Jerónimo, or the 'séptima vieja', Iris Mateluna's dog, her baby, a miraculous child, a papier-mâché head, and even a stain on the wall. Moreover, this presentation is effected via a repertoire of straight narration, stream-of-thought, hallucination, multiple dialogues, baffling changes of person and so on.

The novel, then, is clearly bewildering and designed to be bewildering. The obvious question is: why should this be so? And the obvious answer, quite simply, is that the narrator is mad. Reacting against those realist texts where there was a disjunction between form and content, here the content (a madman's account of his life) is given a suitably 'mad' or 'chaotic' form. Given that the source of the narrative is the insane Mudito/Humberto Peñaloza, it naturally follows that the narration should fall in with the course of the twistings and turnings of Mudito/Humberto's deranged mind.[12] Promis Ojeda and Quinteros use a detail (a passing reference to Jerónimo's former secretary as 'uno como medio enano pero no enano y con el labio leporino mal cosido, y como gibado . . . una calamidad') to suggest that Mudito himself is a disturbed freak who projects his own monstrous deformation onto the very narrative he is recounting.[13] A different explanation is that, as Humberto Peñaloza, he suffers from an identity crisis engendered in him by his father who instilled in him what he knows to be an impossible and contradictory longing to make the transition from being a 'nobody' to becoming a 'somebody'. McMurray regards this familial pressure as the likely catalyst for Humberto's schizophrenic retreat from reality and convincingly details the similarities between the novel's protagonist and a schizophrenic patient.[14] Humberto's condition means that he experiences a sense of power and omnipotence as he assumes a series of protective fantasy masks or personae. But at the same time he feels terror of the outside world which leads to increasing withdrawal and isolation. Both add up to an eventual disintegration of the unity of the personality. This, of course, explains the metamorphic narrative form and the narrator and narrative's self-effacement at the end. Bacarisse takes all this a stage further. Associating Humberto/Mudito's schizophrenic ontological insecurity with the processes of isolation, escape and depersonalisation, she concludes that he is using his writing 'to escape and hide'. In other words: 'the narrator is telling his story so that he will not be understood. It is a process of evasion, not self-revelation.'[15] Thus, she identifies a peculiar inner logic to the novel's multiple contradictions, based on the nature of the narrator's mental condition.

Of course, in the context of the new novel, an 'explanation' of a text based on madness is not, in a sense, necessary. In *Coronación* the crumbling protagonist Andrés remarks that 'el único orden es la locura, porque los locos son los que se han dado cuenta del caos total, de la imposibilidad de explicar, de razonar, de aclarar'.[16] In other words, 'order' is an artificial human construct, an attempt by man to impose a false structure onto reality. 'Reality' itself is fluid, uncertain, ambiguous, subjectively created and impossible to pin down. Therefore the 'mad' form of *El obsceno pájaro* is more authentic than the supposed harmony of the traditional realist text in that its distortions reflect the disunity of external reality and of the minds that internally mould it. Hence Humberto's impatience with the limited 'aspiraciones de estos escritorzuelos que creían en la existencia de *una realidad* que retratar' (p.242) or those of the 'mente tradicional' who, as in a 'pobre historia realista', cling to 'lo que *creen* es la realidad' (pp.137–8, my italics). Hence too the inversion of normality and monstrosity in La Rinconada: 'un único ser normal en un mundo de monstruos adquiere *él* la categoría de fenómeno al ser *anormal*, transformándolos a ustedes (los monstruos) en normales' (p.237). All categories for defining reality are arbitrary mental creations by humans so that reality can never be any more than 'eso que llamaban la realidad' (p.493).

Advancing the argument a stage further, many critics have gone on to reason that if reality cannot be grasped and therefore reflected in literature, then there can be no relationship between the literary text and any external referent. That is to say that ultimately the text (in this case, *El obsceno pájaro*) has nothing to say: the reference in the novel's epigraph to the notion that 'the wolf howls and the obscene bird of night chatters' is, then, merely an allusion to the absence of any meaningful communication in the narrative. These ideas are best developed by Sharon Magnarelli in a series of sophisticated and stimulating articles.[17] For her, just as the Baroque was a reaction against the Renaissance, so too is the twentieth-century neo-baroque of *El obsceno pájaro* a reaction against social realism (with, emblematically, La Rinconada parodying invertedly the traditional order of the 'classical' world). But central features of the Baroque, it is claimed, are its wastefully excessive use of language and its frantic attempts (Magnarelli makes much of the phenomenon of ellipsis) to divert attention away from the centre – the reason being that there is no centre, only surface and appearance. So, taking up the motifs of the package and the game in *El obsceno pájaro*, Magnarelli concludes that 'the word in the novel becomes a game with the discovery of the impossibility of unmasking or unwrapping the essence, with the impossibility of finding a center, a core'.[18]

There are, however, a number of problems with the position of Magnarelli *et al.* and with the critical practice upon which it is based. If language here is merely self-referential, as MacAdam would have it, or merely 'el juego de un sentido por siempre diferente y por siempre diferido' in the words of Martínez,[19] then why should the referentiality of their own language be any less suspect? As Steve Giles has written in his critique of Catherine Belsey's *Critical Practice* (1980): 'if no discourse is privileged over any other, and if there is no order of things or concepts that exists independently of discourse, then the world must be arbitrary and inscrutable, and all modes of action and belief equally acceptable'; 'this set of contentions clearly involves relativism, the view that any one belief or statement is as valid as any other. But in this case *Critical Practice* cannot claim any more validity than any other position.'[20] Moreover, the postulation that Donoso is 'presenting literature and the written word as the principal themes of the novel'[21] is really only a disguised form of the sort of traditional literary criticism these scholars seek to replace. Indeed such a view implies a clear relationship between signifier and signified, text and referent, and may even smack of 'old-fashioned' 'intentionalism'. This can be seen in the way this group of critics claims that certain images, motifs or episodes 'represent' the 'theme' of writing in the same way a traditional critic might claim they represent the 'theme' of social injustice, metaphysical anguish or whatever else. Why should the unwrapping of a package represent man's failure to unravel meaning in a text any more than it should represent man's frustrated quest for existential fulfilment? Why equally should games and the false window represent one of these ideas rather than the other? Why should the transfusion of blood and the transplant of organs necessarily represent the conferral or combination of exhausted linguistic signifiers? Why should an operating theatre represent the blank page and the patient's blood black ink? Why on earth should the dark stain of Mudito's ashes imply he is no more than a black print mark on a white page? The point is that such claims actually subvert from within the critical approach upon which they are based, in so far as they unintentionally mimic and reassert the value of interpretative criticism based on 'meaning'. As Giles says: 'even if one concedes that texts may not possess a unitary determinate meaning, it does not follow that there cannot be a correct or valid reading or interpretation of a text. . . . Furthermore, the fact that texts may not possess unitary meanings does not necessarily imply that texts are therefore open to multiple readings which are mutually undecidable.'[22]

A way forward from this problem is to introduce a social or political dimension into the theoretical framework (which, in fairness, *Critical Practice* and Magnarelli's *The Lost Rib* (1985) attempt to do). Post-structuralist theory, in positing the multiplicity and irreducibility of meaning, actually highlights an important aspect of the socio-political meaning of texts. Catherine Belsey, for instance, usefully shows how the underlying linguistic structures of texts have just as much (or even more) political significance than their content:

The experience of reading a realist text is ultimately reassuring, however harrowing the events of the story, because the world evoked in the fiction, its patterns of cause and effect, of social relationships and moral values, largely confirm the patterns of the world we seem to know.

The strategies of the classic realist text divert the reader from what is contradictory within it to the renewed recognition (misrecognition) of what he or she already 'knows', knows because the myths and signifying systems of the classic realist text represent experience in the ways in which it is conventionally articulated in our society.[23]

So whereas the ('classic') realist text ultimately restores order, leading to closure through disclosure, Benveniste's 'interrogative' text or Bakhtin's 'polyphonic' text draw attention to their own textuality and promote multiple viewpoints and unresolved contradictions. Thus, in the words of Barthes:

> Par là même, la littérature. . ., en refusant d'assigner au texte (et au monde comme texte) un 'secret', c'est-à-dire un sens ultime, libère une activité que l'on pourrait appeler contre-théologique, proprement révolutionnaire, car refuser d'arrêter le sens, c'est finalement refuser Dieu et ses hypotases, la raison, la science, la loi.[24]

This, indeed, is exactly what happens in *El obsceno pájaro*. In rejecting the realist model, it is also rejecting the social and cultural 'norms' of Western society. Decentring the text, unfixing meaning, unseating the notion of a single and authoritative meaning – this is all an attack on the rigidity of prevalent values (be they social, political, religious or whatever). The dislocation of the centre in Donoso's novel is, in effect, a rejection of 'toda una cultura logocéntrica',[25] a rejection of all forms of rationalism and authority. This is the key which links the two main thematic levels of the novel (levels of 'meaning'?): the social and the metaphysical. At both levels, convention is subverted and order is challenged.

The discussion about whether *El obsceno pájaro* and Donoso's other works are fundamentally 'social' or 'metaphysical' novels has been a long-running one.[26] Donoso himself has not helped matters, for his own comments are as contradictory as the contents of his fiction. For example, in interviews published in 1971, he said of *El obsceno pájaro*: 'No tengo ninguna visión social. Es un ejercicio interior. No hay ninguna actitud o propósito mío con respecto a la sociedad'; and, 'Nada me irrita tanto como los críticos que reducen mis novelas a sus elementos sociales, éstos que quieren que yo haya escrito "el canto de cisne" de las clases sociales chilenas.' Yet in 1986, betraying perhaps his characteristic susceptibility to trends and his awareness of the current voguishness of political criticism, he said to me of his work up to 1970: 'Creo que ésas eran desesperanzas sociales, y no desesperanzas metafísicas o de identidad. En el fondo eran novelas políticas ésas. . .'.[27] But, in a sense, and as the earlier quotation from Barthes suggests, the discussion is a false one, for both levels involve the same questioning of conventional views, the same inversion of accepted patterns. In terms of both content and technique, the 'unity' of the novel lies in its negation of approved beliefs and the overturning of the literary structural and linguistic systems that support them.

Before examining the mechanisms through which this process of subversion is executed in the text, it might be best first to sketch a broad outline of the main social and metaphysical concerns of the novel. There are two basic aspects to the novel's social level. Firstly, it is clearly an attack on the injustice of the external social and political structures of Chilean society in particular and Latin American society in general. As with El lugar sin límites, El obsceno pájaro dramatises 'the demise of the feudal aristocracy' in Chile.[28] The crumbling of the harmonious career and marriage of the wealthy don Jerónimo (reflected in the monstrosity of the home he builds for his son, La Rinconada, and in the advancing decrepitude of the Casa, the convent the family acquired to preserve their status) is a metaphor for this decline. His class is repeatedly shown to be shallow and hypocritical so that, for instance, they abuse religion for personal ends via the Casa and via the promotion of the abortive project to secure the beatification of the original Inés de Azcoitía as a means of increasing the family's social and political standing. To expose the falsehood of their social posturing is at least part of the reason for the novel's insistence on the motif of the mask or disguise, while the exact parallel between La Rinconada and the outside world shows up the arbitrariness of the social divisions encouraged by the Azcoitías. The 'monsters' display the same frivolous consumerism and the same need for class hierarchies, suggesting that class is arbitrary and that the outside class system is also monstrous. But it is interesting that the freaks feel the need to mimic their 'normal' masters and that the humble Humberto Peñaloza, though resentful of don Jerónimo, is partly driven by a need to be like him. Since such groups can only identify themselves in terms of the existing system, then if their role-model goes they are plunged into an identity crisis. From this point of view Humberto's mental crisis is not purely psychological but socially generated. Despite its injustice and despite his struggle against it, he is so dependent on the system according to whose structures he defines his own self, that its collapse has catastrophic consequences for him. Hence in order to destroy Jerónimo he must first destroy himself: 'Ahora me eliminaré yo para que te desplomes y te partas en mil fragmentos al caer' (p.471). This recalls the position of Pancho Vega in *El lugar sin límites* who, having liberated himself from the tyranny of his dying former feudal overlord don Alejo, is plunged into an irresolvable existential crisis. Thus, as Rowe points out, 'in both books the transition from feudalism to bourgeois rule emerges as a negative liberation'.[29]

The other principal aspect of the social theme concerns the deeper structures of society. Throughout Donoso's work we see a conflict between instinct on the one hand, and reason and convention on the other, the idea being that man's natural impulses and desires are held excessively in check by the straitjacket of logic and social tradition. The simple illustration of this is the case of the stuffy, middle-aged, middle-class Andrés of *Coronación*, whose life-style is shaken by the arrival of the young country girl Estela with her innocently sensuous peasant vitality. However, the case of tía Matilde, whose humdrum existence in the short story 'Paseo' is given new impetus when she disappears to a shadowy but potentially fulfilling new sphere with a mysterious dog, implies something more: the Surrealists' dream of the transformation of man through the linking of his rational and irrational sides.[30] In *El obsceno pájaro* don Jerónimo clearly represents rationality. This is brought out in the repetition of *Este domingo*'s 'medallones' motif with which he is associated. Basically, Jerónimo's conception of life is compared to a series of interlocking medallions, a series of stages in life fixed by societal formulae rather than in response to individual aspirations, as in the following example:

Inés no alcanzaba a comprender las implicaciones que Jerónimo saboreaba en todo esto. Las reglas y las fórmulas, el ritual tan fijo y tan estilizado como los símbolos de la heráldica, que iban regulando el proceso del noviazgo, inscribían su propia figura y la de Inés, entrelazadas como iban debajo de los árboles cargados de fruta, como en un medallón de piedra: este medallón no era más que una etapa del friso eterno compuestos por muchos medallones, y ellos, los novios, encarnaciones momentáneas de designios mucho más vastos que los detalles de sus sicologías individuales. El cuerpo y el alma de Inés, intactos, esperaban que él la animara para sacarla de ese primer medallón y hacerla ingresar en la suntuosidad del medallón siguiente.

(p.179)

Yet Jerónimo's sense of order is clearly precarious. It is based on social convention and the supremacy of reason, but both of these depend on the suppression of the irrational and the unconventional which constantly threaten to creep to the surface. These menacing forces are represented in the novel by: Inés's friendship with the filthy, ugly old crone Peta Ponce, a relationship which 'no calzaba dentro de ningún medallón de piedra. Y si calzaba en alguno era en la otra serie, en la leyenda enemiga que contradecía a la suya,. . . el mundo de abajo, de la siniestra, del revés' (pp.182–3); Inés and Jerónimo's apparent inability to conceive a child which impedes the natural progression of the 'medallones' towards their 'dicha total' (pp.191–2); and the eventual birth of the grotesquely deformed Boy who is hidden away so as to submerge the truth that 'un hombre tan dotado de armonía como Jerónimo . . . puede contener la semilla de lo monstruoso' (p.162). The fragile unity of Jerónimo's socially-constructed personality eventually collapses altogether when he visits La Rinconada. He sees his reflection in a pool of water which when disturbed transforms his image into that of a monster; overcome by terror he attempts to tear at his reflected face and drowns in the pool. The Rinconada experience is a symbolic dramatisation of the disintegration that follows man's confrontation with the irrational subconscious upon whose suppression the smooth functioning of society depends.

It could be argued, of course, that the corollary of Jerónimo's story is the aforementioned Surrealist proposition that man can achieve greater fulfilment through the liberation of the irrational realm of his psyche. An indication of this is Inés's childhood illness which conventional medicine (the rational world) is unable to cure, but which is eventually remedied by Peta Ponce's witchcraft (the irrational) (p.185). Similarly, it is implied that the only way Inés's inability to have a child will be rectified is with the help of one of Peta's spells (p.215). The positive effects of the freeing of the irrational are thus emphasised. And it is partly a desire to achieve this which prompts Inés to move to the Casa and transform herself into a crazy old woman, for old age is 'una anarquía que todo lo permite, ... es una forma de libertad que yo no podía comprar, seguía esclava de un orden...' (p.399). But does she really accomplish anything? After all, she does not appear terribly happy or fulfilled when she is carted off under heavy sedation to a lunatic asylum. And as for Humberto, the liberation of fantasy seems only to create misery and leads to his ultimate self-destruction. There seems to be no real faith in the Surrealist dream in this novel. Indeed there seems to be no way out at all. As Caviglia says of Humberto: 'the abandonment of the norm ... leads not to unique individuality but to disintegration and chaos'.[31] And Humberto's own comment on his copulation with Peta Ponce – 'fue una pesadilla engendradora de monstruos' (p.228) – recalls Goya's famous caption: 'El sueño de la razón produce monstruos.' The idea is that the rational world is an unstable one and in constant danger from the suppressed irrational world which man keeps at bay in order to survive. The most positive thing one can say about all this is to repeat Wood's comment: 'if our reason were less repressive, its sleep would engender fewer monsters'.[32]

The negative viewpoint and inversion of traditional perceptions which is visible at the novel's social level are also apparent when considering the existential or metaphysical dimension of *El obsceno pájaro*. The conventional notion of God as the source of benevolence and order in the universe is roundly rejected. God is 'un Dios mezquino' (p.155) whose will irrationally provokes cruel acts of nature, such as the still-birth of all Brígida's children: 'así es la vida, Dios lo quiso así' (p.134). Furthermore, God's creation of the universe is mocked symbolically through the opinions of the freaks on Jerónimo's creation of La Rinconada:

Ellos no estaban dispuestos a ser sus instrumentos ni a formar parte de un mundo que a él se le antojaba desbaratar porque sí,... porque ya se había aburrido con sus demás juegos, como un dios un poco inferior que nunca sobrepasó una frívola y antojadiza niñez en que sus juguetes viejos tienen siempre que ser reemplazados por nuevos juguetes que su aburrimiento envejecerá y destruirá . . . como una deidad arteriosclerótica que cometió la estupidez, al crear el mundo, de no ponerse al resguardo de los peligros que podrían gestarse en su propia creación.

(pp.492–3)

The point is that a mad or incompetent creator implies a meaningless, formless creation. In other words, the universe has no ultimate order and, as with the Casa, 'lo que superficialmente podría parecer unidad no es más que un total descuido' (p.350).

Given this wider, metaphysical context Jerónimo's clinging to rationality can now be interpreted as the creation of a false construct, representative of man's need to fabricate an illusion of order to ward off his suppressed fear that life may be senseless, the universe chaotic. Jerónimo's gruesome fate (outlined earlier) and his metamorphosis into 'un ser retorcido, horripilante, monstruoso' (p.506) is therefore symbolic of the collapse of the construct and his awakening to the horrific nature of reality. Practically all of the characters go through this process, their 'immortality myths' – as Scott calls them – being 'ruthlessly shattered'.[33] Inés, for instance, withdraws from her failed marriage (an experience of disorder) to immerse herself in the hopeless beatification project (an unreal alternative order); when she realises this is a lost cause, she sinks into a downhill spiral of hysterectomy, senility and madness marking her absorption into a world of chaos. Similarly, Humberto's desire for identity, a 'máscara definitiva', is symbolic of man's search for fulfilment, but his heady succession of 'disfraces' are mere attempts to fight off the terrifying reality that this is an impossible quest. This is reflected in his obsession with sexuality (representing the myth of potential satisfaction, for desire is always undermined). Hence, despite his oft-stated longing to make love with Inés, this never really happens. As he seduces her she is transformed into the wrinkled and disgusting Peta Ponce, she denies his identity (pp.465–6) and later, when he imagines Inés's return, instead of caressing what he sees as his potent penis this chimerical figure (actually Iris Mateluna) appears to rip it off (p.511). The total hopelessness of the human condition, as reflected in Humberto, is summarised in his final fate: he is destroyed by fire, reduced to sheer nothingness.

The common denominator linking this existential theme to the two elements of social or socio-psychological complaint discussed earlier is the tendency to disrupt orthodox categories of thinking, with one pole of belief (identity, power, convention, rationality, order) dissolving into its opposite (fragmentation, rebellion, instinct, irrationality, chaos). This gives a clue to help identify the actual textual processes through which the 'meanings' considered above are generated. The ideas of French-Bulgarian feminist philosopher Julia Kristeva, as expounded in her *La révolution du langage poétique* (1974), may help clarify this process. Using terms from Lacan, she discusses the child's transition and entry into the so-called 'symbolic order', the 'grown-up' post-Oedipal phase. The formless, rhythmic, bodily 'pulsions' of the infant (an unspoken language she terms the 'semiotic') is repressed and replaced with organised language on entry to the symbolic order. The pre-Oedipal 'semiotic' (associated with the body of the mother) is opposed, then, to the post-Oedipal 'symbolic' (associated with the law of the father). Kristeva sees this language of the semiotic as a means of invading and subverting the symbolic order. In other words, a fluid and contradictory language disrupts fixed meanings and, by extension, fixed ideologies. To quote Terry Eagleton's summary of Kristeva:

> The semiotic throws into confusion all tight divisions between masculine and feminine – it is a 'bisexual' form of writing – and offers to deconstruct all the scrupulous binary oppositions – proper/improper, norm/deviation, sane/mad, mine/yours, authority/obedience – by which societies such as ours survive.[34]

This is not dissimilar to what Donoso was trying to explain to Mercedes San Martín when he said of *El obsceno pájaro*: 'Es una novela en que existe un sistema binario, no unitario. ¡Que no hay maniqueísmo! Es todo lo contrario del maniqueísmo. Entonces, el binarismo como negación del maniqueísmo.'[35] The technique of the novel, therefore, is to establish a chain of binary oppositions but then annul the boundary between each binary element so that one blends into the other and comfortable concepts and distinctions disappear. The basis of all order (be it psychological, social, metaphysical) is now eroded as it becomes contaminated by chaos. The effect is to demonstrate that all order or rationality is a myth for it has always contained the seeds of its own destruction.

Though this pattern is a *feature* of *El obsceno pájaro* rather than an externally imposed *system*, it does seem to embrace virtually every motif of significance in the novel.[36] Given that Kristeva's perspective is essentially (though not necessarily) feminist, it might be useful to start with a male-female binarism. The usual scenario of a male-dominated society with women on the periphery is both re-presented and undermined. Men control the world because 'ellos entienden lo que significa y saben explicarlo', while women always act 'por motivos irracionales, totalmente subjetivos, imposible comprender esos motivos' (pp.376–7). Yet this separation is an illusion, for the 'chaos' of woman can become dominant over the 'order' of man, as is shown when the supposedly passive, weak Inés uses Jerónimo's sexual dependency on women to force him to allow Peta Ponce to remain on the household staff (p.186). This episode links the male-female binarism to further oppositions via the figure of Peta Ponce, namely: youth-age, masters-servants. The old hag is obviously not unlike the demented 'viejas' who inhabit the Casa: 'estos seres anárquicos' whose minds 'se enredaban en una maraña que impedía todo intento de iniciar un orden' (p.529). Moreover, the old women are, like Peta, servants or ex-servants: in doing their masters' dirty work they confront the underbelly of reality their bosses try to ignore, thereby becoming 'algo como una placa negativa' and acquiring 'el reverso del poder' (pp.65–6). These various elements combine in Jerónimo's confrontation with Peta Ponce. As has been seen already, her ugliness and dirtiness threaten the stability of his 'medallions' – yet she is already *within* the household. On top of this, the fact that she gives him a set of perfectly beautiful handkerchiefs 'hizo tastabillar su orden al reconocer en la Peta Ponce a una enemiga poderosa' (p.183). The binary distinction disintegrates here, suggesting that chaos is contained *inside* order. So, it is not surprising that the ragged 'perra amarilla', which is identified with Peta, outwits and steals the meat from Jerónimo's supposedly powerful black dogs. It is important too that the yellow bitch and Peta Ponce are associated with the witch of the legend which is repeated (in varying forms) throughout the novel. The Peta Ponce-Inés relationship has its parallel in the nursemaid-girl relationship in the legend, where the former is thought to have infected the latter with her witchcraft. But the 'niña-bruja' becomes totally confused with the eighteenth-century 'niña-beata' who saves the convent from destruction during an earthquake (though again there is confusion for this could have been an act of saintliness *or* black magic). The point is that the 'bruja'-'beata' duality is fused into a singular: chaos, the irrational, the unacceptable are ever present within the superficial structures of order, reason and social coherence. Indeed, as Magnarelli has pointed out,[37] the witch is actually *part* of the male-dominated society that produces her: a witch is 'created' to explain away the inexplicable. But equally the witch (like the old female servants) is connected with 'knowledge' of the dark side of reality, the side that is ugly or frightening and cannot be rationalised or made acceptable. This is why the male landowner in the legend uses his poncho to cover up the scene between his daughter and the nursemaid-witch. The male represents the need to sustain a false order; the woman, the servant, the witch represent those underlying forces that are always on the verge of exploding that myth of order.

Humberto/Mudito is also involved in this scheme of disintegrating binarisms. His entire crisis manifests itself in terms of an oscillation between the need to become 'alguien' and the desire to be 'nadie', thus provoking a further clash of binary conflicts based on the opposition of power-weakness, expansion-withdrawal, inside-outside. So, for example, he feels his 'mirada cargada de poder' (p.84) controls Jerónimo, but of Iris he says: 'ni siquiera me ibas a conceder existencia con una mirada' (p.76). Indeed he thinks he can dominate Iris and force her into his model Swiss cottage, but shrinks away when she refuses (p.142) and is even compelled to follow her, 'ciego y sin voluntad' (p.82). In sexual terms too, his 'sexo inmenso' (p.269), his 'sexo ... de carne potente' (p.511) can all too easily become a 'trozo de carne inerte' (p.431), 'una cosa inútil' (p.463). The urge for power (an ordered, fixed system) is undermined, then, by the underlying reality of weakness and submission. The recurring symbol of the 'ventana mentirosa que habían colgado para que creyera que existía un afuera' (p.303) implodes the same sort of binary distinction: the illusory, fulfilling, structured world beyond the window does not really exist because the 'outside' is, in fact, an 'inside'. Moreover, Mudito's urge to escape through the window to the outside may be contrasted with his self-immersion in the Casa whose doors and corridors he progressively walls up so as to facilitate even further withdrawal. Both are ways of seeking comfort and order, yet both are opposites: they are therefore arbitrary and cancel each other out. The whole idea of withdrawal is, in fact, itself contradictory. This is reflected in the image of the 'imbunche'. An 'imbunche', from the myths of the Araucanian Indians of Chile, is a child stolen by witches and transformed into a creature whose orifices have been sewn up. The complete withdrawal of becoming an 'imbunche' would be, for Mudito, 'la paz total' (p.288) and he begs to be allowed the freedom of this state so he can at last 'anularme' (p.433). To ease this process, Mudito 'becomes' the 'niño milagroso', the offspring of Iris's alleged virgin birth: he now decreases in size and is wrapped in swaddling-clothes; the clothes get tighter and tighter until he is finally sewn up within layers of sacks and ends up:

> sordo, ciego, mudo, paquetito sin sexo, todo cosido y atado con tiras y cordeles, sacos y más sacos, respiro apenas a través de la trama de las capas sucesivas del yute, aquí adentro se está caliente, no hay necesidad de moverse, no necesito nada, este paquete soy yo entero, reducido, sin depender de nada ni de nadie, oyéndolas dirigirme sus rogativas, posternadas, implorándome porque saben que ahora soy poderoso. . .
>
> (p. 525)

But at this point he panics, especially when the hag comes to carry off the sack:

> sálvenme, no quiero morir, terror, estoy débil, tullido, inutilizado, sin sexo, sin nada, rasado . . . se instaura el terror, la necesidad de ver el rostro de esa sombra que respira y tose tan cerca, recobrar la vista y el afuero (sic), muerdo, masco el saco que tapa mi boca, royendo y royendo para conocer las facciones de esa sombra que existe afuera. . .
>
> (pp.538–9)

Expansion-withdrawal, inside-outside become totally interchangeable here. The binary distinction disappears as chaos and order are shown to be ultimately the same thing. This is a complete overturning – at all levels – of the rational principles upon which existence has traditionally been based. And that process of undermining conventional values is continued into the final page where Mudito is reduced to ashes, mere waste: a negation of life, a negation of all doctrines, a vision of absolute nihilism.

However, in spite of all its apparent radical subversiveness, a question mark remains over *El obsceno pájaro*. Having outlined the ways in which the novel demolishes stock values and practices, it might seem rather churlish to question the integrity of its – in literary terms – 'revolutionary' credentials. Yet even though it seems to break up expected formats and turn on its head the notion of order, there is a good deal of internal coherence in the novel. The binary system implies a pattern of sorts. But also there is a clear skeletal plot (albeit fragmented and inconsistent), there are abundant time references to help us fashion a basic time scheme, there is a broad spatial division (Casa-La Rinconada) to aid a structured reading, and there is a plainly identifiable overall form (described by me elsewhere)[38] tying the novel's parts firmly together. But even more important than all of this is Belsey's comment on Barthes's claims for the 'writerly' polyphonic text: 'The problem here is that it seems that none the less any text can be rendered fit for consumption.'[39] The point is that Western culture tends to *normalise* difficult works. And perhaps (going back to our opening remarks) by the late 1960s–early 1970s the new novel was coming to be normalised. In a sense, then, *El obsceno pájaro* may have been both genuinely subversive but simultaneously conforming to a new type of modernist stereotype. Donoso's striking change in direction after 1970 may well suggest that his greatest novel marks not only a climactic point in the Boom but also the beginnings of its possible exhaustion.

NOTES

1 José Donoso, *Historia personal del 'boom'* (Seix Barral, Barcelona, 1983), p.46.
2 ibid., p.89.
3 José Promis Ojeda, 'La desintegración del orden en la novela de José Donoso', in Antonio Cornejo Polar (ed.), *José Donoso. La destrucción de un mundo* (Fernando García Cambeiro, Buenos Aires, 1975), p.31. My outline here is, of course, a simplification or schematisation of the whole process. Nonetheless, the broad pattern (which is developed in Ch. 11) is thought to be accurate. See Ch. 10 for a slightly different perspective from Pamela Bacarisse.
4 This and other information in this paragraph is from José Donoso, 'Chronology', *Review*, no. 9 (1973), pp.12–19. Also useful for Donoso's life up to the early 1970s are: his *Historia personal del 'boom'*; George R. McMurray, *José Donoso* (Twayne, New York, 1979); Isis Quinteros, *José Donoso: una insurrección contra la realidad* (Hispanova, Madrid, 1978).
5 According to 'Chronology', as a youth Donoso himself seems to have explored the anatomy of one of his family's servants.
6 *Historia personal del 'boom'*, p.32.
7 Donoso was, of course, influenced by American and European writers. Also his work as a journalist and reviewer exposed him to an increasingly wide range of literature.

8 For a more detailed discussion of these ideas, see my 'Donoso and the post-Boom: simplicity and subversion', *Contemporary Literature*, vol. 28, no. 4 (1987), pp.520–9, and my 'Structure and meaning in *La misteriosa desaparición de la marquesita de Loria*', *Bulletin of Hispanic Studies*, vol. 63, no. 3 (1986), pp.247–56. This matter will be returned to in Ch. 11.

9 'A conversation between José Donoso and Marie-Lise Gazarian Gautier', in Guillermo I. Castillo-Feliú (ed.), *The Creative Process in the Works of José Donoso*, Winthrop Studies on Major Modern Writers (Winthrop College, 1982), p.3.

10 Philip Swanson, 'Una entrevista con José Donoso', *Revista Iberoamericana*, vol. 53 (1987), p.67.

11 Russian Formalism is succinctly explained in Ann Jefferson and David Robey (eds), *Modern Literary Theory. A Comparative Introduction* (Batsford Academic, London, 1983), pp.16–37.

12 Though most critics agree that Mudito is the novel's narrator or centre of consciousness, not all do. See, for example: Hugo Achugar, *Ideología y estructuras narrativas en José Donoso (1950–70)* (Centro de estudios latinoamericanos 'Rómulo Gallegos', Caracas, 1979); William Rowe, 'José Donoso: *El obsceno pájaro de la noche* as test case for psychoanalytical interpretation', *Modern Language Review*, vol. 78 (1983), pp.588–96.

13 Quotation from José Donoso, *El obsceno pájaro de la noche*, 6th edn (Seix Barral, Barcelona, 1979), p.395. All subsequent references will be to this edition and will be included in the main body of the text. References to Promis Ojeda and Quinteros are 'La desintegración del orden. . .', p.36 and *José Donoso*, pp.238–9 respectively.

14 McMurray, *José Donoso*, p.110 ff.

15 Pamela Bacarisse, '*El obsceno pájaro de la noche*: a willed process of evasion', in Salvador Bacarisse (ed.), *Contemporary Latin American Fiction* (Scottish Academic Press, Edinburgh, 1980), pp.21, 29.

16 José Donoso, *Coronación*, 2nd edn (Seix Barral, Barcelona, 1981), p.157.

17 Sharon Magnarelli, '*El obsceno pájaro de la noche*: fiction, monsters and packages', *Hispanic Review*, vol. 45 (1977), pp.413–19; 'Amidst the illusory depths: the first person pronoun and *El obsceno pájaro de la noche*', *Modern Language Notes*, vol. 93 (1978), pp.267–84; 'The baroque, the picaresque and *El obsceno pájaro de la noche*', *Hispanic Journal*, vol. 2, no. 2 (1981), pp.81–93; 'José Donoso's *El obsceno pájaro de la noche*: witches everywhere and nowhere', in *The Lost Rib. Female Characters in the Spanish American Novel* (Associated University Presses, London and Toronto, 1985), pp.147–68.

18 'Amidst the illusory depths', pp.271, 272.

19 Alfred J. MacAdam, 'José Donoso: endgame' in *Modern Latin American Narratives* (University of Chicago Press, Chicago and London, 1977), e.g. p.115; Z. Nelly Martínez, '*El obsceno pájaro de la noche*: la productividad del texto', *Revista Iberoamericana*, vol. 46 (1980), p.55.

20 Steve Giles, 'Delimited by discourse: some problems with the new critical practice', *Renaissance and Modern Studies*, vol. 27 (1983), p.144.

21 Magnarelli, 'Amidst the illusory depths', p.289.

22 Giles, 'Delimited by discourse', p.147.
23 Catherine Belsey, *Critical Practice* (Methuen, London and New York, 1985), pp.51 128.
24 Roland Barthes, *Le bruissement de la langue*, Essais critiques IV (Seuil, Paris, 1984), p.66. The references to Émile Benveniste and Mikhail Bakhtin are, respectively, to *Problems in General Linguistics* (University of Miami Press, Miami, 1971) and *Problems of Dostoevsky's Poetics* (Ardis, Ann Arbor, Michigan, 1973). See Belsey, *Critical Practice*, Chs 4.2, 6.2.
25 Martínez, 'La productividad del texto', p.58. Martínez here appears to favour Derrida rather than Bakhtin, stressing the impossibility of establishing meaning.
26 For a summary of this and other critical differences up to the early 1980s, see my 'Concerning the criticism of the work of José Donoso', *Revista Interamericana de Bibliografía*, vol. 33, no. 3 (1983), pp.355–65.
27 Respectively: Guillermo I. Castillo, 'José Donoso y su última novela', *Hispania*, vol. 54, no. 4 (1971), p.958; Anon., 'Entrevista a José Donoso a propósito de *El obsceno pájaro de la noche*', *Libre*, no. 1 (1971), p.74; Swanson, 'Una entrevista con José Donoso', p.997.
28 Charles Michael Tatum, '*El obsceno pájaro de la noche*: the demise of a feudal society', *Latin American Literary Review*, vol. 1, no. 2 (1973), p.100.
29 Rowe, '*El obsceno pájaro* as test case for psychoanalytical interpretation', p.596. The entire article is a very useful discussion of the aforementioned ideas. Also useful here are Achugar, *Ideología y estructuras narrativas* (especially on *El lugar sin límites*) and Hernán Vidal, *José Donoso: surrealismo y rebelión de los instintos* (Aubí, Barcelona, 1972).
30 The more general and more specifically Surrealist aspects of this issue are covered by Vidal and McMurray respectively in their books on Donoso.
31 John Caviglia, 'Tradition and monstrosity in *El obsceno pájaro de la noche*', *Publications of the Modern Language Association of America*, vol. 93 (1978), p.38.
32 Michael Wood, 'José Donoso: where the wolf howls', in John King (ed.), *Modern Latin American Fiction: A Survey* (Faber & Faber, London, 1987), p.238.
33 Robert Scott, 'Heroic illusion and death denial in José Donoso's *El obsceno pájaro de la noche*', *Symposium*, vol. 32 (1978), p.137.
34 Terry Eagleton, *Literary Theory. An Introduction* (Basil Blackwell, Oxford, 1983), p.189. Eagleton provides an excellent summary here of Julia Kristeva's arguments in *La révolution du langage poetique* (Seuil, Paris, 1974).
35 Mercedes San Martín, 'Entretien avec José Donoso', *Caravelle*, vol. 29 (1977), p.201.
36 For a fuller discussion of the binary pattern, see my 'Binary elements in *El obsceno pájaro de la noche*', *Revista de Estudios Hispánicos*, vol. 19, no. 1 (1985), pp.101–16, and Ch. 4 of my *José Donoso: the 'Boom' and Beyond* (Francis Cairns, Liverpool, 1988).
37 Magnarelli's chapter on *El obsceno pájaro* in *The Lost Rib* is central to the

discussion here and is indispensable for an understanding of the function of the witch in the novel.

38 *José Donoso: The 'Boom' and Beyond*, pp.80–7.
39 Belsey, *Critical Practice*, p.129.

10

MANUEL PUIG:
BOQUITAS PINTADAS

PAMELA BACARISSE

The 1960s were almost over when *La traición de Rita Hayworth*, the innovative first novel by an unknown 36-year-old Argentine, Manuel Puig, was published. In 1968, some of the most important works of the creators of the *nueva novela* had still to see the light of day,[1] but critics were quick to produce a new category in which to place Puig, together with several other emerging writers;[2] this was variously – and infelicitously – designated the '*petit*-Boom', the 'Junior Boom', or even the 'post-Boom'.[3] One possible reason for devising this classification may have been that it was erroneously assumed that the principal productive period of the 'new novelists' had ended, but it is more likely that its inventors realised that they were now dealing with a very different kind of writer. Authors such as the Cuban, Severo Sarduy, the Mexican, Gustavo Sainz and, of course, Manuel Puig demonstrated a new approach to the novel; it was clear that they constituted a new generation, though it was not so much a question of age (like Puig, some of those ascribed to the 'Junior Boom' were well into their 30s when their first books came out, older than Mario Vargas Llosa) as of originality. Certainly no one had ever read anything like *La traición de Rita Hayworth* before; initially there was a certain amount of resistance to it and several commentators were guilty of facile judgements and slipshod readings, but when *Boquitas pintadas* appeared a year later, in 1969,[4] Puig's reputation was incontrovertibly established, and many previously hostile critics began to reconsider their view of the first book.

With the first two novels Puig revealed a capacity, unique among contemporary serious authors, to find favour with fairly un-sophisticated audiences, and this talent was again in evidence with the publication of *El beso de la mujer araña* in 1976[5] (*The Buenos Aires*

Affair, which came out in 1973, was less well received). This worked against him to a certain extent: in the beginning it made his writings suspect in the eyes of academics; then, as his fundamental seriousness became increasingly apparent, especially in the last three books,[6] his popularity in the mass market began to wane. The superficial appeal of *La traición de Rita Hayworth* and *Boquitas pintadas* owed much to what was then a completely new authorial technique:[7] the depiction of character and situation by means of correlative Hollywood films of the 1930s and 1940s[8] and romantic fiction in the first book, and the cinema, *radionovelas* and the lyrics of popular songs, particularly tangos, in the second. Furthermore, the full title of *Boquitas pintadas* is *Boquitas pintadas. Folletín*, and Puig originally intended to publish it in instalments, in true novelette fashion. In spite of the book's immediate success, it has to be admitted that at first the author's intentions were largely misunderstood. Even some of those who realised that it was not itself a novelette mistakenly assumed that it must therefore be parodic – one claimed that it was 'el doble irrisorio del folletín'[9] – while others were unable to see that the sentimental values of the characters were being *used* by the author to make a serious statement. While they find consolation in their favourite books, films, plays and songs, they are also being conditioned into continued acceptance of the oppressive patriarchal principles that permeate these. At the same time, their attempts to better themselves result in a *cursilería* which is both ludicrous and pathetic. It would indeed have been easy for a work of this sort to turn into parody, but *Boquitas pintadas* cannot be classified in this way because of the author's attitude towards his creations: he identifies with them, understands them and is never censorious. While it is true that he detests *machismo* and condemns the patriarchal system, he is well aware that there is no easy answer: what lies behind all his novels is a desire to make his readers ask the right questions, together with the hope of some level of improvement. It is not only the confidence of hindsight where this particular society is concerned that prevents him from sharing the utopianism of his characters.

Boquitas pintadas is a continuation of *La traición de Rita Hayworth* (which is an elaborated autobiography),[10] but it also constitutes a move away from it. It is a continuation in that once again its setting is Coronel Vallejos (General Villegas, the small town in the Argentine Pampa where the author was born in 1932), and the period is more or less the same. On the other hand, the format is different, and there is also a change of scene, so to speak, within the spatial confines of the novel which is far more significant than the fact that here some of the characters do actually achieve their ambition of going to a big city, Buenos Aires: this time we are presented with a completely new set of protagonists. Gone are the idiosyncratic, neurotic misfits whose dreams of fulfilment were structured around the escapist fantasy of foreign films and novels. Instead, we meet representatives of the other section of the community, those who are equally impressed and manipulated by romantic values, but who have much narrower cultural, ideological and psychological horizons and – it has to be said – who are generally less intelligent. Frustration, rebelliousness and nonconformity permeate *La traición de Rita Hayworth*, but no one in *Boquitas pintadas* questions or challenges the rules of society. The gulf between the levels of characterisation in the two novels is striking: individualists populate the first, whereas the second is entirely made up of people that the author himself has referred to as *chatos*. There is no point in looking for interesting, quirky, iconoclastic elements in them, for – as he says – they are like chess pieces. It is their trajectory across the chess-board of their lives and the truths that lie behind this that Puig is drawing our attention to.[11] However, in the event these flat and transparent characters contribute to a work that many have judged moving, and it is precisely because of their lack of depth and mystery that it is so easy for the reader to recognise and feel for them. Conformity has resonances for most people, and the characters' fascination actually resides in their emblematic qualities.

Puig's deliberate avoidance of psychological complexity means that the effectiveness of the novel must depend on other factors. The most obvious of these (and this is true of the majority of the so-called *géneros menores*) is the layout and pace of the narrative, but *Boquitas pintadas* has two more features that are of vital importance. One is the insidious, demythifying juxtaposition of mass-media clichés and what actually happens. The other is extraordinary formal variety: any initial impression of unthinking spontaneity in Puig's writing is misleading, for it is made up of a conscious and very knowing technique. Indeed, the word 'narrative' could be judged inappropriate: it is not only individual characterisation that is missing, but also the usual third-person narration of events. Details of these are conveyed indirectly by means of newspaper announcements, letters, diary entries, lists, programmes and stream-of-consciousness passages which ensure that there is never any risk of stylistic monotony. The author himself has admitted to a very low boredom threshold[12] and he always strives for formal variety, embarking on a fresh format with each new book. However, behind these different frameworks – such as that of the detective story in *The Buenos Aires Affair* and the novel-in-dialogue layout of *Maldición eterna a quien lea estas páginas* – lies basic homogeneity, and within each novel the theme is indicated, though not directly expressed, by means of correlative allusions and discourses. In *Boquitas pintadas*, for example, the tango lyrics and the values implicit in *radionovelas* do not actually tell the truth, but suggest where it can be found.

Puig is a novelist who is prepared to take risks in order to achieve his objectives. One striking example is found in his fourth book, *El beso de la mujer araña*, when lengthy footnotes, the relevance of which is not immediately apparent, accompany and interrupt the flow of the main body of the text. Another is when he starts *Boquitas pintadas* with one of its most dramatic narrative climaxes: the death, at only 27, of Juan Carlos Etchepare, an irresistibly handsome man who in a real *folletín* would indubitably be the hero. The possibility of a happy ending is thus eliminated, and the reader cannot dismiss the suspicion that the whole book will look in a backwards direction;[13] this is indeed the case, for almost everything of any importance has already happened. Nevertheless, it is clear that for Puig the potentially negative effect of this opening is counterbalanced by its value as a thematic indicator: in this novel, the region into which his unhappy protagonists (who are all female) yearn to escape is not another country or another culture, with their promise of perfect happiness, but the past, when they could still believe that this could be achieved.

As the text progresses, it is impossible to avoid the realisation that the past that haunts their thinking is as much a manifestation of fantasy and wishful thinking as the Hollywood mythology that plays so prominent a part in *La traición de Rita Hayworth*. In a way, these women have rewritten the story of their lives, but their inability to face up to reality is neither wilful nor self-seeking, and Puig is consistently compassionate towards them. The contrast between their imposed and unchallenged sentimentality and the harsh facts of life is encapsulated in the epigraphs to the book's two parts, elaborations on the title:[14] the first refers to glamorous 'Boquitas pintadas de rojo carmesí'; the second – 'Boquitas azules, violáceas, negras' – indicates the unpalatable truth behind all illusions.

Illusion is the key to the text. The first epigraph, 'Era. . . para mí la vida entera. . .',[15] establishes an appropriate atmosphere for the epistolary opening section in which Nené (Nélida Fernández de Massa, now disenchanted with marriage, motherhood and life in Buenos Aires) looks back with therapeutic longing to the bliss of her relationship with Juan Carlos, the love of her life. The facts are less comfortable, for this disgruntled product of machismo had actually been a promiscuous, deceitful and exploitative Don Juan,[16] 'la vida entera' to a not inconsiderable number of misguided and masochistic Coronel Vallejos women. Nené's innocent and romantic devotion is rekindled on hearing of his death, and in spite of the fact that his mother blamed her for his tubercular state, she decides to write to her in an attempt to recover her love letters. Somewhat to her surprise she receives a reply, and the continuing correspondence encourages her to wallow in misplaced nostalgia, abandon her disappointing husband and go to Cosquín, where Juan Carlos had spent his last days. Her attitude is not atypical. It is repeated in the case of Raba, a servant-girl who is coldly deserted by Juan Carlos's friend, Pancho, when she becomes pregnant, but who consoles herself by fondly imagining all the touching details of the reconciliation that she judges inevitable if he actually sees their son. The other two female characters whose faith in the superiority of men is all too apparent are Mabel, briefly engaged to a dull Englishman but also one of Juan Carlos's conquests, and his long-term mistress, the widow Di Carlo, who selflessly cares for him and supports him when he is dying. All these women cling to their illusions as the reader is gradually made aware of the worthlessness of the object of their affections. Juan Carlos had made no attempt to be faithful to Nené because of her sexual reserve, partly the product of her remorse after a short-lived and guilt-ridden affair with her employer. Then, although he claimed to be committed to Mabel (p.52), this did not prevent simultaneous involvement with several others, including Elsa Di Carlo. She – 'la tranquila', as he called her (p.50) – was his constant refuge, but it never occurred to him to enter into a permanent, exclusive relationship with her. Perhaps she was too 'tranquila'. Both he and Pancho accepted affection, even devotion, but gave nothing.

The tragic dichotomy between what people believe and conflicting facts is never explicitly alluded to. The novel demands the analytic, even judgemental, participation of its readers: only then is the (partially) hidden truth revealed. Given the many changes of emphasis, it is not surprising that when the film version (directed by the late Leopoldo Torre Nilsson) came out in 1974, it was widely misinterpreted. V. S. Naipaul, who saw it in Buenos Aires, dubs it 'aimless' and recalls that for the weeping audience, 'the tragedy lay in the foreseeable death of . . . the poor boy who made his conquests the hard way, by his beauty'.[17] However, there is considerably less danger of this misplaced reaction in the skilfully constructed written text, and reader/author collaboration is not, in fact, taxing. Only the most obtuse could fail to be struck by the incompatibility between the narrative and the style and values of the chapter epigraphs, the interpolated tango lyrics (in the eleventh *entrega*) and the *radionovela* (in the thirteenth *entrega*) that Mabel and Nené listen to together in preference to talking about real life.

To say that these four women are *personajes chatos* does not, of course, mean that they are carbon copies of each other. There are class differences: for example, Mabel comes from a much higher stratum of provincial society than Raba and as a consequence has greater expectations. Then there is the question of sexual activity: Mabel is more experienced and more realistic about sex than either Nené or Raba. And it is hardly worth adding that life deals more harshly with some than with others: Elsa Di Carlo, a widow with a daughter, has in no way caused her own problems. Nevertheless, because of their adhesion to patriarchal ideology, they are stereotypes. This is manifest in two ways: they are aware of the rules of the game[18] and go to great lengths, both practical and psychological, to conceal any failure to observe them; and they are unquestioning believers in male superiority, cherishing unrealistic ambitions where men are concerned. Unsurprisingly, their dreams of bliss come to nothing. Nené's apparently affectionate correspondent turns out to be Juan Carlos's frustrated, jealous and rancorous sister, Celina, who divulges her mental infidelity in an anonymous letter to her husband; her dramatic flight to Cosquín is ludicrously short-lived, and when she dies (significantly, the first and last chapters begin with death announcements), her last wish is that Juan Carlos's love letters, which she had previously wanted buried with her, be destroyed. As for Raba, she does indeed see the elusive Pancho again, but the encounter coincides with his emerging from Mabel's bedroom, and she knifes him; her projected happiness and her ultimate situation contrast sharply – the last piece of information we are given is that she is living 'en concubinato' with a widower, his four children and her own son, and she is pregnant once again. She is still an exploited servant. Mabel, whose engagement is broken off when her father loses all his money, makes her last appearance in the novel on the eve of a loveless marriage. And in 1968, the year of Nené's death, the widow Di Carlo must be elderly if not already dead.

With some justification, one critic has signalled the 'antiheroísmo' of this book: 'antiheroísmo que reina en la vida de la provincia argentina, invadida, como tantas otras zonas del subcontinente, de la nueva mitología de los medios de comunicación de masas'.[19] But though 'antiheroísmo' is unquestionably a key word, it has to be pointed out that the mass media did not invent the pernicious ideology that distorts the characters' vision of their lives, they merely reflect it. Furthermore, although the resulting problems were particularly acute in small provincial Argentine communities in the 1930s and 1940s, they were not confined to that geographical area nor have they entirely disappeared with the passage of time, in spite of the influence of feminism. The culprit is not romantic fiction but the patriarchal system that is observed and mirrored in it, and Argentina is not the only breeding ground for its most extreme and harmful manifestation: machismo. Machismo presupposes that a 'real man' (the definition of which Puig queries in several of his novels) will be strong, powerful, unemotional to the point of callousness, sexually insatiable, concerned about the size of his genitals, aggressive, easily aroused to violence and, within his own social limits, rich; paradoxically – since this ideological structure is so inflexible – he must also see himself as rebellious and individualistic. Moreover, machismo assumes that 'being a man' is far more important than 'being a woman', as is abundantly clear from the implications of the frequently used first phrase (the second is completely devoid of these). The outcome of this collective attitude is the conquest, domination and, ultimately, humiliation of women. Juan Carlos and Pancho are certainly 'antiheroic', if the converse connotes admirable nobility, courage and integrity. On a mythic scale, they contribute nothing to the advancement of the human spirit; at a more pedestrian level, they sully social morality, for their behaviour is egocentric and defensively self-preserving.

213

Traditionally, women are both economically and emotionally dependent on men and since – to quote Kate Millett – 'patriarchy's chief institution is the family', which is 'a patriarchal unit within a patriarchal whole',[20] marriage has always been judged the only acceptable path to female fulfilment. This principle is never challenged by the women in *Boquitas pintadas*. Indeed, spinsterhood is considered shameful, as Elsa Di Carlo's contemptuous (but unspoken) words to the unlovely Celina clearly demonstrate: 'Pescó marido', she says proudly of her grown-up daughter, 'no como vos' (p.191). The options are marriage or failure (the only other alternatives would be to enter a religious order or prostitution), so that in practice there is little choice other than to strive to win a husband and to accept the conditions that he dictates. The problems inherent in the process (including the need to project immaculate virtue *and* sexual promise) are counterbalanced by hope and expectation. With such a prize, no effort or sacrifice is too great: female sexuality is repressed and female masochism indulged as women collude with male-invented rules. All four of the novel's protagonists suffer when these are broken. Nené finds it difficult to live with her conscience after her affair with Dr. Aschero, and it is this reaction that is largely responsible for her insistence on a conventionally pure relationship with Juan Carlos. Raba's whole life is blighted by her relationship with Pancho, for within the code, pregnancy is always the woman's fault. Mabel's promiscuity is the indirect cause of Pancho's death, and then she has to lie and deceive in order to avoid a scandal. And the widow Di Carlo is treated like a pariah by respectable society, as typified by Celina. These women are torn between the needs of their own sexuality, which – of course – coincide with those of the men they are attracted to, and socially-imposed limitations to them. They have been made to feel ashamed of their desires (even after she is married, Nené is shocked by Mabel's frankness on the subject of sex (p.209)), and they clothe them in romantic fantasy, which will inevitably lead to disillusion. They have faith in future happiness, but in fact, the only happiness available to them is that of anticipation. And it is this which is no longer possible once the text starts.

It is tempting to see *Boquitas pintadas* as a feminist novel. Puig's concern for the plight of subservient women is patent (even though few critics have considered it worthy of investigation), and it would not be difficult to construct a kind of vengeance theory around the demise of the unscrupulous hero. This would be a mistake, for the author's antipathy is to the system, and he is convinced that with machismo neither sex is happy or fulfilled: 'I write about people who make mistakes', he says, 'but they always have an alibi: they have been distorted by their environment. And everybody is uncomfortable with machismo. Power is a cross too.'[21] If we divert our attention to the situation of Juan Carlos, or even Pancho, we will find that *Boquitas pintadas* illustrates this thesis; Puig always avoids a manichaean approach.

The system was created by men for men, so that their power is never at risk. Within it, social institutions and practices ensure the survival of universal acceptance of their superiority. 'In one sense', claims a feminist theorist, 'a patriarchal society is organised so that the belief in male supremacy "comes true".'[22] Inflexible role-models for both sexes form part of this plan, and while it is not in doubt that women have the more difficult task in emulating society's ideals (the virgin mother, the self-sacrificing maiden and the complaisant wife, for example) and that they are doomed to disappointment when the anticipated compensatory bliss does not materialise, demands made on men are also daunting. Juan Carlos is also a victim. Like one of his real-life prototypes, he suffers from 'inadaptación al medio',[23] the word 'medio' here being taken to refer to the social climate. It is a constant struggle for any male to preserve a sense of importance in impecunious circumstances, and this is highlighted by the fact that, in the author's own words, Juan Carlos 'está envenenado por un resentimiento' because 'lo han despojado de unas tierras'.[24] He is so shamefully poor, in fact, that shortly before his death he moves from financial dependence on his mother to being kept by Elsa Di Carlo. It is not because of the sexual implications of the liaison that it must be concealed from the *vecinos*. The public image is everything. His problems are further aggravated by his illness: he has to make heroic efforts to keep up the appearance of physical strength, and later he is obliged to write mendacious letters from the sanatorium in order to disguise the gravity of his condition. Indeed, all the rules are difficult to follow. Deep down, he may be more sentimental than is appropriate: we cannot know whether the diary entries that suggest this (p.52) are mere self-deception. He has to cope with the shame of being socially inferior to Mabel – although this, too, is totally artificial: as the widow Di Carlo says to Celina, 'vergüenza es robar' (p.194), and the criminal activities of Mabel's father reveal the hollowness of the family's 'superiority'. In almost all contexts, whenever Juan Carlos feels constrained to do his macho duty and show off, he has to seek the help of others – borrowing cars and money, even getting someone else to write his letters – but this is essential because a man has to *be* somebody, and nothing must be allowed to stand in his way: this principle explains, even if it cannot condone, Pancho's reprehensible behaviour too. Perhaps one of the most distressing aspects of the system is constituted by the occasional doubts that men themselves experience: it is apparent to the reader – or it ought to be – that narcissism, money and arrogance are not ideal criteria on which to base the concept of manhood, but there is a point in *Boquitas pintadas* where the author makes it clear that even Juan Carlos understands this. Like Josemar, the protagonist of *Sangre de amor correspondido*, whose macho image is also precarious, he uses the expression 'hombre de verdad'. 'Prometo ante dios,' he says, 'comportarme como un hombre de verdad. . .' (p.52), and if he had kept his promise, his proposed future conduct would have constituted a complete change in his life.

There is just one area in which Juan Carlos does not have to depend on anybody else. He is extremely attractive, with a 'rostro perfecto', and he is virile. In his sex life there is no risk of humiliation: he can use this power to compensate for any other weaknesses or (undeserved) disadvantages. More than one critic of the novel has referred to the connection between the hero's substantial sexual appetite and his tubercular condition: some, like Sarduy,[25] highlight Puig's subversive intention in contrasting the myth of the consumptive Romantic hero with the real, repulsive symptoms of the disease, thus indicating yet another dissonance. Others confine themselves to a brief mention of the theory that tuberculosis causes a dramatic increase in the libido. This confirms the plausibility of the hero's behaviour, certainly, but more would have been gained if they had not stopped short of asking themselves exactly why Puig should have judged these circumstances particularly appropriate for Juan Carlos; after all, it would be perfectly acceptable from a narrative point of view if a highly-sexed young man had died in an accident. It is Emir Rodríguez Monegal's reference to Juan Carlos's 'voluntad de aniquilarse en el placer'[26] that points us in the direction of a comprehensive explanation. The 'placer' of this phrase is not just the self-gratification found in physical release, but also – and much more importantly – the deeper gratification of the male ego that illness, stupidity and poverty (and, perhaps, indolence) prevent him from achieving in any other way (it is interesting to compare the self-satisfied and sexually cold attitude of Mabel's *novio*, the tedious Cecil, so sure of his social worth). Ironically, his tuberculosis both increases Juan Carlos's desire and gradually reduces his capacity to satisfy it, echoing the feudal lord in a fable recounted in *La traición de Rita Hayworth*, who conditions children into tastes for which he then severely punishes them. In the end, when Juan Carlos is weak and impotent, desire has been stripped bare. The element of fulfilment, which always obscured its nature, is now absent, and it is seen for what it always was: an expression of the struggle of human beings to recognise and assert their individuality. For women, the means to self-discovery is seen as love, but for men it is the knowledge that society classifies them as 'hombres de verdad'. Both views are unexceptionable, even admirable, but Puig is at pains to point out – however indirectly – that love is not what the women in *Boquitas pintadas* think it is, and that it is profoundly disturbing that Juan Carlos's machismo should inspire social indulgence, to say nothing of approbation. Even more distressing is the ineluctable atmosphere of failure that haunts the novel from the very beginning. The reader brings to the text the knowledge that there is no possibility of anything else: the myths that clothe the *Weltanschauung* of the female characters are gradually shown to be false and, on a narrative level, the hero is dead. His ambitions, as well as those of the women (which he signified), belong to the past. Then, with Nené's death, the circle closes. All illusions have been shattered. Puig includes many factual details in his text: we are always aware of the date, for example, and when Nené dies, her exact age is given. His purpose is not to achieve a kind of Borgesian spurious authenticity in his writings, but to clarify the hidden narrative and, even more important, the truth behind it. In *Boquitas pintadas*, the thematic relevance of the dates is twofold. They indicate the passage of time and the inevitable decline in the hopes and optimism of the characters ('Lo que han hecho no es nunca importante,' admits the author, 'pero al final la suma de esas banalidades significa algo'[27]), and they also signal the epoch during which pernicious social attitudes were most prevalent. In this context, for a woman to die at the menopausal age of 53 can be judged symbolic: if the only source of female happiness is romance and the past cannot be recaptured, her life is effectively over in any case.

Demythification, like satire, suggests that its perpetrator is in possession of 'the right answer', and this in its turn implies an unsympathetic, even arrogant, authorial stance. However, it is perhaps worth repeating that Manuel Puig never provides solutions and, furthermore, his tenderness towards his creations is never in doubt. He is always personally involved in their problems, and he has emphatically declared that it is never his intention to mock them: 'Cuando escribo una carta de Nené, me identifico con ella al punto de sentir lo mismo que ella'; he finds *cursilería* touching, because it is born of 'el afán de ser mejor',[28] and though his writings are often ironic, he employs what I have seen as 'non-distanced irony'.[29] In spite of everything, he even sympathises with the fact that countless generations of women have derived pleasure and happiness from their belief in male superiority and he realises that the female unconscious is 'peuplé d'images fascinantes du machisme,' as he put it when discussing his fifth novel, *Pubis angelical*. 'Le grand avantage de la femme soumise,' he went on to explain, 'c'était d'avoir droit à une grande aventure de l'imagination.'[30] He reproduces what he understands.

His total lack of sentimentality has been seen as the main objection to classifying *Boquitas pintadas* itself as a *folletín*.[31] There are many others.[32] However, there are implications in his experimental use of certain aspects of the *folletín* format which should not be ignored. The first provides yet another piece of evidence to support the claim that, in spite of what some critics have said, Puig never distances himself from his characters. This is that he actually shares their taste for what are so often designated *géneros menores*, seeing the dichotomy between popular culture and so-called High Art as artificial and coinciding with the current school of theorists which denies the validity of this cultural hierarchy. 'Tengo la impresión', says Puig, 'de que hay un paralelismo entre los géneros menores y la situación de la mujer en los países machistas: todos gozan con ellas, pero nadie las respeta.'[33] We have already seen that the sentimental values of popular culture influence, even create, those of the characters, but the author's comments on the enjoyment that it provides for so many people opens up a whole new area of thought about why this should be so. One explanation is that the apparent unassailability of these values is consolatory; another, that they are expressed clearly, often melodramatically, with no danger of any disturbing ambiguity. And (to return to a point made very much

earlier) where fiction is concerned, the skilful disposition of the
narrative is all-important: characters are schematic, description is
kept to a minimum, the author is never intrusive and the values are
prefabricated, so that emphasis is inevitably on what happens next
and on creating an emotional reaction in the reader by means of
what are usually referred to as 'mini-climaxes'. The brilliance of
Boquitas pintadas lies in the author's capacity to construct a narrative
of this sort while at the same time ignoring the rules. It is not only
where fantasy and reality are juxtaposed that he is subversive. He
eschews linear narration, employs different linguistic patterns[34] (the
style of the novelette is invariably homogeneous) and although he
follows the convention of introducing 'mini-climaxes', these often
look backwards – as does the novel itself – theoretically precluding
the possibility of sustained interest on the part of the audience. Yet
the enormous popular success of the novel is testimony to the
efficacy of the plot and the pleasure it has afforded to many who
have not delved beneath the surface of this variation on a narrative-
heavy *genre*.

It was Freud who distinguished between the accidental and the
constitutional factors that make up the human psyche: accidental
elements are susceptible to change, whereas – it goes without saying
– those that are constitutionally based are not. This theory is
singularly appropriate when it comes to determining the ideology
that lies behind all Puig's novels, especially if it is applied
collectively. There was much to deplore in the society that provides
the setting for *Boquitas pintadas*, and the author is sure that much of
this was 'accidental', particularly machismo. For him, machismo has
overwhelming significance; 'Sexual oppression,' he has said, 'is the
school of all other oppressions',[35] and if it could be eliminated,
human suffering would be reduced in most areas of life. The
difficulty, of course, lies in distinguishing between what is accidental
and what is constitutional, and Puig would be the last to deny the
value of fantasy and the imagination or the power of the emotions.
In *Boquitas pintadas*, the role of the reader, which has been described
as 'de enorme, si no total importancia en la novela',[36] not only
involves deciphering a question, but also the search for an answer.

NOTES

1 For example, Gabriel García Márquez's *El otoño del patriarca* (1975), Carlos Fuentes's *Terra nostra* (1975) and *Conversación en la Catedral* (1969), by Mario Vargas Llosa.

2 Usually included in this category are Fernando del Paso (Mexico, b.1935), Gustavo Sainz (Mexico, b.1940), Salvador Elizondo (Mexico, b.1932), Severo Sarduy (Cuba, b.1937), Reinaldo Arenas (Cuba, b.1943), Salvador Garmendia (Venezuela, b.1924), Adriano González León (Venezuela, b.1931), Enrique Congrains Martín (Peru, b.1932), Alfredo Bryce Echenique (Peru, b.1939), David Viñas (Argentina, b.1929), Néstor Sánchez (Argentina, b.1935) and Jorge Edwards (Chile, b.1931), among others.

3 The so-called post-Boom is approached with a different emphasis by Philip Swanson, partially in Ch. 9, but more particularly in Ch. 11.

4 All references in this study will be to Manuel Puig, *Boquitas pintadas. Folletín* (Seix Barral, Barcelona, 1982).

5 The theatrical version was published in 1983, and the film (for which William Hurt won an Oscar in 1986) was directed by Héctor Babenco.

6 *Pubis angelical* (1979), *Maldición eterna a quien lea estas páginas* (1980), *Sangre de amor correspondido* (1982).

7 Since then several authors have used mass-media clichés in their work. In Great Britain, for example, the most successful has been Dennis Potter.

8 For an excellent analysis of the relationship between the cinema and *La traición de Rita Hayworth*, see René Alberto Campos, *Espejos. La textura cinemática en La traición de Rita Hayworth* (Pliegos, Madrid, 1985).

9 Severo Sarduy, 'Notas a las notas a las notas. . . a propósito de Manuel Puig', *Revista Iberoamericana*, vol. 37 (1971), pp.555–67. I consider the question of the *folletín* in more detail in my chapter on *Boquitas pintadas* in *The Necessary Dream. A Study of the Novels of Manuel Puig* (University of Wales Press, Cardiff, 1988).

10 See the author's interview with Jean-Michel Fossey in *Galaxia latinoamericana* (Inventarios Provisionales, Las Palmas, 1973).

11 See the interview with Emir Rodríguez Monegal, 'El folletín rescatado', *Revista de la Universidad de México*, vol. 27, no. 2 (October, 1972), pp.25–35.

12 He also said, 'Lo que me parece inmoral es el aburrimiento', to Elisabeth Pérez Luna, 'Con Manuel Puig en Nueva York', *Hombre de Mundo*, vol. 3, no. 8 (1978), pp.69–107.

13 The epigraph ('Era. . .para mí la vida entera. . .') also looks backwards, while at the same time establishing the 'heroic' role of Juan Carlos.

14 The title comes from a foxtrot sung by Carlos Gardel in the film *El tango en Broadway* (1935).

15 From the tango 'Cuesta abajo' (1934), lyric by Alfredo Le Pera, music by Carlos Gardel.

16 For an analysis of the Don Juan element in Juan Carlos, see Lucille Kerr's chapter on *Boquitas pintadas* 'A succession of popular designs', in

Suspended Fictions. Reading Novels by Manuel Puig (University of Illinois Press, Urbana and Chicago, 1987).

17 V. S. Naipaul, *The return of Eva Perón* (Penguin, Harmondsworth, 1981), p.150.

18 My chapter on this novel in *The Necessary Dream* is called 'The rules of the game'.

19 Juan Manuel García Ramos, *La narrativa de Manuel Puig (por una crítica en libertad)* (Universidad de La Laguna, La Laguna, 1982), pp.192–3.

20 Kate Millett, *Sexual Politics* (1969) (Virago, London, 1985), p.33. It first came out in 1969.

21 In conversation with the present author (Rio de Janeiro, August 1987).

22 Dale Spender, *Man Made Language*, 2nd edn (Routledge & Kegan Paul, London, 1985), p.1.

23 Rodríguez Monegal, 'El folletín', p.26.

24 Ibid. The same problem is found in *Sangre de amor correspondido*.

25 Sarduy, 'Notas', p.564.

26 Rodríguez Monegal, 'El folletín', p.28.

27 ibid.

28 ibid., p.29.

29 See *The Necessary Dream*.

30 J.-Michel Quiblier and J.-Pierre Joecker, 'Entretien avec Manuel Puig', *Masques: revue des homosexualités*, vol. 11 (1981), pp.29–32.

31 Margery A. Safir, 'Mitología: otro nivel de metalenguaje en *Boquitas pintadas*', *Revista Iberoamericana*, vol. 41 (1975), pp.47–58.

32 See *The Necessary Dream*.

33 Pérez Luna, 'Con Manuel Puig', p.104.

34 See Iris Josefina Ludmer, '*Boquitas pintadas*: siete recorridos', *Actual* (Jan.–Dec. 1971), for a breakdown of the various styles. This is reproduced in García Ramos, *La narrativa*.

35 In conversation, August 1987.

36 Safir, 'Mitología', p.56.

CONCLUSION: AFTER THE BOOM

PHILIP SWANSON

The word Boom implies temporality, a sudden and rapid development of finite proportions. As has been demonstrated in the previous chapters, the Boom in the Latin American new novel occurred basically in the 1960s building on the foundations laid by major experimental works in the 1940s and 1950s, themselves anticipated by even earlier narratives. This Boom was helped by the Cuban Revolution (which gave the writers of the time a sense of unity and turned world attention to Latin America) and by the growth of the Spanish publishing industry (which was keen on promoting the 'new' and 'different' Latin American novel). But the end of the 1960s and the beginning of the 1970s saw a damaging split in the Barcelona-based Seix Barral publishing house and the arrest of Cuban poet Heberto Padilla: both factors could be said to mark a break in the cohesion of the Boom. The Boom was certainly not over and a number of significant works were still to come, but from now on clear changes could begin to be perceived in the actual nature of modern Latin American fiction. Many established writers were seen to adopt a new style: the most obvious examples are the switch to greater accessibility and, above all, humour in Vargas Llosa and the return to apparently straightforward story-telling in Donoso. Moreover, a new generation of novelists (or at least a new type of novelist) had already started to emerge in the late 1960s. Puig in many ways marks the transition, but also significant are, for instance, Cuba's Reinaldo Arenas (b.1943), Guillermo Cabrera Infante (b.1929) and Severo Sarduy (b.1937), Mexico's Salvador Elizondo (b.1932), Fernando del Paso (b.1935) and Gustavo Sainz (b.1940), and Peru's Alfredo Bryce Echenique (b.1939). Though some of them have greater reputations than others, these are all fairly familiar names by now. More recently, other authors have appeared or have been the subject of critical attention; amongst them are Argentina's Jorge Asís (b.1946), Mempo Giardinelli (b.1947) and Luisa Valenzuela (b.1938), Chile's Isabel Allende (b.1942) and Antonio Skármeta (b.1940), and Uruguay's Saúl Ibargoyen (b.1932). So, while some critics might nit-pick over the terminology, it nonetheless seems clear that a new phase has been in operation since (roughly) the late 1960s or early 1970s, and this is now commonly referred to as the post-Boom.[1]

Having adopted, for working purposes at least, the term post-Boom, the questions remain as to what it is and why it happened. That is: in what ways does the post-Boom differ from the Boom and why did the transition take place? At this stage of research into a very recent phenomenon, answers have to be, at best, tentative. However, it is becoming clear that a number of broad aspects can be identified and it is hoped to illustrate these via both a general survey and a more detailed look at some of the more established authors.

The first point to be made is that the post-Boom is in part a reaction against the neo-conventionalism of the Boom. What this means is that though the new novel was essentially a response to the conventions of traditional realism, by the end of the 1960s, it had replaced those conventions with new ones of its own. Long, tortuous, fragmented, baroque novels were simply not unusual or challenging any more and were close to becoming as stereotyped as the forms they claimed to have overthrown. One novelist who has honestly and consistently confronted this fact is José Donoso. Having worked towards the publication of a great and typical 'new novel' in 1970 with *El obsceno pájaro de la noche*, he turned his back on the previous trend in his career to produce instead works written in a seemingly traditional or self-consciously artificial style like *Casa de campo* (1980) and *El jardín de al lado* (1981). He explained his position with these words:

> Lo que me interesa . . . es hacer una batida contra la aceptada novela clásica: no la novela clásica antigua sino la contemporánea. Digamos, la novela del buen gusto contemporáneo. Es decir la novela que bajo el disfraz de una libertad narrativa forja una serie de reglas de las cuales no es posible prescindir. Por ejemplo, todas las reglas terribles que me parece que usa Cortázar: *Rayuela* es un muestrario de reglas encubiertas que forjan toda una teoría de la novela: esta teoría pretende destruir la novela clásica pero forja otra novela clásica.[2]

A related point here is that post-Boom fiction is also a reaction against the scale or 'totalising' tendency of the new novel. It rejects grandiose efforts to capture in writing a total picture of Latin American reality. González Echevarría therefore comments that 'lo que la narrativa postmoderna hace es abolir la nostalgia de totalización' and that 'la novela del post-Boom abandona la saudade de la identidad'.[3] Donoso, again, has said the same thing:

> Es increíble que hasta novelas que no se pueden considerar de primera categoría . . . adolezcan de esta ambición totalizadora que en un momento del cercanísimo pasado consideramos como la marca registrada sobresaliente y gloriosa de la novela de este continente, pero que nos está pesando un poco. . . ¿No ha llegado un momento de ruptura para la novela latinoamericana, de cambio, para renacer de las cenizas de tantas y tantas novelas totalizadoras, agobiantes de significado, ahogantes de experimentos, que se imprimen todos los días y que pretenden honradamente y a veces brillantemente desentreñar las verdades de nuestro destino general?[4]

Implicit in all of this is a certain renunciation of the commercialisation of the new novel. Some of the Boom novelists (like Fuentes, García Márquez and Vargas Llosa) had effectively become superstars. A type of novel which was once difficult and subversive had now been normalised by the system which had exploited it, marketed it and turned it into a consumer good. Indeed the very 'modernity' of these novels may not have had the 'revolutionary' impact which is often supposed but may have been used (or abused) to consolidate faith in the value of 'modernisation', of the mechanical, technological, consumerist world of advanced capitalism. Ortega, for example, has commented that:

> esos mecanismos de producción y consumo terminarían ilustrando la conversión del escritor, quien de su función marginada e independientemente crítica, pasó a una función profesionalizada, convertido en vocero de opinión, como un especialista certificado precisamente en la 'opinión pública', o sea en el pacto social controlado por las burguesías nacionales.[5]

One thinks here, in particular, of Vargas Llosa who has made the transition from notorious left-wing critic in *La ciudad y los perros*

(1962) and *Conversación en la Catedral* (1969) to a right-leaning public figure and virtual reactionary in novels like *La guerra del fin del mundo* (1981) and *Historia de Mayta* (1984). In fact, Marcos rather aggressively claims that Vargas Llosa, Fuentes, Borges and others 'han propagado la imagen narcisista de una escritura lujosa, cosmopolita y elaborada', while Franco insisted in 1976 that 'it is also crucially important, at the present juncture, for literature to break out of the cultural ghetto of the avant-garde where it has been reduced to technique or hedonism'.[6]

There are obvious political implications here. The suggestion is that the new novel had become elitist: a middle-class medium for a middle-class audience. But also its universalising tendencies and existential pessimism were leading it away from specifically Latin American issues and the social and political struggle. Hence Carpentier, looking forward to the future awaiting the Latin American novel in the 1980s, abandoned his past adhesion to technical virtuosity and argued for fiction dealing with social issues and aimed at the ordinary individual, incorporating melodrama, colloquial and peculiarly Latin American language and a clear political stance.[7] He had already partially attempted to put this theory into practice in 1978 with his own barnstorming glorification of the Cuban Revolution, *La consagración de la primavera*.

One further factor which may have helped promote change is the growth of interest in literary theory in recent years. Modern literary theory has exercised a considerable influence on the literature it is meant to describe, modifying in the process the nature of that literature. One of Britain's best-known theorists, Terry Eagleton, who argues with Michel Foucault for the study of 'discursive practices' rather than the study of 'good literature' (the latter being basically an elitist concept based on the fact that the academic establishment tells us it is 'good' rather than on any real, objective criteria) has commented that: 'critical discourse . . . is the power of policing writing itself, classifying it into the "literary" and non-literary, the enduringly great and the ephemerally popular'.[8] This general tendency to reassess what, in fact, constitutes literature (and, in particular, 'good' literature) may account for the emergence or re-emergence in Latin America of forms and styles not hitherto viewed as acceptable by the literary and academic powers-that-be. At the same time, modern literary theory has problematised the whole question not only of literature but of language itself, encouraging

tives that consciously break down the relationship between uistic sign and external referent (as in Sarduy) or expose the litical implications of attempting to fix meanings in essentially open texts (as in the later Roa Bastos). So, while literary theory has certainly transformed the criticism of the Boom, it may also have contributed to the transformation of the subject of that criticism.

But if these are all possible reasons for a reaction against the Boom, specifically what type of fiction did they cause the post-Boom to produce? To be sure, there is no simple answer, for a considerable variety of features (often meaning different things for different authors) can be identified. However, there are some basic, often shared characteristics which can be outlined. Firstly, there is a reduction in scale. Donoso says that after the Boom:

> la obra de arte es la anti-totalidad. La obra de arte es la existencia. La esencia de la obra de arte es lo particular. Implica particularidad. La obra de arte que se plantea a sí misma como la historia de la humanidad, es una mierda.[9]

This attitude is exemplified in his own small-scale, largely psychological realist 'novela de la persona',[10] *El jardín de al lado*, and even in more social-cum-historical novels like, say, Fuentes's *Gringo viejo* (1985) or Isabel Allende's *Eva Luna* (1987). Tied in with this tendency is the trend towards simple, traditional, essentially realist narrative forms, following the exhaustion of the technical wizardry of the Boom. One could mention here García Márquez's *El amor en los tiempos del cólera* (1985), the later Donoso, the historical novels of Vargas Llosa, the work of Allende, Giardinelli, Skármeta and many others (not forgetting, of course, the upsurge in documentary narrative from people like Mexico's Elena Poniatowska (b.1933) and Chile's Hernán Valdés (b.1943)).[11]

This return to a kind of realism makes much post-Boom fiction more accessible than many of its predecessors and this accessibility or popularity is one of its central features. Humour, for instance, is a major element: Vargas Llosa's 1973 and 1977 novels *Pantaleón y las visitadoras* and *La tía Julia y el escribidor* attract a much wider readership than his previous uniformly serious productions. His compatriot Bryce Echenique similarly scored a hit with the comic social satire *Un mundo para Julius* (1970) and has gone on to produce a string of popular successes. Gustavo Sainz, meantime, appears to revel in the fun-world of youth culture in *Gazapo* (1965) and the hilariously readable *La princesa del palacio de hierro* (1974). Many post-Boom texts actually adopt or exploit various forms of popular culture. Fuentes's *La cabeza de la hidra* (1978) is a spy story; Giardinelli's *Luna caliente* (1983) is a detective novel; García Márquez's *Crónica de una muerte anunciada* (1981) and Donoso's *La misteriosa desaparición de la marquesita de Loria* (1981) owe something to the same genre, as well as to popular erotic or pornographic fiction in the case of the latter novel; Luisa Valenzuela unpretentiously parodies the *novela rosa*; and Puig systematically uses Hollywood B-Movies, tangos and boleros, radio soap operas (as does Vargas Llosa in *La tía Julia*) and, more recently, science fiction. A parallel development in this regard is a renewed interest in popular language: as Marcos has noted, the hybrid Spanish-Portuguese of the border area in Ibargoyen's *La sangre interminable* (1982) or the mixture of Mexicanisms and Argentinianisms in Giardinelli's *El cielo con las manos* (1981) constitute a real attempt to 'revalorar el habla de sectores populares injustamente menospreciados'.[12]

This last point by Marcos carries with it the suggestion that after the narcissism, as he sees it, of the Boom, the narrative of the post-Boom is more at the service of the people, using straightforward, popular formats to transmit clear, optimistic, humanitarian social and political messages to the readership. This is true of many post-Boom authors. Skármeta's 1981 novel on Nicaragua, *La insurrección*, is a good example, dealing as it does with the collective struggle of the people of León against the injustice of the Somoza regime. However, the later works of Vargas Llosa, though more accessible, might not prove so appetising to Marcos: in them collective action often smacks of dangerous fanaticism. As for Puig, his novels – though imbued with an underlying radicalism – show a much more complex political position and positionality than is suggested of other authors by Marcos. Moreover, quite a number of the writers associated with the post-Boom betray few obvious signs of politicisation at all. The picture, then, is much more problematic than it might at first seem.

This is also true of some of the other aspects of the post-Boom commented upon here. In particular, the idea that the post-Boom novel is straightforward and uncomplicated has to be put into a proper perspective. Popular culture does not always mean simplicity. Puig's work is simultaneously sentimental and ironic: it is often difficult to draw a clear distinction between the sense of enjoyment and re-evaluation of popular culture and the feeling that it represses the individual by moulding his life-style and expectations according to meaningless norms. And though there is a clear wave of solidarity running through the popularism of Giardinelli, Skármeta *et al.*, one cannot help wondering if the sudden discovery of popular forms by certain other authors is not somehow related to the expanded market it provides for their works. Moreover, the tendency to stress the rediscovered realism of the post-Boom can, in some cases, be misleading. As I have argued elsewhere, the realism of Donoso's later works is often only apparent. The real effectiveness of his post-Boom technique lies not in a simple return to traditionalism but in a more subtle subversion of realist conventions, with the texts overturning their own apparent pattern of development from within. This accounts for the narrative interference in *Casa de campo*, the way Blanca's jovial sex romps give way to barely fathomable canine symbolism and an unexplained disappearance in *La marquesita de Loria*, and the sudden revelation at the end of *El jardín de al lado* that the narrator is not who we thought it was.[13] But in any case many novels linked to the post-Boom could never be described as even remotely traditional or realistic in the first place. Arenas's *El mundo alucinante* (1965) with its varying narrators and extravagant fantasies on the life of Fray Servando Teresa de Mier is, as its title suggests, completely anti-realist. Del Paso's vast *Palinuro de México* (1975) betrays 'totalising' tendencies and is characterised by tortuous, baroque linguistic games. Language (exploited less exuberantly) is also important in the work of Elizondo, where characters are unreal entities concocted out of words and the novels become a demanding and often baffling sortie in search of a new dimension.

The idea of playing with language provides an important link between Del Paso and Elizondo and some more solidly established figures such as Cabrera Infante and Sarduy. Both Cubans use popular sources and toy with language (albeit in different ways), but despite their playfulness are by no means traditional or straightforward novelists. In a sense they continue the complexity of the Boom novel but take themselves less seriously in the process. This ludic exploitation is a significant feature in a group of writers who link the Boom to the post-Boom and are, in some ways, the latter's major representatives. Given their importance, it seems appropriate to consider their principal works in greater detail than has been offered in the general survey so far.

The aforementioned fascination with language is probably most clearly in evidence in the work of Cuba's most famous writer since Carpentier, Cabrera Infante. His magnum opus, *Tres tristes tigres* dates as far back as 1965 (though 1967 is usually given as the publication date). These dates alert us again to the necessary fluidity of any distinction to be drawn between the Boom and the post-Boom. Though *Cien años de soledad* was published in 1967, Cabrera Infante is still generally associated with the new direction we have been calling the post-Boom. He himself has said quite explicitly that 'I don't see I have much in common with the so-called Boom . . . I've always felt more comfortable with Severo Sarduy and Manuel Puig.'[14]

On one level his work is plainly an exercise in nostalgia. This is evident from the epigraph from Lewis Carroll which introduces *Tres tristes tigres*: 'Y trató de imaginar cómo se vería la luz de una vela cuando está apagada.' Hence, his 1979 novel *La Habana para un Infante difunto* expresses the struggle of memory against the passing of time as it evokes the author's own adolescence in the Havana of the 1940s, with the glorification of eroticism and pop culture serving as a kind of lament for bygone times. *Tres tristes tigres*, meanwhile, concentrates on Havana in the 1950s. In particular it deals with the late 1950s just before the coming of the revolutionary government in January 1959. It becomes a kind of elegy for a dying era as it strives to capture the atmosphere of the night-life, the bars, clubs, characters and language of the period.

The nostalgia, however, is – though affectionate – also ambivalent. The notion of decline implies an element of sadness or even pessimism. There is a political element here. Laura's dream of the dirty-grey, red-eyed dog who, unlike the other dogs, is able, when set free by her, to drag a dead dog from the bonfire and take it back to the house may be a reference to Castro's displacement of Batista. And Arsenio Cué's statement that 'el español al revés es ruso'[15] has clear political overtones in the Cuban context.[16] But, unlike Roa Bastos's *Yo el Supremo* (1974), as we shall see, the novel's main emphasis is by no means political. As Isabel Álvarez-Borland has pointed out, the depressing raving of the anonymous madwoman in the epilogue unites 'la falta de libertad política . . . con el caos existencial'.[17] The pattern of decay in the novel reflects the lack of permanence and stability in life. By the end the positive characters Bustrófedon and La Estrella are dead, while the careers of Cué,

Códac and Eribó are going downhill and Silvestre is losing his sight. Moreover, the sheer arbitrariness of events (and their consequences) and the lack of causal links suggest that life is without any fundamental order or meaning.

However, the absurdity of life can be challenged, it seems, by play and creativity. So, nightclubs, women, fast cars, films, jokes are all – though escapes – alternatives to sterility (in particular the mystery and attractions of the night as set against the drudgery of the working day). The writer Silvestre, the actor Cué, the photographer Códac and the musician Eribó all follow careers which imply both escapism and creativity. But, above all, it is Bustrófedon and La Estrella who represent full authenticity. The fat, ugly La Estrella is contrasted with the glamorous Cuba Venegas: the latter depends on a well-packaged physical appearance and a good backing band, while the former sings unaccompanied, relying solely on the wondrous quality of her voice. If La Estrella embodies authenticity of sound, then Bustrófedon epitomises spontaneity and creativity in language. His uninhibited and often nonsensical linguistic games constitute, according to Souza, an appreciation of the potentiality of language which is 'the key to a method of building a new society'.[18] Art or language, then, provide a kind of alternative order or anti-order to a transient, ephemeral existence. Having said that, though, both Bustrófedon and La Estrella die (and die rather ordinary deaths at that) showing that their originality is equally subject to the ravages of time. Nonetheless, their memory survives and casts its glow over the entire narrative: this 'accentuates a dynamic process instead of a static state' and shows that 'significance is not found in the permanence of being but in the process of becoming'.[19] This explains the restlessness of the characters and the constant transformation in the text at the level of language and structure: life is a game of chance and it is only through ludic creativity that man can renovate existence – though ultimately even the linguistic game masks nothing of substance.

In a sense, *Tres tristes tigres* continues in the vein of the typical new novel of the Boom. The ludic element is a development to some degree; but this was already present in Borges, and the displacement in the penultimate sequence of the orderly music of Bach with the game or joke of the 'Bachata' has its precedent in *Rayuela*'s displacement of novel with anti-novel. What is different is the freedom and exuberance of the humour, the inclusion of trivia, the enjoyment of popular culture (especially films and song) and the *centrality* of the role of language and linguistic processes. These are the factors which account for Cabrera Infante's association with Puig, Sarduy and the post-Boom.

However, before turning to Sarduy, it is necessary first to consider an important influence on him – that of another Cuban, José Lezama Lima. It might seem strange to include a writer who was born in 1910 and died in 1976 and whose major novel, *Paradiso*, was published in 1966 in a section dealing with the post-Boom. Equally, it might seem odd to present a Catholic writer whose work is essentially optimistic as an influence on an author as subversive as Sarduy considers himself to be. The problem is that *Paradiso* is a novel which is very difficult to classify. In a sense it seems a traditionally-written third-person novel which charts a young man's apprenticeship in life in a very local, Cuban context; but at the same time it is bafflingly complex, contains a vast range of pseudo-erudite allusions, is stylistically incredibly elaborate and, at times, quite experimental. Although hailed by many of the new novelists, notably Cortázar and Vargas Llosa, *Paradiso* is not, then, a typical novel of the Boom. Its fascination with language (and Orientalism) links it more with the work of certain post-Boom writers like Sarduy. Indeed it is a key work in the development of the so-called neo-baroque in Latin America. In Cuban terms this stretches back to the ornate prose of Carpentier; but it is really from Lezama Lima through to Sarduy that the potentiality of language is most fully explored.

Some kind of understanding of *Paradiso* can perhaps be achieved by a consideration of one of its most bizarre elements, the unusual twelfth chapter. This chapter abandons the more or less chronological narrative on the life of the Cemí family in the late nineteenth and early twentieth century, and instead offers us four separate stories unrelated to the main plot (one even goes back to Roman times in the second century BC) and a little sketch. Though it is beyond the scope of this survey to examine each of these stories in detail, what is notable about them is the way their apparently unrelated events all begin to merge as the different characters come together and reveal themselves as symbols of different aspects of time. Souza, tying this to the theme of the sketch, concludes that 'a chapter that deals with man's war against time and his thirst for eternity ends with affirmation of the creative process. . . . The essence of life then is to create rather than preserve what was.'[20] This process is paralleled

231

by the technique of the chapter which gradually fuses disparate elements into a unified, coherent whole. This is, in effect, the technique and the point of the entire novel: poetry and creativity offer a glimpse of the potential harmony man can achieve once he has found his way on the road of life and overcome the chaos of experience.

The protagonist José Cemí's journey through life essentially re-enacts this pattern. In particular, sexuality is used as a means of exemplifying the apprenticeship-of-life idea. José's two friends, Foción and Fronesis, represent two aspects of sexuality. Foción's sexual turmoil (he embraces homosexuality and becomes obsessed by Fronesis) represents chaos and disorder, while Fronesis (who overcomes his early sexual difficulties with the opposite sex) stands for the possibility of initiating order. The point is that the creative impulse has to be channelled in the right direction and this is the lesson that José gradually learns. Above all, this lesson is taught to him by his mentor, Oppiano Licario (the subject and title of Lezama's unfinished second novel, published posthumously in 1977). When José visits Licario's apartment, the following exchange takes place:

> –Veo, señor–le dijo Cemí–, que usted mantiene la tradición del *ethos* musical de los pitagóricos, los acompañamientos musicales del culto de Dionisos. –Veo –le dijo Licario con cierta malicia que no pudo evitar–, que ha pasado del estilo sistáltico, o de las pasiones tumultuosas, al estilo hesicástico, o del equilibrio anímico, en muy breve tiempo.
>
> Licario golpeó de nuevo el triángulo con la varilla y dijo: Entonces, podemos ya empezar.[21]

In fact, the novel ends, echoing this scene, with the words 'podemos empezar' (p.653). The clear implication is that José has learnt how to deal with the creative urge, that he has now ordered the chaos of existence and, in this sense, is now ready really to begin life.

This transition from chaos to order is expressed in the novel by the imagery of the square becoming a circle, of a spiral leading to an ideal state.[22] But this use of imagery returns us once again to the centrality of poetic expression or creativity: for what Licario introduces José to is the world of 'la imagen'. Interaction with the poetic image, it seems, is a means of getting closer to the essences of existence. The link between language and creativity goes much

232

further here than with Cabrera Infante: for Lezama Lima, language or, specifically, poetry is a means of integration with the universe. It is not so much this quasi-religious quality of poetry which accounts for the importance of Lezama Lima for his fellow Cuban Severo Sarduy, but rather the former's employment of a tortuously-wrought baroque artistic style. But language is not an issue for Lezama in the sense that it is for Sarduy. Equally, though language is important for Cabrera Infante, for Sarduy it is *everything*. In the view of González Echevarría, the essential concern of Sarduy is 'la autonomía de la escritura, o sea, la escritura como sistema específico sujeto a sus propios leyes, no circunscrita a un significado, sino abierta a una multiplicidad de significados.'[23] Sarduy, who was a student of Roland Barthes, has been clearly influenced by structuralism and post-structuralism whose theories provide the basis for his fictional as well as his essayistic writing. For him, it seems, language is a mere sign-system marking only an absence of meaning; writing therefore reflects no more than 'el acto de escribir'.[24] This also links in with the element of eroticism in Sarduy's narratives. Sarduy rejects the bourgeois conception of sexuality as a means of reproduction and language as a means of communication, replacing both with non-functional ludic eroticism and artificiality – that is, a 'juego cuya finalidad está en sí mismo y cuyo propósito no es la conducción de un mensaje . . ., sino su desperdicio en función del placer'.[25] This also explains why Sarduy is generally thought of as the epitome of the neo-baroque writer of Latin America. In a sense (for Sarduy at least), the essence of the Baroque is excess: in writing, it signals a squandering, wasteful, non-utilitarian use of language for the sake of pleasure. But also the Baroque, as well as mixing different periods and cultures, often depends on ellipsis: a stream of signifiers deflects attention from a central signified, but only to call attention to the fact that behind the signifiers there is therefore nothing and, indeed, ultimately only an absence at the centre. This is exactly the narrative technique of Sarduy where the gap between what signifiers *signify* on the one hand and *allude to* on the other is exploited to rupture the process of revelation of 'meaning'.[26]

This theoretical stance has led Sarduy to produce a series of novels which defy categorisation and interpretation and which will leave the reader either challenged or frustrated (as will much of the barely penetrable criticism his work has provoked). For basically, his fiction has no narrative quality: plot, such as there is, is 'distorted and dictated by phonetic associations or by the internal logic of language itself'.[27] The reason why Sarduy's second novel, *De donde son los cantantes* (1967), is so confusing is that its surreal, mutating structure is simply a reflection of the fact that characters like Auxilio and Socorro are, as MacAdam reminds us, mere incarnations of 'the signs of language, the signifiers chasing after or searching in vain for meaning'.[28] But Auxilio's desire that 'tendré sentido' is hopeless, because meaning is 'siempre ausente'.[29] It follows then that 'the drama of the signs, their being doomed to a permanent state of emptiness, their being condemned to exist as surfaces, points out to the reader that what is at stake in the text is language itself, that there is nothing hidden here, that the surface, or a palimpsest-like series of surfaces, is all'.[30]

The same notions underlie what, along with *De donde son los cantantes*, is probably Sarduy's most widely-known novel and usually considered his best, *Cobra* (1972). Again the narrative (dealing with a transvestite show-girl or prostitute, male or female, wax doll become human, dead then alive, who travels from Europe to India with a kinky motorcycle gang to join up with an oriental deity) is hardly worth summarising. *Cobra*'s operation and changes of identity show the fluidity of any given signifier. The text's overall pattern of movement and transformation implies the flight of signifiers (flight is to become central in *Colibrí* (1984)) which points to a lack of fixed, final meaning. The emphasis on rituals in the novel suggests much the same thing: writing ritualistically acts out a system of surface relations between signs without conferring any new, original meaning. Hence, as González Echevarría points out, the novel's structure undermines progress: 'the exile of the motorcycle gang (from Europe) corresponds to the return of the monks (to Tibet), and this double movement cancels the sense of progression implicit in the pilgrimage', while the final section which carries the title 'Diario Indio', the name of Columbus's diary, marks a new era, a new beginning, but comes at the end.[31] Just as the spiritual quest is mocked in *Maitreya* (1978), so too here the Orient is not a Utopia and the novel ends in whiteness – a blankness, an absence of meaning.[32]

The question remains of where all this situates Sarduy in relation to the Boom. Again, though his first novel *Gestos* appeared in 1963, he is really generally regarded as one of the major figures of the post-Boom. Certainly, as with Cabrera Infante, there is a reaction against the 'seriousness' of many of the novels of the Boom and a new interest in the ludic, camp, pop culture and so on. Moreover, the baring of the fictional process (evident in Macedonio Fernández and *Rayuela*, but coming into its own with Donoso's *Casa de campo*, Elizondo's novels and, to some degree perhaps, Vargas Llosa's *La tía Julia y el escribidor*) reaches an extreme in Sarduy where linguistic connections determine the course of the action. Clearly Sarduy regards himself as writing beyond the limits of the Boom and in *Cobra* he addresses the reader who may be having difficulties (a 'tarado lector') and advises him: 'abandona esta novela y dedícate al templete o a leer las del Boom, que son mucho más claras'.[33] González Echevarría, who likewise sees *Cobra* as 'a work of the anti-Boom', makes a more serious point. He argues that many novels of the Boom retain traditional elements in that the characters' thoughts and actions are all ultimately explicable in terms of the cultural tradition to which they belong. This is not the case with Sarduy, whose characters are often only functions of rhetoric and whose language is grossly artificial, thereby exposing how cultural identity is an illusion, for values are forged by language. In this sense, Sarduy's work is 'nothing less than the subconscious of the Latin American narrative', for it – in true post-structuralist style – shows up the lacunae or repressions hidden by the previous generation of authors.[34]

There is, of course, a political dimension to all of this. Sarduy's work (and that of others such as Elizondo or Argentina's Néstor Sánchez (b.1935)) seems revolutionary in that it exposes the ways in which conventional narratives reproduce structurally the values of conventional society and it is a kind of writing which, being unclassifiable and irreducible, is resistant to institutionalisation by that society. However, there are difficulties with this position. Franco sums up the problem succinctly:

Even if we set aside the elitist nature of texts which are addressed to readers already schooled in certain literary antecedents (especially Octavio Paz and contemporary French critics), their subversive potential rests on disputable premises. Firstly, these are said to reveal their own production process and hence to show the underlying ideological structure of traditional narrative. Secondly, because they constitute closed sign systems, they are said to defy a society which is bent on reducing everything to signs and messages and which institutionalises art. Yet if the texts merely reveal their own self-constitution, they become little more than technical *tours de force* and their authors 'move into the proximity of industrial technocrats'. Further, far from being irrecuperable by society, their very 'neutrality' makes them eminently suitable for recuperation by university departments of literature, since established literary criticism has long defended the autonomy of art. And, as the case of Borges shows, authors of self-referential texts may even be useful cult figures in the service of reactionary governments.[35]

Basically, critics like Franco believe that an over-reaction to the inertia of realist fiction has led to the creation of modernist texts which are empty politically. She would argue therefore for a new kind of non-elitist political narrative. A key work for her in this respect, one of the most remarkable novels to appear in the 1970s, is *Yo el Supremo* (1974) by the Paraguayan Augusto Roa Bastos (b.1918). This novel continues the characteristic experimentation of the new novel and indulges in the linguistic play of the post-Boom without falling prey to the dangers of commercialisation and normalisation. For Franco therefore it is a kind of model by following which 'radical writing and criticism can begin to separate itself both from the passive model implied by realism and the vacuity of the modernizing avant-garde'.[36] Equally it provides a clear link between the Boom and the post-Boom in that it is, according to Martin, 'a novel which constituted a vast watershed, incorporating all the currents of the past and opening out a whole network of new channels into the future'.[37] Indeed, the Paraguayan's previous novel, *Hijo de hombre*, was published in 1960 on the threshold of the Boom; and though there are obvious connections between the two works, the later text is worlds apart in terms of technical sophistication and really marks a dramatic new appearance by Roa Bastos on the literary scene.[38]

   To facilitate a compact approach to this vastly demanding novel, it is useful to consider it in terms of two levels, the historical and the literary (both of which are ultimately intrinsically linked politically). On the historical level, the novel appears to be a fictional autobiography of Dr. José Gaspar Rodríguez de Francia, known as 'el Supremo', whose reign of absolute dictatorship ('Dictadura Perpetua') lasted in Paraguay from 1814 to 1840. But this superficial impression of a historical novel quickly dissolves into a complex web of contradictions and ambiguities. The author presents himself as a mere 'compiler' of historical records and the novel seems to be made up of documents such as: notes dictated to Francia's secretary, the Supremo's private diary, the circulars he produces for his staff, footnotes or glosses, and sundry other items like a log-book, official declarations, a poster and so on. However, there are all sorts of complications with this spuriously objective process. For instance, the dictations contain lots of incidental dialogue and asides which the secretary could not possibly have taken down; the *Cuaderno Privado* (despite being locked away with seven keys) has been violated by comments in an unknown handwriting (as has the *Cuaderno Privado*); Francia's words, in any case, emanate from the perspective of death, since they often cover events going up to the 1970s; the footnotes, though usually authentic, sometimes contain suspicious elements and often contradict other parts of the text; and the compiler himself does not always maintain his separation from the 'documents' and becomes confused with the fiction. Thus there is no clear viewpoint on Dr. Francia and no clear distinction between history and fiction. The novel, then, deconstructs history and official discourse, suggesting – in the words of Marcos – that 'la escritura imaginativa es menos engañosa que las crónicas consagradas por la cultura dominante' and projecting 'el texto como una forma de pulverizar ideológicamente los valores consagrados'.[39]

All of this relates to the novel's literary level. There is an obvious parallel between the political idea of a 'dictator' and the literary act of 'dictation'. In a sense, by dictating to his secretary and his subjects Francia controls both language and history: and the style of the novel, transcending narrow referentiality and capturing the dynamism of oral communication, seeks to create a kind of 'supreme' or absolute language. But this is an impossible quest, for 'meaning' is constantly obstructed by the Supremo's linguistic excesses, the punning and word play, his regular reassessments of his own statements, while gaps in meaning are indicated by the references to the secretary's misunderstandings, the illegibility of the writing, the fact that parts of the manuscript are torn or burnt, and so on. Indeed, Foster identifies the novel with the false or absent meanings of myths – ultimately no more than 'luxuriant verbal artefacts'.[40] But the idea of myth implies a collective enterprise which calls to mind the role of the compiler. Roa himself has said of *Yo el Supremo* that 'el designio de permutar la función tradicional de autor por la de compilador representó el núcleo generador inicial'.[41] The point is, as Milagros Ezquerro has explained, that:

> la función del compilador sugiere que el sujeto productor de una obra literaria no se considera como 'original creador', sino como el artesano que elabora una obra a partir de materiales que son propiedad de una colectividad: una lengua, una Historia, unos mitos, una literatura, toda una herencia cultural... En tal perspectiva, la obra no se puede considerar como propiedad exclusiva e inalienable de un individuo, sino como un objeto autónomo destinado a lectores qua deben apropiárselo en un acto de lectura activo y productor de sentido.[42]

In other words, a compiler represents a rejection of fixed, given ideology in favour of free production of meaning. It is in this sense that we can understand Martin's claim that the novel's 'greatest triumph . . . is to have found a means of fusing "literary revolution" with "revolutionary literature" '.[43]

From a political standpoint, there can be little question, then, that Roa's linguistic games are less vacuous than those of, say, Sarduy. And, as has already been mentioned, a direct or popular form of social or political denunciation is an increasing feature of post-Boom fiction as it turns its back on totalisation and stylistic excess. Yet Roa's novel can hardly be described as 'popular'. Marcos, who repeatedly identifies Roa as the central figure of the post-Boom, argues, with Antonio Gramsci, that 'la nueva literatura debe hundir sus raíces en el *humus* de la cultura popular' and against 'el falso dilema de elegir entre un arte demagógico y barato, de contenido vulgar y reaccionario, o un arte sofisticado y elitista, cuyo mensaje, revolucionario en esencia, resulta sin embargo poco accesible a las masas, por su alto grado de rarificación expresiva'.[44] But surely *Yo el Supremo*, however much critics acclaim it, falls into this latter category. Despite its oral quality and its humour, it is in many ways a massively difficult and irritating novel; and in this sense it is linked to certain novels of the Boom and to Sarduy. The exploitation of the 'popular' for a social critique is certainly a feature of the post-Boom, but Roa Bastos is at one end of the scale of difficulty, with someone like Puig in the middle and other more recently discovered writers at the other end. Indeed, if Roa is, as Marcos would have it, the father of the post-Boom, then somebody like Isabel Allende must be its daughter. She is the only member of the more recent group to establish genuine success and has done so principally via her masterly first novel *La casa de los espíritus* (1982), which manages tremendous political power via a combination of the popular and the sophisticated which has pleased public and critics alike.

La casa de los espíritus has been compared repeatedly to *Cien años de soledad*, and it is pretty plain that Allende does, in fact, owe García Márquez a great debt. In both novels, Latin American history is explored through the medium of a lengthy family saga; the characters' lives are punctuated by fantastic or improbable occurrences; the style of both works has been described as magical realist; and there are more specific parallels between Rosa la bella and Remedios la Bella, tío Marcos's obsession with progress and inventions and that of several members of the Buendía family, Alba's work with her mother's writing and the attempts of several Buendías to decipher Melquíades's manuscripts, and so on and so forth. However, it would be unfair to condemn the novel on the grounds of its derivativeness, for in several ways it goes against the García Márquez grain and may be even parodying it. What is different is that *La casa de los espíritus* refers clearly and unequivocally to a specific reality, while *Cien años de soledad* offers allegorical glimpses of a wider reality from the refuge of patent unreality. In Allende's work, the references to twentieth-century Chile are unmistakable and the story of the Trueba family does not so much 'stand for' or 'represent' the Chilean experience but actually takes place in the modern Chilean context and is shaped by it. There is, in short, a greater 'realism' about the more recent novel. It is significant that the central character upon whose 'diaries' the text is based is called Clara. Her name implies the need for clarity, as does her choice of names for her children and grandchildren: 'no era partidaria de repetir los nombres en la familia, porque eso siembra confusión en los cuadernos de anotar la vida'.[45] This, of course, is the opposite of García Márquez's tendency to obfuscate via the repetition of family names. The point is that *La casa de los espíritus* is, to borrow Earle's phrase, a 'celebration of *reality*' (my italics)[46] and much of the novel's power – especially in the latter part – comes from its close fidelity to the Latin American referent.

Having said all that, Chile is never mentioned by name in the novel. The point is that this is not simply '*traditional* realism' – it is more a question of the family saga having a concrete link to a specific 'reality'. The story's underlying humanitarianism is relevant to all of Latin America and the world as a whole. However, beneath the generalities of the story it is clear that the scene is modern Chile and we are taken through the heyday of *latifundismo*, the growth of capitalism, the politicisation of workers and peasants, the election of socialist Salvador Allende (Isabel's uncle) and the brutal Pinochet coup. There is a marked change in tone in the final chapters dealing with the coup and its aftermath. The gentle humour and irony used to describe the daily life of the inhabitants of the house of spirits gives way to something close to the fierce denunciation of testimonial literature. In the words of Jara:

> Quizás el Golpe no podía ser narrado de otra manera, tal vez necesite del dramatismo estólido de la épica para cronicar la brutalidad de su ocurrencia. El Golpe, al fin y al cabo, significó el colapso de la cotidianidad; hasta los fantasmas dejan de hablar por un rato. Dentro del modo épico a que se acoge entonces el discurso de Isabel Allende, la ficción del testimonio parece ser la forma más apropiada de narrar ese hecho traumático y de transmitir, al mismo tiempo, el vacío de significación que produjo.[47]

There is, in fact, an inversion here, for the earlier fantastic stories of spirits are turned inside-out: now, to quote Rojas, 'ocurren hechos de inverosímil ficción, pero reconocidos por el lector como terrible realidad histórica'.[48] What the change of tone really shows is the inevitably disastrous consequences of injustice. Esteban Trueba's gleeful sexual abuse of the women on his estate produces the resentful bastard child Esteban García who will one day join the *carabineros* and vengefully torture Trueba's granddaughter. Similarly, most of the novel deals humorously and entertainingly with the activities of the Trueba family, as the head of the household moves from successful entrepreneur to Conservative politician; but the shocking violence of the final chapters indicates the unavoidable dangers of an anti-democratic and unfair system. In fact, Trueba's commercial and political climbing is matched at every stage by a decline in his emotional fortunes: his paternalistic vision is ultimately a myth.

There is a further social or political aspect to *La casa de los espíritus* (which is quite absent from García Márquez) and that is its feminism. While cynics may suggest that Isabel Allende's career has benefited from the novelty of her name and her sex, she has proved that she is not only the single most significant female novelist to emerge from Latin America, but also offers, importantly, a definite woman's perspective on reality. Though Esteban Trueba provides a narrative backbone to the novel, his emblematic patriarchy is really a counterpoint to the activities of the female characters. Of them, Allende has said:

> Todas las mujeres de mi libro son femenistas a su modo, es decir abogan por ser personas libres y completas, por realizarse, por no depender del hombre. Cada una lucha de acuerdo a su carácter y a la época en que lo tocó vivir.[49]

Moreover, not only do they achieve increasing independence, they also represent an increasing integration of the women's struggle with the class struggle. Taking them chronologically, then, Nívea is a suffragette, but well-off and not genuinely in touch with the working classes; her daughter Clara defies her husband, avoids domesticity, spurns jewellery and fashion, devoting instead much time to looking after the poor, though realising that 'no necesitan caridad, sino justicia' (p.124); her daughter Blanca stands up to her father's authority, brings up an illegitimate child and has a lasting love affair with a peasant leader and revolutionary singer; finally her daughter Alba joins the student movement, has a relationship with a guerrilla leader, finds herself a victim of torture, and ends up finding solidarity with ordinary women in a prison camp and, later, a shanty town.

This positive development of progressiveness in the female characters is linked to the theme of creativity. Rosa sews, Clara writes, Blanca makes clay figures and Alba paints her wall and later writes as well. It is significant that the creatures portrayed by the women's art work are bizarre hybrids and that Blanca's fairy tales tell of 'un príncipe que durmió cien años, de doncellas que peleaban cuerpo a cuerpo con los dragones, de un lobo perdido en el bosque a quien una niña destripó sin razón alguna' (p.269): these all invert traditional roles and disrupt the system of binary distinctions upon which society bases itself. This is also, as Agosín has explained,[50] the function of Clara's silence: she converts the traditional concept of feminine coyness and passivity into an act of will (in the case of her husband) when she refuses to speak. What is more, this silent withdrawal encourages her imagination and her writing (further acts of subversion), but the manuscripts she produces are non-chrono-logical and full of fantastic events. The point is that Clara's vision of events is anti-establishment: it challenges the 'official version', fixed ideology and rigid social hierarchies. Her liberation of spirits in the patriarchal Trueba's house is therefore symbolic of the potential overturning of the fixed and iniquitous system he supports.

The dissolution of binarisms helps explain why the novel is ultimately positive. The women's names (Nívea, Clara, Blanca, Alba) connote growing brightness or luminosity. The culmination is Alba, suggesting the hope of a new dawn amidst all the darkness and despair. And significantly in this respect, Allende's second novel is called *De amor y de sombra* (1984) and tells of a journalist and photographer's growing love as they sink deeper into a dangerous investigation into killings under the Pinochet regime. Allende's feminism deconstructs black-and-white binarisms rather than rein-forces them. Hence Alba discovers that through reading her grandmother's notes her desire for vengeance has gone: 'busco mi odio y no puedo encontrarlo' (p.379). Hence also Esteban Trueba, thanks to the example of his daughter's love, ends up hugging Pedro Tercero García, the enemy he had once tried to kill (p.346). This is not, then, simply a clear-cut struggle between two extremes, for there remains the conviction that people retain within them the capacity for love and that they will one day each learn to set it free.

The combination of optimism and political realism visible in Allende's work is a pointer to the general direction of much post-Boom fiction. The pessimism and metaphysical contemplation associated with much of the *nueva narrativa* is on the wane and instead of elaborate and grandiose explorations the post-Boom novel restores (often via the use of popular forms) the centrality of the Latin American referent, broaching the subcontinent's political tragedies in a direct and meaningful manner, and ultimately offering hope for the future. But, again, it must be emphasised that this is only a partial picture. As has been said, not all the fiction is political and not all of it is more 'realistic'. The linguistic, stylistic and structural games of many post-Boom novels – even where they depart from the 'seriousness' and self-importance of some of the novels of the Boom – have their roots in the technical experiments of the Boom and are often extensions or reworkings of them. Moreover, there are often differences within the work of a single writer: for instance, the gloomy monologue at the heart of Sainz's *Obsesivos días circulares*

(1969) seems an attempt to ape the conventions of the *nueva novela*, while his comic youth-novel *La princesa del palacio de hierro* is very much of the more popularly oriented post-Boom. The point is that the sheer variety of the post-Boom means that it cannot be reduced to a single formula. What the Boom did was to create a market for the Latin American novel and further its professionalisation. The legacy was a generation (or generations) of writers who would, with inherited expertise, continue, expand upon or develop alternatives to the narrative trends of the new novel alongside the already established authors.

However, a question remains about the present and the future of the Latin American novel. Professionalisation and the creation of a market have brought undoubted benefits to Latin American writers, but have equally exposed them to the risk of producing well-packaged mediocrities, while leaving many not-so-big names banished to less-well-known publishing houses. It would be sad if the supply and demand generated by the growth of the Latin American novel in the 1960s were to lead in the 1980s and after to an industry primarily concerned with promoting slick and exotic entertainments for the international market. Having said that, as long as there are novels like *La casa de los espíritus*, there is still hope that the drift in this direction can continue to produce meaningful results.

NOTES

1 The question of a transition from Boom to post-Boom is also raised in Chapters 9 and 10 of this book. The best available attempt to categorise the post-Boom is: Donald Shaw, 'Towards a description of the post-Boom', *Bulletin of Hispanic Studies*, vol. 66, no. 1 (1989) pp.87–94. I have also found useful: Juan Manuel Marcos, *De García Márquez al postboom* (Orígenes, Madrid, n.d.); David William Foster, *Alternate Voices in the Contemporary Latin American Narrative* (University of Missouri Press, Columbia, 1985). For a discussion of the post-Boom in Mexico, see J. Ann Duncan, *Voices, Visions and a New Reality: Mexican Fiction since 1970* (University of Pittsburgh Press, Pittsburgh, 1986).
2 Interview with Z. Nelly Martínez, *Hispamérica*, no. 21 (1978), p.53.
3 Roberto González Echevarría, *La ruta de Severo Sarduy* (Ediciones del Norte, Hanover NH, 1987), pp.249, 251. Here he is essentially using the term 'post-modern' as a synonym for 'post-Boom'.
4 José Donoso, 'Dos mundos americanos', *El Mercurio (Artes y Letras)*, 14 Nov. 1982, p.1.
5 Julio Ortega, 'La literatura latinoamericana en la década del 80', *Eco*, no. 215 (1979), p.537.

6 Marcos, *De García Márquez al postboom*, p.9; Jean Franco, 'From modernization to resistance: Latin American literature 1959–1976', *Latin American Perspectives*, vol. 5, no. 1 (1978), p.93.

7 See Alejo Carpentier, *La novela latinoamericana en vísperas de un nuevo siglo y otros ensayos* (Siglo XXI, Mexico, 1981).

8 Terry Eagleton, *Literary Theory. An Introduction* (Basil Blackwell, Oxford, 1983), p.203.

9 Martínez interview, p.60.

10 Donoso, 'Dos mundos americanos', p.1.

11 There is a chapter on documentary narrative in Foster, *Alternate Voices*.

12 Marcos, *De García Márquez al postboom*, p.54.

13 For a fuller discussion of this aspect of Donoso, see my: 'Structure and meaning in *La misteriosa desaparición de la marquesita de Loria*', *Bulletin of Hispanic Studies*, vol. 63, no. 3 (1986), pp.247–56; 'Donoso and the post-Boom: simplicity and subversion', *Contemporary Literature*, vol. 28, no. 4 (1987), pp.520–9; *José Donoso: the 'Boom' and Beyond* (Francis Cairns, Liverpool, 1988).

14 'Guillermo Cabrera Infante: an interview in a summer manner with Jason Wilson' in John King (ed.), *Modern Latin American Fiction: A Survey* (Faber & Faber, London, 1987), p.316.

15 Guillermo Cabrera Infante, *Tres tristes tigres* (Seix Barral, Barcelona, 1983), p.360.

16 Both these observations are made by William L. Siemens in *Worlds Reborn: The Hero in the Modern Spanish American Novel* (West Virginia University Press, Morgantown, 1984), pp.164, 156.

17 Isabel Álvarez-Borland, *Discontinuidad y ruptura en Guillermo Cabrera Infante* (Hispamérica, Gaithersburg MD, n.d.), p.113.

18 Raymond D. Souza, *Major Cuban Novelists: Innovation and Tradition* (University of Missouri Press, Columbia and London, 1976), p.85.

19 ibid., p.87.

20 ibid., pp.70–1. Souza's discussion of Chapter 12 (pp.66–71) has been extremely useful here, as has his entire chapter on Lezama Lima.

21 José Lezama Lima, *Paradiso* (Cátedra, Madrid, 1980), p.606. Any subsequent reference will be to this edition and included in the text.

22 Again, see Souza, *Major Cuban Novelists* for an illuminating explanation of this process.

23 Roberto González Echevarría, 'Són de la Habana: la ruta de Severo Sarduy', *Revista Iberoamericana*, vol. 37 (1971), p.731.

24 Interview with Emir Rodríguez Monegal, *Mundo Nuevo*, vol. 2 (1966), p.25.

25 Severo Sarduy, 'El barroco y el neobarroco' in César Fernández Moreno (ed.), *América latina en su literatura* (Siglo XXI, Mexico, 1972), p.182.

26 This is summarised in fairly clear terms by Alicia Rivero Potter in her 'Algunas metáforas somáticas – erótico-escripturales – en *De donde son los cantantes* y *Cobra*', *Revista Iberoamericana*, vol. 49 (1983), pp.498–9.

27 Ronald Schwartz, *Nomads, Exiles and Emigrés. The Rebirth of the Latin American Narrative, 1960–80* (Scarecrow Press, Metuchen, NJ, and London, 1980), p.99.

28 Alfred J. MacAdam, *Modern Latin American Narratives* (University of Chicago Press, Chicago and London, 1977), p.47.

29 Severo Sarduy, *De donde son los cantantes* (Seix Barral, Barcelona, 1980), pp.11–12.

30 MacAdam, *Modern Latin American Narratives*, p.48.

31 Roberto González Echevarría, 'Plain song: Sarduy's *Cobra*', *Contemporary Literature*, vol. 28, no. 4 (1987), pp.450–1.

32 See ibid., p.455.

33 Severo Sarduy, *Cobra* (Sudamericana, Buenos Aires, 1972), p.66.

34 See González Echevarría, 'Plain song', especially pp.445–6, 458–9.

35 Franco, 'From modernization to resistance', pp.90–1. The quotation in inverted commas is from H.M. Enzensberger, *The Consciousness Industry* (Seabury Press, New York, 1974), p.88.

36 Franco, 'From modernization to resistance', p.94.

37 Gerald Martin, '*Yo el Supremo*: the dictator and his script' in Salvador Bacarisse (ed.), *Contemporary Latin American Fiction* (Scottish Academic Press, Edinburgh, 1980), p.73.

38 For this reason *Hijo de hombre* was considered separately in the opening chapter of this book.

39 Juan Manuel Marcos, *Roa Bastos, precursor del post-boom* (Katún, Mexico, 1983), pp.70, 67.

40 David William Foster, *Augusto Roa Bastos* (Twayne, Boston, 1978), p.107.

41 Augusto Roa Bastos, 'Algunos núcleos generadores de un texto narrativo' in *L'idéologique dans le texte*, XVI (Travaux de l'Université, Toulouse, 1978), p.86.

42 Milagros Ezquerro in her introduction to Augusto Roa Bastos, *Yo el Supremo* (Cátedra, Madrid, 1983), pp.64–5.

43 Martin, '*Yo el Supremo*', p.84.

44 Marcos, *De García Márquez al postboom*, pp.107–8.

45 Isabel Allende, *La casa de los espíritus* (Plaza y Janés, Barcelona, 1985), p.233. All subsequent references will be to this edition and will be included in the text.

46 See Peter G. Earle, 'Literature as survival: Allende's *The House of the Spirits*', *Contemporary Literature*, vol. 28, no. 4 (1987), pp.543–54.

47 René Jara, *Los límites de la representación* (Fundación Instituto Shakespeare/Instituto de Cine y Radio-Televisión/Ediciones Hiperión, Madrid/Valencia, 1985), p.26.

48 Mario A. Rojas, '*La casa de los espíritus*, de Isabel Allende: un caleidoscopo de espejos desordenados', *Revista Iberoamericana*, vol. 51 (1985), p.919.

49 Quoted by Marjorie Agosín in her 'Isabel Allende: *La casa de los espíritus*', *Revista Interamericana de Bibliografía*, vol. 35 (1985), p.452.

50 See Agosín, 'Isabel Allende: *La casa de los espíritus*', p.450 ff. for a useful discussion of the role of Clara.

SELECT BIBLIOGRAPHY

What follows is a list of basic further reading on the nine texts considered in the central chapters of this book. The selection in each case is that of the author of the chapter on the text concerned.

Two useful and accessible surveys of modern Latin American fiction are: John King (ed.), *Modern Latin American Fiction: A Survey* (Faber & Faber, London, 1987) and D.L. Shaw, *Nueva narrativa hispanoamericana* (Cátedra, Madrid, 1981). Both books have handy bibliographies. For a guide to bibliographies on Latin American authors, see David Zubatsky, *Latin American Literary Authors: An Annotated Guide to Bibliographies* (Scarecrow Press, Metuchen, NJ, and London, 1986). Further up-to-date bibliographical information can be obtained by consulting *The Year's Work in Modern Language Studies* (produced by The Modern Humanities Research Association, Great Britain) and *The Modern Language Association of America International Bibliography*, both published yearly.

2 BORGES: *FICCIONES*

Alazraki, J. (1968) *La prosa narrativa de Jorge Luis Borges*, Gredos, Madrid.
—— (ed.) (1976) *Jorge Luis Borges*, Taurus, Madrid.
—— (1977) *Versiones. Inversiones. Reversiones*, Gredos, Madrid.
Barrenechea, A.M. (1965) *Borges the Labyrinth Maker*, New York University Press, New York. Spanish version (1967) *La expresión de la irrealidad en la obra de Jorge Luis Borges*, 2nd edn, Paidós, Buenos Aires.
Christ, R. (1969) *The Narrow Act*, New York University Press, New York.
Dunham, L. and Ivask, I. (eds) (1971) *The Cardinal Points of Borges*, University of Oklahoma Press, Norman.
Ferrer, M. (1971) *Borges y la nada*, Tamesis Books Ltd,. London.
McMurray, G. (1980) *Jorge Luis Borges*, Ungar, New York.
Modern Fiction Studies (1973), vol. 19, no. 3.
Pérez, A. (1971) *Realidad y suprarrealidad en los cuentos fantásticos de Jorge Luis Borges*, Universal, Miami.
Rodríguez Monegal, E. (1978) *Jorge Luis Borges. A Literary Biography*, Dutton, New York.
Shaw, D.L. (1976) *Borges: 'Ficciones'*, Grant & Cutler, London. Spanish version (1986) *Jorge Luis Borges: 'Ficciones'*, Laia, Barcelona.

Tri-Quarterly (1972), no. 25.
Wheelock, C. (1969) *The Mythmaker*, University of Texas Press, Austin.

3 ASTURIAS: *EL SEÑOR PRESIDENTE*

Bellini, G. (1969) *La narrativa de Miguel Ángel Asturias*, Losada, Buenos Aires.
Callan, R. (1970) *Miguel Ángel Asturias*, Twayne, New York.
Cheymol, M. (1987) *Miguel Ángel Asturias dans le Paris des années folles*, Presses Universitaires de Grenoble, Grenoble.
Couffon, C. (1970) *Miguel Ángel Asturias*, Seghers, Paris.
López Álvarez, L. (1974) *Conversaciones con Miguel Ángel Asturias*, Magisterio Español, Madrid.
Menton, S. (1960) *Historia crítica de la novela guatemalteca*, Editorial Universitaria, Guatemala.
Sáenz, J. (1975) *Genio y figura de Miguel Ángel Asturias*, Eudeba, Buenos Aires.
Verdugo, I. (1968) *El carácter de la literatura hispanoamericana y la novelística de M.A. Asturias*, Editorial Universitaria, Guatemala.

4 RULFO: *PEDRO PÁRAMO*

Álvarez, N.E. (1983) *Análisis arquetípico, mítico y simbológico de 'Pedro Páramo'*, Ediciones Universal, Miami.
Benítez Rojo, A. (ed.) (1969) *Recopilación de textos sobre Juan Rulfo*, Casa de las Américas, Havana. In particular items by Harss, Frenk, Leal and Estrada.
Boldy, S. (1983) 'The use of ambiguity and the death(s) of Bartolomé San Juan in Rulfo's *Pedro Páramo*', *Forum for Modern Language Studies*, vol. 19, no. 3, pp.224–35.
Freeman, G.R. (1970) *Paradise and Fall in Rulfo's 'Pedro Páramo: Archetype and Structural Unity*, CIDOC, Cuaderno núm. 47, Cuernavaca (Mexico).
Galindo, L.O. (1984) *Expresión y sentido de Juan Rulfo*, José Porrúa Turanzas, S.A., Madrid.
Giacoman, H.F. (ed.) (1974) *Homenaje a Juan Rulfo*, Las Américas, New York. In particular items by Leal, Coddou, Ortega, Dorfman, Pupo Walker, Freeman, O'Neill, Sacoto Salamea.
González Boixo, J.C. (1980) *Claves narrativas de Juan Rulfo*, Colegio Universitario de León, León (Spain).
Luraschi, I.A. (1976) 'Narradores en la obra de Juan Rulfo: estudio de sus funciones y efectos', *Cuadernos Hispanoamericanos*, no. 308, pp.5–29.
Peralta, V. and Befumo Boschi, L. (1975) *Rulfo. La soledad creadora*, Fernando García Cambeiro, Buenos Aires.
Portal, M. (1981) *Análisis semiológico de Pedro Páramo*, Narcea, S.A. de Ediciones, Madrid.
Rodríguez Alcalá, H. (1965) *El arte de Juan Rulfo*, INBA, Mexico.
Rodríguez Monagal, E. (1974) 'Relectura de *Pedro Páramo*' in *Narradores de esta América*, vol. 2, Alfa, Buenos Aires.
Roffé, R. (1973) *Juan Rulfo. Autobiografía armada*, Corregidor, Buenos Aires.

Sommers, J. (ed.) (1976) *La narrativa de Juan Rulfo*, Sep/Setentas, Mexico. In particular items by Blanco Aguinaga, Sommers, Leal, Ortega and Frenk.

Stanton, A. (1988), 'Estructuras antropológicas en *Pedro Páramo*', *Nueva Revista de Filología Hispánica*, vol. 36 (page numbers unavailable).

5 FUENTES: *LA MUERTE DE ARTEMIO CRUZ*

Boldy, S. (1984) 'Fathers and sons in Fuentes' *La muerte de Artemio Cruz*', *Bulletin of Hispanic Studies*, vol. 61, pp.31–40.

—— (1987) 'Carlos Fuentes' in J. King (ed.) *Modern Latin American Fiction: A Survey*, Faber & Faber, London, pp.155–72.

Befumo Boschi, L. and Calabrese, E. (1974) *Nostalgia del futuro en la obra de Carlos Fuentes*, Fernando García Cambeiro, Buenos Aires.

'Carlos Fuentes at UCLA: an interview' (1982), *Mester*, vol. 11, no. 1, pp. 3–15.

Faris, W. (1982) *Carlos Fuentes*, Ungar, New York.

Fouques, B. (1975) 'El espacio órfico en la novela en *La muerte de Artemio Cruz*', *Revista Iberoamericana*, vol. 41, pp. 19–48.

González Echevarría, R. (1971), '*La muerte de Artemio Cruz* y Unamuno fuente de Fuentes', *Cuadernos Americanos*, vol. 177, no. 4, pp.197–207.

Gyurko, L. (1980) 'Structure and theme in *La muerte de Artemio Cruz*', *Symposium*, vol. 34, pp.29–41.

—— (1982) '*La muerte de Artemio Cruz* and *Citizen Kane*: a comparative analysis' in R. Brody and C. Rossman (eds) *Carlos Fuentes, a Critical View*, University of Texas Press, Austin, pp.64–94.

Osorio, N. (1971) 'Un aspecto de la estructura de *La muerte de Artemio Cruz*' in H. Giacoman (ed.) *Homenaje a Carlos Fuentes*, Las Américas, New York, pp.125–46.

Shaw, D.L. (1980) 'Narrative arrangement in *La muerte de Artemio Cruz*' in S. Bacarisse (ed.) *Contemporary Latin American Fiction*, Scottish Academic Press, Edinburgh, pp.34–47.

Stoopen, M. (1982) *La muerte de Artemio Cruz: una novela de denuncia y traición*, UNAM, Mexico.

Vidal, H. (1976) 'El modo narrativo en *La muerte de Artemio Cruz*', *Thesaurus*, vol. 31, pp.300–26.

6 CORTÁZAR: *RAYUELA*

Alazraki, J. and Ivask, I. (eds) (1978) *The Final Island: The Fiction of Julio Cortázar*, University of Oklahoma Press, Norman.

Barrenechea, A.M. (1983) 'Estudio preliminar' in J. Cortázar and A.M. Barrenechea, *Cuaderno de bitácora de 'Rayuela'*, Sudamericana, Buenos Aires.

Boldy, S. (1981) *The Novels of Julio Cortázar*, Cambridge University Press, Cambridge.

Burgos, F. (ed.) (1987) *Los ochenta mundos de Julio Cortázar: ensayos*, Edi-6, Madrid.

Curutchet, J.C. (1972) *Julio Cortázar o la crítica de la razón pragmática*, Nacional, Madrid.
García Canclini, N. (1968) *Cortázar: una antropología poética*, Nova, Buenos Aires.
González Bermejo, E. (1978) *Conversaciones con Cortázar*, Edhasa, Barcelona
Hernández del Castillo, A. (1981) *Keats, Poe, and the Shaping of Cortázar's Mythopoesis*, John Benjamins, Amsterdam.
Picon Garfield, E. (1981) *Cortázar por Cortázar*, Universidad Veracruzana, Xalapa.
Fuentes, C. (1972) 'Cortázar: la caja de Pandora', in *La nueva novela hispanoamericana*, Joaquín Mortiz, Mexico, pp.67–77.
Giacoman, H.F. (ed.) (1972) *Homenaje a Julio Cortázar*, Las Américas, New York.
Harss, L. (1983) 'Julio Cortázar o la bofetada metafísica', in *Los nuestros*, Sudamericana, Buenos Aires, pp.252–300.
Lastra, P. (ed.) (1981) *Julio Cortázar*, Taurus, Madrid.
Revista Iberoamericana (1973), vol. 39.
Roy, J. (1974) *Julio Cortázar ante su sociedad*, Península, Barcelona.
Sola, G. de (1968) *Julio Cortázar o el hombre nuevo*, Sudamericana, Buenos Aires.
Sosnowski, S. (1973) *Julio Cortázar: una búsqueda mítica*, Noé, Buenos Aires.
Viñas, D. (1971) *De Sarmiento a Cortázar: literatura argentina y realidad política*, Siglo XX, Buenos Aires.
Yurkievich, S. (1987) *Julio Cortázar: al calor de tu sombra*, Legasa, Buenos Aires.

7 GARCÍA MÁRQUEZ: *CIEN AÑOS DE SOLEDAD*

Arnau, C. (1971) *El mundo mítico de Gabriel García Márquez*, Península, Barcelona.
Earle, P.G, (ed.) (1981) *Gabriel García Márquez*, Taurus, Madrid.
Giacoman, H.G. (ed.) (1972) *Homenaje a Gabriel García Márquez*, Las Américas, New York.
González Echevarría, R. (1984) '*Cien años de soledad*: the novel as myth and archive', *Modern Language Notes*, vol. 99, no. 2, pp.358–80.
Levine, S.J. (1975) *El espejo hablado: un estudio de 'Cien años de soledad'*, Monte Ávila, Caracas.
Ludmer, J. (1972), '*Cien años de soledad': una interpretación*, Editorial Tiempo Contemporáneo, Buenos Aires.
McGuirk, B. and Cardwell, R. (eds) (1987) *Gabriel García Marquez: New Readings*, Cambridge University Press, Cambridge.
McMurray, G.R. (1977) *Gabriel García Márquez*, Ungar, New York.
Maturo, G. (1977) *Claves simbólicas de García Márquez*, 2nd edn, Fernando García Cambeiro, Buenos Aires.
Mena, L.I. (1979) *La función de la historia en 'Cien años de soledad'*, Plaza y Janés, Barcelona.
Mendoza, P.A. and García Márquez, G. (1982) *El olor de la guayaba*, Bruguera, Barcelona; English version (1983) *The Fragrance of Guava*,

trans. A. Wright, Verso, London.

Minta, S. (1987) *Gabriel García Márquez*, Cape, London.

Palencia-Roth, M. (1983) *Gabriel García Márquez. La línea, el circulo y las metamorfosis del mito*, Gredos, Madrid.

Shaw, D.L. (1977) 'Concerning the interpretation of *Cien años de soledad*', *Ibero-Amerikanisches Archiv*, vol. 3, no. 4, pp.317–29.

Sims, R.L. (1981) *The Evolution of Myth in García Marquez from 'La hojarasca' to 'Cien años de soledad'*, Universal, Miami.

Vargas Llosa, M. (1971) *Gabriel García Márquez: historia de un deicidio*, Barral, Barcelona.

Williams, R.L. (1984) *Gabriel García Márquez*, Twayne, Boston.

8 VARGAS LLOSA: *LA CASA VERDE*

Anon. (1971) *Agresión a la realidad: Mario Vargas Llosa*, Inventarios Provisionales, Las Palmas.

Boldori de Baldussi, R. (1974) *Vargas Llosa: un narrador y sus demonios*, Fernando García Cambeiro, Buenos Aires.

Díez, L.A. (1972) *Mario Vargas Llosa's Pursuit of the Total Novel*, CIDOC, Cuernavaca, Mexico.

—— (ed.) (1972) *Asedios a Vargas Llosa*, Editorial Universitaria, Santiago de Chile.

Enkvist, I. (1987) *Las técnicas narrativas de Vargas Llosa*, Acta Universitatis Gothobergensis, Gothemberg.

Fernández, C.M. (1977) *Aproximación formal a la novelística de Vargas Llosa*, Editorial Nacional, Madrid.

Giacoman, H.F. and Oviedo, J.M. (eds) (1971) *Homenaje a Mario Vargas Llosa*, Las Américas, New York.

Lewis, M.A. (1983) *From Lima to Leticia*, University Press of America, Lanham.

Martín, J.L. (1974) *La narrativa de Mario Vargas Llosa: acercamiento estilístico*, Gredos, Madrid.

Oviedo, J.M. (1970) *Mario Vargas Llosa: La invención de una realidad*, Seix Barral, Madrid.

—— (ed.) (1981) *Mario Vargas Llosa*, Taurus, Madrid.

Pereira, A. (1981) *La concepción literaria de Mario Vargas Llosa*, UNAM, Mexico.

Texas Studies in Language and Literature (1977), vol. 19, no. 4. Reappears as C. Rossman and A.W. Friedman (eds) (1978) *Mario Vargas Llosa: A Collection of Critical Essays*, University of Texas Press, Austin.

World Literature Today (1978), vol. 52, no. 1.

9 DONOSO: *EL OBSCENO PÁJARO DE LA NOCHE*

Achugar, H. (1979) *Ideología y estructuras narrativas en José Donoso (1950–70)*, Centro de estudios latinoamericanos 'Rómulo Gallegos', Caracas.

Bacarisse, P. (1980) '*El obsceno pájaro de la noche*: a willed process of evasion', in Salvador Bacarisse (ed.) *Contemporary Latin American Fiction*, Scottish

Academic Press, Edinburgh.
Borinsky, A. (1973) 'Repeticiones y máscaras: *El obsceno pájaro de la noche*', *Modern Language Notes*, vol. 88, pp.281–94.
Cornejo Polar, A. (ed.) (1975) *José Donoso. La destrucción de un mundo*, Fernando García Cambeiro, Buenos Aires.
Gutiérrez Mouat, R. (1983) *José Donoso: impostura e impostación. La modelización lúdica y carnavalesca de una producción literaria*, Hispamérica, Gaithersburg.
Magnarelli, S. (1978) 'Amidst the illusory depths: the first person pronoun and *El obsceno pájaro de la noche*', *Modern Language Notes*, vol. 93, pp.267–84.
—— (1985) *The Lost Rib. Female Characters in the Spanish-American Novel*, Associated University Presses, London and Toronto, pp.147–68.
Martínez, Z.N. (1980) '*El obsceno pájaro de la noche*: la productividad del texto', *Revista Iberoamericana*, vol. 46, pp.51–65.
McMurray, G.R. (1979) *José Donoso*, Twayne, New York.
Pujals, J.A. (1981) *El bosque indomado donde chilla el obsceno pájaro de la noche. Un estudio sobre la novela de José Donoso*, Universal, Miami.
Quinteros, I. (1978) *José Donoso: una insurrección contra la realidad*, Hispanova, Madrid.
Review (1973), no. 9.
Rowe, W. 'José Donoso: *El obsceno pájaro de la noche* as test case for psychoanalytical interpretation', *Modern Language Review*, vol. 78 no. 3, pp.588–96.
Solotorevsky, M. (1983) *José Donoso: incursiones en su producción novelesca*, Universidad de Valparaíso, Valparaíso.
Swanson, P. (1988) *José Donoso: The 'Boom' and Beyond*, Francis Cairns, Liverpool.
Vidal, H. (1972) *José Donoso: surrealismo y rebelión de los instintos*, Aubí, Barcelona.

10 PUIG: *BOQUITAS PINTADAS*

Bacarisse, P. (1978) 'The first four novels of Manuel Puig: parts of a whole?', *Ibero-Amerikanisches Archiv*, vol. 4, no. 4, pp.253–63.
—— (1988) *The Necessary Dream. A Study of the Novels of Manuel Puig*, University of Wales Press, Cardiff.
Borinsky, A. (1975) 'Castración y lujos', *Revista Iberoamericana*, vol. 41, pp.29–45.
García Ramos, J.M. (1982) *La narrativa de Manuel Puig (por una crítica en libertad)*, Universidad de La Laguna, La Laguna.
Kerr, L. (1987) *Suspended Fictions. Reading Novels by Manuel Puig*, University of Illinois Press, Urbana and Chicago.
—— (1982) 'The fiction of popular design and desire: Manuel Puig's *Boquitas pintadas*', *Modern Language Notes*, vol. 97, pp.411–21.
McCracken, E. (1980–81) 'Manuel Puig's *Heartbreak Tango*: women and mass culture', *Latin American Literary Review*, vol. 18, pp.27–36.
Morello-Frosch, M. (1975) 'La sexualidad opresiva en las obras de Manuel Puig', *Nueva Narrativa Hispanoamericana*, vol. 5, pp. 151–8.

Rodríguez Monegal, E. (1972) 'El folletín rescatado', *Revista de la Universidad de México*, vol. 27, no. 2, pp.27–35.

Safir, M.A. (1975) 'Mitología: otro nivel de metalenguaje en *Boquitas pintadas*', *Revista Iberoamericana*, vol. 41, pp.47–58.

Sarduy, S. (1971) 'Notas a las notas a las notas. . . a propósito de Manuel Puig', *Revista Iberoamericana*, vol. 37, pp.555–67.

Solotorevsky, M. (1984) 'El cliché en *Pubis angelical* y *Boquitas pintadas*: desgaste y creatividad', *Hispamérica*, vol 13, no. 38, pp.3–18.

Triviños, G. (1976) 'La destrucción del verosímil folletinesco en *Boquitas pintadas*', *Texto Crítico*, vol. 9, pp.117–30.

Weiss, J. (1974) 'Dynamic correlations in *Heartbreak Tango*', *Latin American Literary Review*, vol. 3, no. 5, pp.137–41.

INDEX